Acclaim for Maria Hinojosa and *Raising Raul*

"This book, witty and knowing, is a Latina version of Anne Lamott's bestselling memoir about first-time motherhood, *Operating Instructions*."
—*Newsweek*

"Hinojosa is very much a postmodern heroine."
—*Miami Herald*

"How a woman of many cultures and great self-awareness meets life's trials is the heart of *Raising Raul*."
—*Fort Worth Star Telegram*

"*Raising Raul* is not just for mothers but for all of us who are challenged to combine the best of our traditions with the new selves we become as we grow beyond our roots. Maria Hinojosa is sassy, soulful and intensely, intimately honest with herself and her readers. All readers will find themselves in this book. All readers will add her familia to their family."
—Julia Alvarez, author of *How the Garcia Girls Lost their Accents*, *Yo!*, and *Something to Declare*

"*Raising Raul* reads as if Maria dipped her pen into salsa to write it. It's spunky, spicy, and full of joy. Raul is lucky to have a mom so exuberantly loving and determined—with just the dash of nerves that make her sublimely human. I love this book for the world it opens up, and for letting me spend such tangy time with its author."
—Susan Stamberg, Special Correspondent, National Public Radio

"*Raising Raul* is a brutally honest but wildly entertaining account of motherhood and womanhood today. Maria Hinojosa has written an insightful, emotional, and funny book."
—Linda Villarosa, author of *Body & Soul* and co-author of *The Black Parenting Book*

PENGUIN BOOKS

RAISING RAUL

Maria Hinojosa is an urban affairs correspondent for CNN. From 1990–1996 she was a correspondent for National Public Radio. She continues to host NPR's nationally broadcast *Latino USA*. In 1995, *Hispanic Business Magazine* named her as one of the one hundred most influential Latinos in the United States and in 1999 *Working Mother Magazine* named her one of the year's twenty-five most influential mothers. She has won numerous awards including the Robert F. Kennedy Award, an Associated Press Award, and La Raza's Ruben Salazar Award. Hinojosa resides in New York City with her husband, her son, Raul, and her daughter, Yurema.

Raising Raul

ADVENTURES RAISING MYSELF AND MY SON

Maria Hinojosa

PENGUIN BOOKS

PENGUIN BOOKS
Published by the Penguin Group
Penguin Putnam Inc., 375 Hudson Street,
New York, New York 10014, U.S.A.
Penguin Books Ltd, 27 Wrights Lane, London W8 5TZ, England
Penguin Books Australia Ltd, Ringwood, Victoria, Australia
Penguin Books Canada Ltd, 10 Alcorn Avenue,
Toronto, Ontario, Canada M4V 3B2
Penguin Books (N.Z.) Ltd, 182–190 Wairau Road,
Auckland 10, New Zealand

Penguin Books Ltd, Registered Offices:
Harmondsworth, Middlesex, England

First published in the United States of America by Viking Penguin,
a member of Penguin Putnam Inc. 1999
Published in Penguin Books 2000

1 3 5 7 9 10 8 6 4 2

Grateful acknowledgment is made for permission to reprint an excerpt from
"Welcome to the World" by David Hershey-Webb. © David Hershey-Webb, 1997.

THE LIBRARY OF CONGRESS HAS CATALOGED
THE HARDCOVER EDITION AS FOLLOWS:
Hinojosa, Maria.
Raising Raul/by Maria Hinojosa.
p. cm.
ISBN 0-670-88445-6 (hc.)
ISBN 0 14 02.9636 0 (pbk.)
1. Motherhood—New York (State)—New York case studies.
2. Mothers—New York (State)—New York case studies.   3. Child
rearing—New York (State)—New York case studies.   4. Hinojosa, Maria.
5. Journalists—New York (State)—New York biography.   6. Women journalists—
New York (State)—New York biography.   7. Mexican American women—
New York (State)—New York biography.   I. Title.
HQ759.H667   1999   99–39593
306.874'3—dc21

Printed in the United States of America
Set in Perpetua
Designed by Betty Lew

To the men in my life—Gérman and Raul Ariel—
for helping me to be the woman I am becoming.
And to Yurema, for closing the circle of the
Perez–Hinojosa clan.

Acknowledgments

Gracias to Papi, Mom, Bertha Elena, Raul, and Jorge for giving me life, love, and support and for letting me tell the cuentos I've told. I love you all. And to Dennis, Scott, Christen, Paula, and Marcel for being familia. For sisterhood and spirit and much more—thank you Sandy. To Ceci for twenty years of the strongest kind of friendship and cariño. Gracias to Ro, my Bronx girl whose lessons and power I cherish.

There are many amigos who inhabit my life (and this book) and fill me with joy—Rain in de Face, Graci, Victor, Nico, Erasmo, Mandalit, Franc, Guadalupe, Pedro Julio, Beatriz—and D.H.W. Andaye has always been my most beloved teacher of life. Maria Martin, Angie, and the Latino USA grupo showed the utmost of patience for putting up with my wild schedule and I will never forget that. Mil gracias to Gabby and Paty por el amor a mí familia y por ser grandes mujeres. To my querida reader Sara, my hermanita, and to Santiago, mi hermanito. Thank you, Dr. Mark, for being a friend I will always trust for so many things and thank you, Dr. Larry Levitan, for bringing new lives into this world. I couldn't have written this book if it weren't for the SIPA library cubicles at Columbia and for the Barnard office, thank you, Judith Shapiro. Susan Hans O'Connor made it all sing and Jill Bialosky moved me in the right direction, and John Jusino for catching all the little things. Mi tía Gloria, Maritere, mi tía Licha, Berta Alicia, and the bola de primos, tíos, tías, y abuelitos de la madre patria have always been at the heart of my Mexican soul. Thank you, Stuart and Mary Ellen, for watching out for me. For their support during the time of birthing babies and books I thank my jefes and jefas at CNN—Edith, Mary Ann, Nancy, Keith, David, Gail—and to Rose, for watching out for el duo dinámico, thank you. Gracias a las Lipsters, Las Chicas del Poder, for the hermandad. Janet Goldstein is the best editor a writer could ever want. Thank you for seeing this book even before I did. Susan Bergholz, you are the person most responsible for all of this. Gracias for believing in me more than I often have believed in myself. Eres una angelita.

And for Ingrid Washinawatock. En memoria. Your spirit lives on.

AUTHOR'S NOTE

In certain instances names and identities of specific individuals have been changed to protect their privacy.

CONTENTS

Raising Raul

Wanting It All

At thirty-three, I thought I was finally coming to terms with who I had become. A Latina gringa. This crazy mixture of Azteca-New Yorker-salsa-dancing, goddess-worshipping, hard-hitting journalist, Ivy League–educated, Chicago-raised, barrio-living woman. I often wondered what I would have been like as a born-and-raised-in-Mexico Latina. Traditional? Rebellious? Iconoclast? Nun? I would never know. What mattered was that I was making a life for myself that fit—though my own father still questioned himself every day about whether he had made the right decision in bringing his family to the United States.

But while Papi was missing Mexico I was missing something else.

Now I wanted to become a mom. And the most overused phrase of late-twentieth-century gringo-landia summed up my life at that moment. *I wanted it all.* Yes! I wanted it all—just like every other woman in gringo-landia.

Even though I grew up seeing myself as different from everyone around me, I suddenly realized that I wanted what everyone else had. I wanted to be a full, well-rounded, accomplished woman. And though I had achieved a lot in my life, I couldn't get away from the Mexican yardstick for measuring womanhood—becoming a mother.

For the past ten years, I had been climbing the proverbial modern woman's ladder. Get a college degree. Next. Do the career thing. Next. Meet the right man (finally!). Next. Time to become a mom—and a *real* woman. For me, it was not a matter of if I would have children. It was a matter of when.

Gérman, my wise husband, would always warn me, "You talk about having a baby as if it's just one more number you've got to fill on your life's scorecard. That's not what it's about."

"How can you think of me that way?" I would answer him in my most dramatic horrified-face look. "I want to be an earth mamá, not a score-keeper!"

"La vida is not about keeping a tally. You better be ready for what you are asking for. Having children is not easy," Gérman would say, shaking his head.

I figured he was talking about raising kids or birthing babies. I knew that would be hard, but it didn't overwhelm me. But what I never imagined was that *conceiving* kids could be so difficult.

I thought I was ready to be a mamá because I was convinced I was *already* a woman. I never considered that my secret little life scorecard was about to get scribbled on and trampled upon and thrown in the trash. I had no inkling that I was about to embark on a journey of becoming a woman like the women I had always admired. Women who had stories to tell, mujeres que habían sufrido y triunfado, women who had suffered and triumphed. Women who had balls, or rather, ovaries. *Big* ovaries.

Gérman was the love of my life, a gorgeous Afro-Taino from the Dominican Republic. I fell truly in love with him when I saw his paintings that warm spring day back in 1988 when I walked up four flights of that awful pee-in-the-hallways-smelling building and opened the door to his apartment and saw the magic of the Caribbean hanging on the walls. He was living in a tenement in the Dominican barrio of New York so he could save money and paint. But as soon as I saw the mystery and innocence he was able to capture on the canvas (a kind of Caribbean Chagall, I thought to myself), I ran straight out of his apartment and down the four flights of stairs and didn't answer his phone calls for two years. I was terrified of my emotions, scared to feel so out of control, worried that this might be the real thing. And since I had never before had the real thing, I didn't know if now I wanted it.

In my mind, I excused my running away by blaming it on something else.

How could I fall in love with this stunning man, with long, black curls, who was an artist and a *Dominican?* I convinced myself that these were the three biggest strikes against him—gorgeous, artist, Dominican. No way! I was sure he had to be a mujeriego, a womanizer. I chose to believe everything that my New York Latina hermanas had said to me about Dominican men. "They are more machos than Mexicanos," they wound rant. "Stay away from them!" And so I did.

Thank god Gérman was as stubborn as they come. He never gave up hope that one day I would at least speak to him again and become if not his lover, then at least his friend. Two years later, he showed up at a Village Gate salsa-meets-jazz concert and saw me sway my caderas the way my Puerto Rican and Dominican girlfriends had taught me—with measured but potent moves that I hoped expressed mysterious sensuality. Gérman came and stood next to me on the dance floor until I literally bumped into him. I then had no excuse for saying no when he asked me to dance. When he wrapped his arms around my waist and pressed his hips against mine, I trembled and felt my heart fall straight from my chest into the cradle of the most intimate part of my body. I accidentally brushed my hand against his chest and I shuddered to recollect myself. I felt something like a slab of cement, and then I asked, innocently, "Is that a book in your shirt pocket?" and he said, "No, that's just me." Dios mío! A flesh-and-blood Adonis in my midst (not like the flabby guys I had been with before). I just about melted right there and then. I spent the next hours on the dance floor grilling him, asking a slew of rapid-fire questions—my public radio experience had me well trained in news conferences—about his lifestyle and what he did and who he knew, who had his girlfriends been and what his dreams were. In between salsa moves and Dizzy on the trumpet, he answered my interrogation with the kind of patience I had never experienced in a man. And when later he looked me in the eyes and asked if he could take care of *me* (I never knew relationships like that existed in real life), well, that was it. We were married a year later in 105 degree heat in Central Park, two blocks away from where we live now.

I was thirty when we got married, una vieja, an old woman, according to all my Mexican cousins. I didn't care what they thought. I was just so elated to have finally found the man I had been asking for since I was old enough to dream about men and marriage. For me, that started when I was about six. It's all I saw around me. Parejas. Couples. Moms and Dads who looked as if they had been together forever and who would stay together forever as well. Y nada más.

I had dreamt about a man who would take care of me and love me and hug me and kiss me and tell me he loved me more than anything else in the world. I wanted a man who would stay by my side forever and never leave me. Just as I saw with my parents and all of my tías and tíos and grandparents. (Of course, I was too young to realize that my grandfather *had* left my abuela for another woman years before I was even born. My family was good at keeping secrets. Grandpa was always around my grandmother during the day, so it never occurred to me to ask where he went to *sleep* at night.)

Gérman and I spent the first years of our life together in full urban bliss. We were living in the most exciting city in the world and each working hard on our careers, I as a journalist, he as a painter. I had started out in 1985 as a production assistant at National Public Radio in Washington, D.C., with the dream that I would one day become a reporter. After five years and a lot of hard work, climbing up the career ladder and paying my dues, my dream had come true and I was finally working as a reporter for NPR in New York. I became a journalist because I wanted to tell stories about the America that I had grown up in but that I never saw in the media. I wanted to tell untold stories about real people in the neighborhoods that many journalists never ventured into. I wanted to tell stories that meant something, that would make people feel things deeply. In my college philosophy classes I had labeled myself an existentialist. As a journalist, I finally had a way to give my angst an expression. I wanted to find the humanity in all kinds of people—whether they were gang members, skinheads, teenage moms, new immigrants, battered women, or artists and writers. I took this phrase very much to heart: *I wanted to give voice to the voiceless.*

And Gérman wanted to bring beauty into the world because he had grown up seeing so much sadness. This was his way of communicating humanity and hope. He had been raised in poverty in the Dominican Republic, abused by his father. As a teenager he had seen people shot for no reason other than protesting against a miserable minimum wage. He went to college and worked as an architect designing housing for the poor and the mentally ill. He rebelled against his parents, who had wanted him to become an engineer. Then for several years he worked as a filmmaker and photographer, but he knew there was something else he was meant to do with his life. He sold everything he had, came to New York, and committed himself to paint the poetry of life.

During those first years of our marriage, as I struggled to define my voice as an urban affairs reporter, I would come home from interviewing kids who had shot other kids with machine guns or who were serving time and I would see cream-colored canvases transformed into art so beautiful that there were no words to describe what it did to my soul. The beauty he captured fed my heart and his mindful words and strong arms made me feel safe enough to go back out on the street and find the humanity that I knew was there but was so often buried in sadness or violence.

We also had a great time just living life and adoring each other, making passionate love, sleeping late, going out to see music and theater and movies, and because we both lived far from our familias, we made it a point to create a sense of community with our friends. We had huge parties with two hundred people crammed into our small two-bedroom loft, and when no more could squeeze in, we'd open up the roof and everyone would mingle under the stars and the skyrises. There were people dancing and playing drums and music until five in the morning, and then a bunch of us would go to Chinatown for dim sum to cut the cruda, the hangover. We traveled to Mexico and the D.R. (short for the Dominican Republic) and saw family and friends and bought lots of masks and artesanía for our apartment. We transformed our space into a wildly colorful combination of Frida Kahlo's studio and an island paradise. There were Mexican-blue walls with rows of masks, altars with flowers and fruits and goblets of water on white lace, La Virgen de Guadalupe candles, Ché ashtrays from Cuba, Mayan sculptures, African drums, Yemanya and Oshun santos, and the smell of yucca, tortillas, cilantro, queso frito, and chile. Our house was our first Domini-Mex production. People would come over and say they couldn't believe they were in New York City. And I would say, "This *is* New York City. This is the future!"

Gérman and I knew that at some point we would have another major Domini-Mex production. A child. But we didn't talk about it much. We just knew it wasn't time. Yet.

Since I was about seventeen I had been doing mental calculations of when would be the best time to have children. I started thinking about this at seventeen because that was how old my mother was when she got married, so my life was always measured against her time line: If mom had my older sister when she was eighteen, and she was done having children by the time she was twenty-five, well, then, I guess I could start having my kids when I turned twenty-five. That felt about right. It was a completely arbitrary process. But twenty-five sounded like a good solid number. Of course, as I got closer to twenty-five, my personal baby-deadline began to extend itself. Okay, twenty-eight sounds like a better age to have kids. Twenty-five was too young. Definitely. Soon, thirty began to sound like a good round number. But when I was just getting married at thirty I realized I needed some more time. So the next best number to thirty was, of course, thirty-three. El año de Cristo, when he died on the cross. Not that I am all that religious, in the strict Catholic sense, but thirty-three is one of those numbers that I had been hearing about since I was a little girl. El año de Cristo, the age of Christ, I often heard my family in Mexico remark. Thirty-three had a nice ring to it. So, thirty-three it was. That was the cutoff. And it would work perfectly because I would have my first at thirty-three, my second at thirty-five, and my third at thirty-seven. Perfect! My Latina self was pleased that I would finally assume this predestined role in life, and my gringa self was happy because I had it all figured out—timed out even to the month that I wanted to get pregnant. September. That way my first baby would be born in June/July, a Cancer, just like my sister and me.

Way back when, during the days when a child was just a figment of my imagination, I used to dream about giving birth in my homeland, en la madre patria. My children, I had decided, were going to be *born in Mexico,* just as I was. I had it all planned out. I would leave the country two months before my due date and I would hang out in Mexico City, and I would go to the same hospital where I was born and deliver my baby there. Yes, all of my children would be born in Mexico. Just like my brothers and sister and me. My children would be able to carry around their green Mexican passports and when arriving in this country, could stand proudly in the line that says FOREIGNERS. They would always know what their roots were and if they ever forgot they could go and pull out their passports from the bottom of a drawer and read the small print over and over again, "*La persona que tiene este pasaporte es de nacionalidad Mexicana—The person who holds this passport is a Mexican citizen*—just as I used to do as a child growing up in Chicago.

I was convinced that I would be helping my children so much by doing this. They would not be confused about who they were. They would be *Mexicanos!* Simple as that. Their identity issues would be solved.

Of course, when I married my Dominican husband it complicated things a little bit, but not to worry. After some thought I had recalculated everything—I would alternate countries. I would give birth to one child in Mexico, one in the Dominican Republic, one in Mexico, and maybe even one more in the D.R. Perfect!

The day I let my husband in on my little plan he looked at me and said, unequivocally, "*Tú estás loca.*"

I was devastated!

The Latina part of me (corazón, emoción) started whimpering, crushed that I might not be able to guarantee getting my babies the *written documentation* (their passports and birth certificates) that would no doubt clear up any of their future questions about where they came from and, as a result, who they were. The gringa part of me (order and control) just couldn't believe that my premeditated plans for life were being disrupted. And by the way, wasn't this a feminist issue? Women have a right to control their bodies and to control . . . what country their babies are born in, right?

Gérman, in his unflinching, self-assured way, just watched me as I went through my mental and emotional gymnastics. And then, with one simple statement he tore down everything that I had built up in my prefabricated identity-problems-solved plan.

"Maria," he said to me calmly, "nosotros *somos* Americanos! And our children will be Americans, too. This *is* our home. We aren't going *back* to anywhere! This *is* our country, too!

"And besides," he said, adding a little reality check, "remember Altagracia's sister who just died in the D.R.? She died after she gave birth to her daughter because of an infection she developed in the hospital when the power went down in the middle of her cesarean. I am not going to lose you just so you can give this child a couple of ridiculous pieces of paper as if this would somehow assure that he or she will not be confused about his or her *roots*. Estás loca, mi amor, pero te adoro. Our children will be born here in Nueva York and they'll be New York Latinos or whatever else you want to call them."

And just as my father used to say when he had decided that a discussion was over, Gérman let it be known that, no hay nada más que discutir. There is nothing left to talk about. No Dominican- or Mexican-born babies in this family. They will be Norte Americanos! Punto. End of discussion. Se acabó. Finished.

For a minute I had this conversation with myself as I pouted, sitting cross-legged on the edge of our bed: *This* is what you get for marrying a Latino. Their machismo is so imbedded that they think they can arbitrarily determine when a conversation is over. It's why I hated having disagreements with Papi. It was so frustrating when he would say "se acabó" and I would feel like a mute child. I would sit there and mope over whatever I was being deprived of—like the time with that sleep-over party (where the plan was to let the boys come by . . .). But then I remembered how often Papi was right and how much I really didn't want to go to that sleep-over anyway because how was I going to say no to those boys. So, maybe Gérman was right, too. It really is crazy to fly in an airplane eight months pregnant. Maybe it really isn't such a smart idea after all. Maybe I should accept that I *am* an Americana after all and stop fighting this secret internal identity battle. I *hate* it when I give in to *se acabó*. I realized I had a lot of rethinking to do. And not just about where I would give birth to my children.

Becoming a mom was the last thing on my mind the night I got a phone call from the office saying the Crown Heights section of Brooklyn was exploding in anger and I was assigned to get out there as fast as I could to cover the story. That was the night a young African American, Gavin Cato, was killed in a car accident involving Hasidic Jews, and Crown Heights had become the scene of furious protests. It was the most challenging "breaking news" reporting I had had to do, and I was anxious—yet in that strange reporter-way, I was exhilarated, too. I spent one night during the ensuing riots inside a Hasidic community center, crouching underneath windows, talking to men and women as they looked out onto their streets in horror, capturing on tape their fear and shock that even though this was modern-day America, they still felt they were being attacked because of their religion. The next night I was out on the street, in the middle of swarms of bitter young Black men upset because a child had been killed, taking out their rage about their lack of representation in any halls of power against the people with whom they shared their same neighborhood. I found myself in the middle of all of this. I was being threatened and pushed around by the protesters who saw the media as the enemy, getting hassled by the police for trying to do my job, hissed at by teenage Hasidic boys, and for the first time, receiving many nasty letters at the office from listeners who accused me of being either anti-Semitic or anti-Black. And Gérman was at home worried sick about me, cursing my bosses for sending me out there in the first place. It was bad. Whatever plans I had about motherhood went out the window—this was a story that was gripping my life, and my career was in full throttle. I was hoping that my coverage of this story would finally convince my bosses that I could cover breaking news and cover it well. This story might solidify my goal of being promoted to correspondent. Even though I had won several awards for my feature reporting, I still felt I had to jump through hoops to prove myself to some of my impossible-to-please bosses.

After several weeks of working on the Crown Heights story, the craziness finally died down. A couple of weeks later I went back to the neighborhood to do a story about how families, both Hasidic and African American, were trying to pick up the pieces and re-create a sense of community from the remnants of violence.

While I was researching the story I met Rebecca. Soft-spoken with soothing light-brown eyes, Rebecca lived in Crown Heights with her eleven children and her husband. I had never been inside a Hasidic home, so when I rang her doorbell I wasn't sure what to expect.

I walked inside and Rebecca gave me a warm greeting, holding my hand tightly as she introduced herself. Her home looked just like ours did when we were growing up in Chicago. Children everywhere, commotion, toys, kids' art hanging up on the refrigerator. The only difference was that instead of four kids as in my family, here there were eleven, ranging from two to fifteen years old. And there were lots of photos of Rabbi Menachem Shneerson, the man who this Hasidic sect believed was the saviour.

We sat down in her cozy living room and nestled into a soft, toffee-colored couch. She held her youngest in her arms and stroked his hair softly as we spoke. There was a motherly calmness about her, and I wanted to lay my head down in her lap, too. But I kept my reporter's distance while longing inside for the warmth Rebecca had created in her home.

As more of her children came home from school (one after another after another after another), they would plop their heavy backpacks on the floor and throw themselves into her arms. She would kiss them several times, hug them, and look deeply into their eyes, giving them affection and security, letting them know that she was right there with them—that nothing in this world was more important than them at that precise moment in time.

After our "work" talk was over, what had begun as a straight reporter's grill had now become a conversation between women. Rebecca showed me a picture of her husband. I showed her one of mine. I asked her how she did it, with eleven children, looking so absolutely composed and peaceful. "In our belief, children are the center of our world. They bring us peace, they bring us all the joy we need to live," she said, sitting her two-year-old on her lap. "Isn't it the same for you?" she asked quietly.

"Yes," I said, nodding my head slowly, thinking about all of the Catholicism that I had long since abandoned—thinking about my grandmother who had five children, my aunt who had seven, my great-grandmother who had ten, and Mom who had four.

"So you're planning on having children?" she asked, still stroking her youngest son's blond hair.

"Oh sure, we're thinking about it," I said. And then there was quiet.

"I don't mean to be rude, Maria," Rebecca said, finally breaking the silence, and suddenly I felt a little anxious, as if the visible difference between us was about to shatter the cozy space we had created, like a lightening bolt splitting a tree right down the middle. She continued. "But what are you waiting for?"

I was silenced. No one had ever asked me this so directly. I thought hard. And I realized there really was no good answer, there was no good reason. My career, my time, the lack-of-money thing—none of that could really be more important than creating a family with the man whom I loved more than anyone else in the world. It was as if I had a revelation.

Right then and there I suddenly realized, *It's time for me to have a baby.*

That evening back at home, I told Gérman what had happened and hinted that I was getting closer to making the decision about having a child. Obviously he was a bit in shock that I would come home from working on my Crown Heights story with this announcement. "You left the house this morning and everything was fine. And now you come home with this?" he laughed. "We will know when the time is right, Malu," he said, hugging me. "You don't have to rely on some stranger to let you know that."

But the procreation seed had been planted and I started making my prepregnancy calculations, figuring out when I would have to get pregnant to have a Cancer baby. No matter how many times Gérman told me that life was unplannable, I couldn't stop making to-do lists. So I just put "get pregnant" on my to-do list for that year.

I hadn't told anyone in my family about my pregnancy plan. I hadn't told my mom who was a social worker or my dad who was a research scientist. Not my sister, Bertha Elena, who taught special education and lived in a Chicago suburb with her husband and two kids. I hadn't told Jorge, my brother who was living in Tijuana doing human rights and cultural work, or my other brother, Raul, who was a professor at UCLA. I hadn't even told my two dearest friends—Ceci, my New Jersey–raised, Argentinian-born journalist friend who was now living in Chicago with her new husband; or Sandy, the woman I call my Amazon sistah, who was a media executive in D.C. And I hadn't told Ro, my only real New Yawker–Puerto Rican friend, also a journalist.

The only people I did tell were Graci and Victor, our close friends and surrogate parents. The Penchas had left Buenos Aires at the height of the military dictatorship because although they were both in the medical field, they had also been activists on their university campus. If Victor had left the country only one day later, he might not have lived. He would have been one more desaparecido.

Victor and Graci were hooked up. I mean, they were hip enough to hang out with but old enough to have a "grown-up lifestyle." They had a fabulous apartment in New York, and they had recently bought a big red cottage in Bethlehem, Connecticut. Most weekends they would invite lots of people and everyone would camp out on the floors and drink wine with soda water—a lo Argentino—and make huge asados, grilling great big slabs of meat. Everyone would lounge around talking about politics, from New York to Nicaragua to Buenos Aires to the barrio. Late at night when the rest of Bethlehem was quiet, Gérman would take out his guitar and we'd sit on the outdoor deck and sing "Gracias a la Vida" or some Silvio Rodríguez nueva trova song, and the sounds of Spanish would echo across the lake and over the cornfields of their neighbors. In the mornings, everyone would drink café con leche and eat toast with dulce de leche and read the Sunday *New York Times* with Bach playing in the background. Graci and Victor had named their house in Connecticut "Rayuela," after the book by Julio Cortázar, and Graci would always joke about how we were integrating Bethlehem.

Gérman and I looked up to los Penchas for guidance and as role models. And I flattered myself to think that their two kids, who were finishing college and starting their own careers, looked up to Gérman and me as their role models.

So one lazy afternoon at the end of July, while Graci and I were sitting under the sun drinking Argentinian maté, I told her that we were planning on "doing it."

"Les vamos a decir ciao a los condones," I said as I sipped through the silver straw, "Bye, bye al látex!"

"No me digas, ché!" she said in her elegant porteño accent. "That's fabulous!"

"Yeah, but I don't think we'll start trying until September. I want to have a Cancer baby. If I time it right maybe it'll be born on my birthday. How cool!"

I now think Graci must have been laughing inside, listening to me talk this way.

"Pues sí. I figure I'll get pregnant in September and we'll take a vacation in December and then I'll have all of spring to get ready. I'm so excited."

"Ché, you never know if you'll get pregnant just like that. You know it could take a few tries. Why don't you start trying now? What's the worst that can happen? Either you'll get pregnant or at least you'll have a lot of fun trying! Making love to make a baby is exquisito—exquisite. Go ahead and start and have a good time."

Why not? I thought. So what if the baby turns out to be a Gemini and not a Cancer? Ceci was a Gemini, so was my father, and so was an ex-lover . . . oh, well, two out of three ain't bad. Geminis are intense albeit divided figures. Cancers were delectably emotional and loved to mother. I figured either one of those signs would be good. So sure, we could start tonight, I convinced myself. It's just one month earlier than I had figured. I could fudge my life schedule a little bit. . . .

And so we said adiós to the Trojans and just as I had planned, I got pregnant that very first time we tried. My two selves were entirely happy, entirely entrelazados, intertwined. I was in control, everything was on schedule, and I was finally going to come into my *madre* self. My Latina mothering instinct (which I had rarely, if ever, felt) would surely be born right alongside my child.

Life was fabuloso.

But as salsero Rubén Blades sings, la vida te da sorpresas, sorpresas te da la vida, ay Dios. Life gives you surprises. And my god, I never expected this one. I had been given a gift and it was about to be taken away, and all of my gringa calculating and all of my Latina prayers were not going to be able to save me from this life lesson, this horrible, horrifying, painful life lesson.

Paying My Debt

I found out about that first pregnancy at the end of steamy August when I looked at my calendar and realized, joyfully, that I was late.

First one day, then two days, then three days went by and no sign of my period. I had a glib self-confidence. It was just me and my body walking around with this little secret. I hadn't even told Gérman. I was allowing myself this time to "get in touch with my feelings" as a future mother. My predestined role in life was finally in progress.

But along with the predictable gushiness, I also felt a little catty. Not that anyone else cared. I mean, they didn't even know I was pregnant so how could they? I remember feeling like a girl who had just gotten a new doll and was anxious to get to school to show it off and rub it in the other girls' faces and then say, "You can't touch it! It's mine!" I flashed back to a memory of myself as a scrawny high school senior standing in line at the cafeteria after just coming back from Mexico where I had finally "done it" and was itching to tell all of my girlfriends that I, too, was no longer a virgin. Hell, wasn't peer pressure supposed to lessen after adolescence? But at thirty-three I was a victim of the peer pressure to get pregnant and now that I was, I wanted to show off. I wanted to prove to everyone that I had "done it." I was so happy that now no one would ever ask me again in that judgmental tone we've all heard that follows that question: "So, when are *you* going to have kids?" Now I could finally say, "I'm pregnant!" End of discussion.

I kept my excitement subdued and silent. I immersed myself in a story I was working on that was more depressing than hopeful. I had spent several days in the Pennsylvania countryside hanging out with skinheads. Even though I had interviewed gang members and had been in the middle of riots, this was the first time in my career that I was really and truly scared. (Well, except for the time in El Salvador during a guerrilla offensive when a huge military helicopter was hovering above our heads and a peasant told us that those were the same helicopters that had been shooting machine guns on their houses.) I interviewed a muscle-man skinhead who had a tattoo of Hitler on his neck. The skinhead told me that because he thought I was a nice person—even though I was a Mexican—he was going to give me a piece of friendly advice. "You should leave the country now. You never know when the race war is going to explode," he said nonchalantly.

Back in the office in my typical fashion, I spent days consumed with the piece and agonizing over my script. The day I finished, a week after my missed period, I left work and on my way home from the subway stopped at the drugstore and bought a pregnancy test.

"Nineteen ninety-five?" I gawked when the woman rang it up. But then I remembered I was supposed to be happy, so I plastered a smile on my face and walked home.

I skipped up the five flights to our apartment, slipped into the john, and, of course, peed all over my hand—but luckily, just enough on the test stick, and then waited the magic few minutes, never taking my eyes off the plastic window. Finally, the little pink line appeared and I ran up to Gérman, kissed him lusciously on the lips, and said, "Estamos embarazados! We're pregnant!"

Gérman was joyful but subdued. Those were the times when I really had trouble with his stoicism, when the secure rootedness that I loved about him drove me crazy.

He gave me a tight hug and said, "Felicidades, mamita! I am so happy! I love you."

I wanted him to run out with me and buy maternity clothes right then and there. I wanted him to stop painting and start redecorating the second bedroom. I wanted to talk about nothing else except the pregnancy for the next twenty-four hours.

Gérman wanted to keep on living life. Normally. From his point of view, though this was a gift from the Gods, it wasn't as if we had just won a twenty-million-dollar lottery. This was a normal, natural part of life.

So I, of course, picked up my trusty telephone and spent the weekend dialing furiously and began telling everyone. I called Mom and Dad first.

"Ay, qué bueno, *mi'jita!* Ay, qué lindo," sang my mom into the phone. And then my dad said flatly, "Estás segura? Are you sure? Did you do the test right? Have you seen the doctor? You better make an appointment right away. Is your insurance in order?"

Papi was great at bringing me down from my highs. He was so serious all the time. And his being a doctor and medical researcher meant that anything having to do with health immediately meant you had to go to the hospital, see a specialist, have tests done. Natural childbirth, natural medicine, natural anything—no way! Medical professionals were the only ones who could be trusted. Not those over-the-counter plastic tests they sell nowadays.

I barked at him, "Why can't you just be happy, Papi, instead of worrying already? Why can't you just congratulate me y ya?"

I don't even know why I asked. His reaction reminded me of that day four years earlier when, on a visit to Mexico, I announced to Papi that Gérman and I were going to get married. Granted, he had only met Gérman three days before, and all he knew about him was that he was an artist with long hair who came from one of the islands in the Caribbean where they speak, as Papi said, "broken Spanish." On that day, Papi was so floored by our announcement that all he could say was that he didn't think he was going to be able to make it to the wedding because he had a conference to go to on the planned date. I stormed out of the room and we flew back to New York. A day later, after my mother, sister, and brother jumped all over him, he called me up to apologize.

Anyway, unlike Gérman, who saw my pregnancy as the most natural of things, I knew for my father it was a "medical condition." And that meant doctors had to be involved sooner rather than later.

When I next called Bertha Elena, my sister, she started crying and so did I. We both knew that this change in my life was going to bring us close once again, and I think we were both equally happy about that. For many years now, my brothers and I had distanced ourselves from Bertha Elena because she had married a gringo and moved out to the suburbs, and we were upset by how she had been transformed from this gung-ho anthropologist hippy living in a Central American jungle excavating ruins to a totally traditional American wife with two kids, a dog, and two cars in the garage, including a minivan and a truck. We all felt she had turned her back on her roots. And she hadn't even taught her children Spanish. Plus she had given them English names. My brothers and I were so hard on her (as if we had the right to think of ourselves as more Latino than she). After I had gotten married I realized how ridiculous I had been acting and I softened on my sister. I apologized for isolating her in the past and started to seek her out more for advice. I was the youngest child and she the eldest, and Bertha Elena had been my idol. Now finally we were seeing each other as equals, and becoming a mother could only solidify my relationship with her.

My brothers were happy when I called to tell them about the pregnancy, but I think deep inside they felt as if they were going to lose their other sister to mommyhood. I would have less time to talk work and politics and less time to party with them. I think they saw it more as their loss.

By Saturday afternoon, I had been on the phone for hours and Gérman told me I should stop talking and start thinking about putting some food in my stomach. We walked over to Broadway and went to the local Italian place where the waiters are all Mexicanos. I was friends with most of them. And so, of course, I told them the good news.

The next morning when I woke up I kissed Gérman and climbed down the loft bed and made him some café con leche and then I picked up right where I had left off. I called Sandy, my friend in D.C., and she was elated. Then I called Ceci, who was also ecstatic but just a bit distant. Our lives had been so parallel—graduating college at the same time, starting our careers at the same time—but Ceci had just gotten married and babies weren't in the picture yet. I think we were both concerned that this might let us drift apart.

Gérman got up and showered, turned on some music, threw on his shorts and sleeveless T-shirt, and started painting. He was working on this gorgeous and mystical blue piece with an adorable horned creature who was floating on the ocean dragging a little island with a palm tree. In between my personal-pregnancy-phone-tree calls, I would take a break and watch him paint for a few minutes while I rested my voice.

I wanted everyone who was close to me to know that I had finally reached this milestone. Even though I knew the conventional wisdom was to wait for the first trimester to end, I thought it would jinx the pregnancy to treat it as a secret. Keeping quiet was simply not part of my plan.

I called Victor and Graci and then Ro (who was ecstatic that now I could join her and her newborn and be part of the mommy club), and before the day was over I squeezed in even some more calls to a few other girlfriends, most of whom were single and in their late thirties. I sensed happiness from them but their responses were tinged with something else—a kind of selfish self-protection and envy. I could sense a turning point in our friendships that only time would help sort out.

On Monday morning, I followed Papi's advice and made an appointment to see the doctor.

Because of some of my medical history my gynecologist thought it would be good to get a sonogram, which was easy to do right in her office. So there I was with my feet hooked into those icy stirrups and my knees holding up that hideous white paper gown that never drapes over you but instead falls stiffly against the most intimate parts of your body.

But I was an elated mother-to-be, so not the stirrups or the paper covering or the strange machine that looked like a tiny TV set was going to bother me. No, the thing that was going to bother me the most was the sonogram technician who was as icy as the foot holders. You know what I mean: She barely said hello, and then just flicked off the lights, put a plastic sheath and some goop on the dildolike protrusion that was connected to the sonogram machine, and told me to lay on my back and relax. Yeah, right.

Not a word from her until she mumbled, "So how far along are you supposed to be?"

"Well, I know I got pregnant on such and such a date so I know I am about three weeks, but the way you doctors measure it I guess that means I am really five weeks pregnant," I said, feeling so proud because I could remember the exact day and time that this miracle occurred.

"Hmmmmmmm," was all she said. "Are you sure?" And all during this she kept prodding and pushing inside of me while clicking the machine and peering into the TV set as if I wasn't even there.

I grew anxious. "Yes, I am sure. What's wrong?"

"Well, you look a little bit small. According to our computer, your embryonic sac should be just a little bit bigger to conform to the number of days of your pregnancy."

What?! Never in my life had I heard that they had measurements for the exact size an embryonic sac should be. I didn't realize, nor could I believe, that something like this could be measured so perfectly or that you had to conform to some kind of size requirement. It reminded me of all the seemingly millions of times when I was growing up when I never quite measured up: I was always the smallest in my class, always the last one to get picked for volleyball and basketball, always the shortest, the tiniest, the weakest. There was only one time when there was a smaller kid in my class and that was when a Japanese girl moved into the neighborhood when I was nine years old. I felt bad for her but I finally had moved up in the world. Although she and I became instant friends (we always stood together in our recess lines), she moved away almost as quickly as she arrived, and it was Maria the shorty all over again.

And I knew why I was so small. It was because I was a Mexican. Mexican's had indigenous roots, was what my mother always used to say. "Look at the size of the doorways that the Aztecs and Mayans built for their pyramids," she would point out. But after my mom had given me the native-roots lecture she would always say, "Pero mi'jita, don't worry, your growing spurt just hasn't started yet." (I remember being eighteen and she was still talking about the famoso growing spurt that hadn't started.)

So there I was again, this time as an adult, being told that I was too small—that I just didn't conform to the standards of mainstream-American-baby-production-quality-and-size specifications.

I was now panicked and angry and I knew exactly what I wanted to say to this technician. I had it on the tip of my tongue, but there I was in a doctor's office feeling completely powerless, voiceless, and just plain stupid. The educated, professional, hard-hitting journalist had become, simply, an unquestioning patient.

So I took a deep breath and asked, "What does it mean?"

"Oh, probably nothing," she answered, now happy and smiling. "Go ahead and get dressed, and I will pass this on to your doctor," she said, starting to hum a tune to herself. And so, I started doing that. But she stayed in the room and while she was cleaning up her equipment, the previously icy woman became a fountain of conversation even though now I wasn't asking any questions.

"It will probably be nothing," she said, "the fact that your sac is a little small. And it is still too early for a heartbeat. But you know the saddest thing happened to me the other day with a patient. This other woman, who was a little old for her first pregnancy, had a small sac, too, and everything was okay and then when she came in for a sonogram at nine weeks . . . well, can you believe that the sac was not only small but that it was empty! It's called blighted ovum, and what happens is that there is a sac and there is a pregnancy but instead of cells multiplying to form an embryo the cells are just reproducing into nothing but a mass of empty cells. There is just nothing there. Anyway, they had to perform an abortion on her that same day. Poor lady, she really felt like she was pregnant and everything, but the sac was empty. Too bad for her, huh? Anyway, I'll pass this on to your doctor. Have a nice day and see you next time, dear."

Dear? Who is she calling "dear"? I wanted to kick her in the ovaries but she left me standing there with my mouth wide open and my pants hanging on my knees just like a good little Mexican girl who felt too small to talk.

My doctor tried to comfort me and said it was too soon to tell anything, but what I really wanted to do was sue her office for the emotional roller coaster they had put me on. My husband talked me out of it and instead we found a new doctor. He was a friend of Victor's from the same hospital where he worked, and Victor said he was very nice and a great doctor and so I went in a week later to meet him for my first appointment.

When I walked into his Park Avenue office for my first appointment, I was uncomfortable with my own un-PC reaction. To my surprise there were three Hasidic couples sitting in the waiting room. (I wondered if this was some kind of Crown Heights/Rebecca sign.) Hasidic women always seemed so different from me and yet here we were all women in the same predicament, looking and feeling concerned, nauseated, bloated, tired, and ecstatic all at the same time.

I told this new doctor that because my husband was out of town I was not interested in having any sonograms until he came back. (Gérman had gone to the Dominican Republic, where he had an upcoming show.) The doctor told me everything appeared to be okay for my pregnancy but that I should take a progesterone supplement just to make sure the embryo implants. I agreed, but after three days I decided to follow my natural mama's instinct and since I felt perfectly pregnant, I got rid of the medicine. A week later I arranged for a few weeks off. I got on a plane and went to visit my husband in Santo Domingo. I knew I felt pregnant and I knew that both my Latina and gringa selves felt both in control and emotionally centered. So I gave into my Latina self and repeated those words that I so often cringed at when I heard them coming out of the mouths of women who acted as if they could control nothing in their lives. Here I was saying the same thing. *Que sea lo que Dios mande.* This is in God's hands; or, more literally, It will be whatever God orders. Of course, "Dios" for me is a woman—or, rather, many women—La Virgen de Guadalupe; Oshun, the Yoruba goddess of sensuality and fertility; and Yemanya, the goddess of the oceans. So, now I was the one throwing up my arms and saying que sea lo que la Diosa manda. I got on the plane and went off to paradise to meet my husband.

In the Dominican Republic, Gérman's friends were all having babies. I wanted to be part of the club so I told them about my pregnancy. Even though Gérman's women friends were really sweet to me, there was no doubt that I was a mainland outsider who had stolen one of the island's most-sought-after single men. Informing them I was carrying his child was a sure way to let them all know that this relationship was for good. It also showed that I was being una buena mujer, bearing his children. I couldn't believe I was having such medieval, territorial, machista sentiments. But there I was. I blamed it on the pregnancy hormones.

When I came back after two weeks I was ten weeks pregnant and feeling fine. A week later Gérman returned. So I was eleven weeks pregnant when we went to the doctor to have the sonogram and to hear the heartbeat of this tiny baby I was carrying inside of me, making my belly protrude just a bit. I was nervous, although I kept telling myself que todo iba salir bien, that everything was going to be fine. Inside the doctor's office, I held my husband's and the Russian nurse's hands. Jenya was a warm, round woman with red-orange hair, and we had taken a liking to each other. Jenya was a nurse, but she was also like a mother, unafraid to touch you, hug you, or give you a kiss. Good qualities for a nurse to have, I thought.

So I held both of their hands tight and the doctor turned off the lights and flipped on the sonogram monitor. For some reason I was scared to look for myself so I turned my head and stared into my husband's eyes to watch his reaction. After a few seconds of silence while the doctor moved the sonogram stick around my belly, I saw Gérman's face suddenly lose all of the electricity it had been glowing with up until then.

"I'm sorry, Maria," the doctor said quietly. "There is no heartbeat. There is no baby."

I closed my eyes and felt myself go into a space I had never been before. A place where there was nothing, just darkness and silence, a place where I was alone and falling quickly, down a deep, dark ditch. I opened my eyes, calmed my dizziness even though I was still lying down, and then turned my head and looked at the monitor myself. And there it was. Nothingness embodied. A little round sac that was inside of me but empty, filled with nothing. Empty and black. Empty of life. It was a blighted ovum.

I felt as if I lost something precious and innocent right then, on that doctor's table, lying on the sheet of white paper. And although my husband was right there beside me, I felt completely alone, because the baby that was supposed to be a part of me had deserted me. I was breeding nothingness. I was bloated and pregnant with a mass of cells. And no one else was crying in that room except the woman who had once again become that little Mexican girl who never quite measured up. So being that good little girl I sucked back my tears, sucked them in deep, deep into my womb of nothingness. I had failed at this thing that I had always been told I would be, a mamá.

To make things even worse, that evening I had to do a TV show. For the past two years I had been hosting a half-hour program about Latinos on one of the local networks, and that night I was scheduled to do an interview with then New York City mayor David Dinkins. There was no way I could cancel. We had been trying to get him on my show for two months. On the way back home from the doctor's office, I sat in the car weeping, wondering how it could be possible that I could be sitting there in the front seat, feeling pregnant, and yet carrying nothing inside of me but a bunch of cells. And in low groans I cried out a throaty *no, please,* no. Why me?

A few hours and two coats of makeup later, I interviewed the mayor in the TV studio and for thirty minutes pressed him on what he, as an African American mayor, had done and would do for New York's Latino community. All that mattered at that moment was being able to juggle the racial politics of the city and stand up to the mayor with quick follow-up questions. I knew many people would be watching this interview and that it wasn't only the mayor who was going to be judged. People were going to be rating me too. I put all of my emotions into a well-sealed box behind my heart and went into performance mode. No one suspected anything.

At home, hours later, in the middle of the night, I began to miscarry. I paced the length of our living room for hours and bled and bled and held the womb that was plunging my body into pain. Even though I felt terribly lonely, I let Gérman sleep. What could he do for me now? I felt like this was something I could do only on my own, a hurt that was profoundly intimate. So I muffled my tears and paced. Finally, the sun came up, and even though I had been carrying something empty inside of me, I still kept bleeding. The doctor said it was an emergency. We went down to his office and he performed a D & C on me. (Hell, in reality, it was an abortion.) Back at home, at the end of the day, I knew what empty really was. There was nothing left of me but my bones and my alma, a soul, as far as I was concerned, that felt as if it had just gone to the underworld.

Gérman didn't know what to do. He had never seen me so miserable and weak, and he was frightened. He had been through so much sadness in his life growing up as a lonely child, fearful of his father, that mourning as an adult was not a part of his psyche. But after years of therapy, I had come to a point in my life where I didn't want to hide my emotions, but rather "own" them, as my therapist Adaluz used to tell me. So I was owning my sadness. I lay in bed for three days, propped up by pillows, mindlessly channel surfing through Oprah, Sally, Cristina, and the news. I looked around my surroundings. Yes, I did indeed have much to be thankful for. I had a husband. We owned our little beautiful apartment. I had domestic conveniences, and a steady job. I had reached a level of comfort that before I only dreamt about. I had become a grown-up. In some ways. But those days after the miscarriage and the D & C, I spent a lot of time searching for answers.

In my emotional state of weakness, my years of Catholic training and sensibilities began to take over. Going over my loss again and again in my mind, I thought I now understood why this miscarriage had happened to me. This had happened because it was my castigo. I was being punished. And I knew what for. A little girl's voice said inside of me, sooner or later, you have to pay. And I was paying. Dearly.

It all began with an innocent mistake I made my third year of college. I ended up in school in New York, with my parents' worries and blessings, because I wanted to become an actress and a dancer. I had applied to Barnard because I knew it was a small women's college, it was in the Big Apple, and it was part of Columbia University (famous for its student activism in the late sixties and early seventies and I was in-trigued). But mostly, I arrived at Barnard because a friend of mine had gone there. So when I realized a few days after my arrival that this was a prestigious "seven sisters" school, I was taken aback. How was I going to survive in this place that had nothing to do with my life?

I had this grand scheme about studying full-time and going to theater auditions in my free time. But that dream evaporated after my first month in New York. I had *no* time. And the one time I did go for an au-dition and saw the kind of cattle calls that they were, (rows of stunning, multitalented actors standing in long lines, all holding their little port-folios with their headshots and résumés), I lost my nerve. After doing an audition that one time, the director said to me, "You're not tall enough and you're not short enough. You're not street enough but not sophisticated, either. You're not Latina enough, but you're not white enough. I just don't get you." I lost my nerve and let my dream of be-coming an actress burst like a little cartoon bubble over my head. Lucky for me I got involved with the college radio station, instead.

It was during my first week in college that I met Ceci. I was unpack-ing my stuff in the suite I was to share with four other girls—my Mex-ican ponchos and carpets, my Ché posters, my Rolling Stones, Led Zeppelin, and Inti-Illimani records—when I saw her walk in. She was eye-catchingly beautiful. Her shoulder-length sunflower-blond hair framed her round but chiseled face, and she had these terrific Brooke Shields–type eyebrows. Her smooth, tanned, caramel-colored legs stretched out long from her white tennis shorts and cream-colored short-sleeved turtleneck. Her air of sophistication threatened me. I thought, "Oh my God. I'm gonna have to share my suite with a bona fide New York beauty." I quickly became defensive. Fearing I couldn't com-pete for looks, or class, or maybe even brains, I took the offensive and put on my tough-street-girl act. At our first suite meeting, I wore my raggedy overalls and baseball cap and made obnoxious comments. She flipped her nose at me and turned away in disgust.

Good. That will keep her out of my hair.

A couple of hours after our meeting I was back in my dorm room when the suite phone rang. "Cecilia! It's for you," I yelled and left the phone dangling. I turned my back and then I couldn't believe what I heard through my half-open door.

"Mamita! Cómo estás? No, no te preocupes. Yo estoy bien. Estoy feliz, Mamita, pero requete contenta!"

She hung up the phone and I almost pounced on her.

"Hey, where are you from?" I asked excitedly. My first Latina friend
in college! An hermana! Someone who could understand me and my bi-
cultural angst. Yipee!

"Me?" she said, flatly. "I'm from New Jersey."

"What? No, no, no, no! I mean, what are your roots? De donde eres?
De donde vienes?"

"Oh, my parents are from Argentina," she said, totally detached.

"Well, that means *you're* from Argentina. That's your blood! You
want to go get a café con leche?"

Our friendship was rocky at first, but as we overcame our differences
we came to love each other like sisters, albeit competitive hermanas.
Our histories were strangely similar. She had been born in Latin America, the youngest of four, just like me. And she had arrived in the U.S.
when she was only a year old, just like me. She had a rebellious brother
and a sister who had married a gringo and moved to the suburbs, just
like mine. We grew up together in college on the wonderful Upper
West Side.

We studied Latin America together, perfected our Spanish, read Ed-
uardo Galeano's *Las venas abiertas de América Latina,* and cried about it together. We got involved with solidarity work with Central America and
became convinced we were little revolucionarias, following in Ché's
footsteps (with the tiny difference of being in New York City and not the
mountains of Cuba). And of course, we found ourselves men—the first
real Latino boyfriends either one of us had had. She hooked up with an
Argentine folk-singer-former-veterinarian. I got together with a Sal-
vadoran who had come to the States on a baseball scholarship but who
was now doing political organizing with Central American refugees.

Ceci and I spent our junior year in college going to political meetings, studying third-world feminism, going to demonstrations and An-
dean music concerts. We talked about our boyfriends and the plans we
had to go back and live in Latin America. We dreamt about raising our
children there while we worked for women's rights and economic development in pueblitos.

Sometimes I was such a little dogmatic feminista guerrillera it even made Ceci crazy. But for all of my feminism, I was totally out of touch with my body—always wrestling with my Latina guilt about not being a virgin. So sex with my boyfriend was often strained or bland. There were occasional moments of passion. One of those dark nights, instead of reaching for the spermicide gel for my diaphragm, I grabbed some other tube that was in my top drawer and put that in my diaphragm instead.

Three weeks later, I discovered I was pregnant. And even though I had a steady boyfriend, I knew I had no choice of what to do.

It was a wintery Saturday morning when my boyfriend and I walked into an office building on the ritzy east side of Manhattan. The building was empty except for the second floor, where there was a lot of activity. But everything was hushed. Teenaged girls, middle-aged women, some looked rich, others not at all, every skin color imaginable was there. Some with men by their side, others with girlfriends, some with their moms. Our names were called four at a time, and we walked in a line through some doors into another waiting room. No one spoke to one another while the nurses there drew our blood and took our vital signs. Then we each went into rooms that were as tiny as closets and changed into stiff blue-paper robes and brown-paper slippers. In my group of four there was me, two others, and a young Asian woman (who, oddly enough, I had seen on campus).

I tried not to look around too much, and I remember wishing they had given me total anesthesia from the minute I walked in the door so I wouldn't have to see anything. Not the faces of the other women or of the doctors, or the nasty brown-paper slippers or the gowns that inevitably didn't cover the part of your body that you most wanted to cover, not the blood or the needles, the gray hallways or the garbage cans, or the faces of the people in the waiting room who looked as blank as we all felt.

I didn't feel anything thanks to the anesthesia. Then all I remember is waking up in a large white room, feeling like herded cattle, my stretcher squeezed into a long line of beds, while some nurses talked loudly to one another, as if on purpose, to make sure we didn't sleep any longer than we already had because we had to make room for the next batch of women who needed our space in this recovery room. I opened my eyes and heard groaning, my own and that of other women. I heard someone say, "No, don't get up yet! You're still bleeding." I saw white lights and a clock. And then I realized where I was and what I had just been through and I started crying, my hands instantly reaching down to my womb. I heard someone who sounded just like me, someone who had the same kind of deep moans and sobs. And then I saw a hand lift up from the stretcher right next to mine and I grabbed it and we held on to each other, and said nothing. Finally, I lifted my head and saw it was the student from my college I had seen before. We just held on to each other, sharing this feeling of emptiness and desolation, of tristeza profunda, of get-me-out-of-here-please, let me have the strength to walk out of here and not see any more blood or faces or tears or nurses or paper slippers.

It was over, finally. I knew this was the most painful experience I had ever been through, and I vowed never to have to go through it again.

But five months later, even though I was still using my diaphragm, I got pregnant again. I don't know how it is that I don't remember anything, absolutely anything, about that second clinic experience except that the day after I had to go to my waitressing job to work a Sunday brunch. And I did. That was the way I dealt with my pain—I blocked it all out, pushed it deep into the "empty" memory file, and as quickly as I could, tried to get back to my normal life. I also immediately went on the pill and never told anyone except for Ceci and my then boyfriend—and much later, Gérman—what I had been through.

So now ten years later, I thought I understood the karma behind my first miscarriage. Payback. Punishment. Retribution. The world goes in circles—life is yin and yang. Once you're baptized, Jesús Cristo has got his reins on you even if you're not a believer anymore. My dormant Catholic self was reawakening, and I convinced myself I was paying for my life mistakes, paying for being a sinner. Paying my debt. Pagando la deuda de la vida.

I knew this retribution stuff could be dangerous. If I was going to let myself go that route, then I knew that before we could have a child, I was going to have to pay some more. I wanted to get these thoughts out of my head. Gérman probably would say that I always looked at the negative part of life and set myself up for expecting the worst, instead of appreciating what life has given me. So I was alone. Alone with my memories. Alone with my mourning. Alone with all of my fear. If my pregnancy failed ten years almost to the month after my first abortion, then what would happen with my next pregnancy attempt—if I even dared to try?

Those first few weeks after my miscarriage were the most difficult. How stupid of me to have babbled about the pregnancy. My big mouth came back to haunt me day after day. People I barely knew would see me and say, "Hey, how's that belly coming?" And before I could answer they would say something stupid like "Wow, you're not even showing! That baby is going to be a chaparita just like you!" Then when I would tell them that I lost it they would say brilliant things like "Oh, this is your first miscarriage? I had three before I finally could stay pregnant. Just forget about it."

Thanks a lot, jerk, I would feel like answering, but instead I would paint a half smile across my face and wonder why it was that people who I thought were so smart scored zero on tact.

I immersed myself in work, but I fell back into my old habits of second-guessing myself on everything I wrote. One of my bosses was pressuring me about my productivity levels. The last big piece I had done, on the skinheads, had gotten positive feedback, but had taken me two weeks to do. It seemed like with every good story I did, he would come down on me with some kind of criticism. I didn't understand. The more I excelled the more I felt as if he wanted to stifle my creativity. And this was the boss who had only a year or two ago been my greatest supporter. Why was he now my biggest roadblock? Whatever it was, he was doing a good job of shaking my self-confidence. I felt insecure about everything I wrote and every idea I came up with. And even though I wanted to respond to him, I withered in the face of his authority. Dad had taught me to fear and respect authority, and so here I was, a grown woman, unable to challenge my boss.

Soon afterward, I got the assignment to go to Cuba to cover the exodus of refugees who were throwing themselves into the ocean in tiny rafts. I hadn't been to the island in ten years (I had gotten the chance to go there once before to collect music for my college radio station). Gérman had been to Cuba only a few years earlier, and he knew that the Cuba I was going to see was a different one than that of ten years earlier. The Russians had pulled out and the promises of socialism and equality and justice were unraveling in the crisis.

Gérman spent a few days with me in Santo Domingo before I took off for Havana from the Dominican Republic. He suggested I meet with all of his friends who had recently visited the island so they could prepare me for what I was going to see. They told me that their Cuban friends all looked like scarecrows because there was nothing to eat on the island.

I saw the most incredible, saddening things in Havana during my ten days of reporting there. It was a surrealistic scene of people, entire families sometimes, jumping desperately into rafts that looked as if they would sink in a swimming pool. Italian filmmakers with lights and expensive cameras were documenting this, and crowds of people would form and cheer the balseros, but it was as if people were cheering as they committed suicide. The police just watched indifferently. One night one of the balseros even made a pass at me: "Chica, si tú no quieres que me vaya, dímelo y me voy contigo." I looked at him stunned. And as groups of people waited for the tide to lower so they could set off in their rafts, they would be playing music and dancing under the moonlight.

"La revolución y la igualdad ya se fueron en una balsa," one young mother waiting to leave told me. The revolution and equality have already left on the rafts. "That's why I'm leaving," she said, shaking her head slowly.

I came home totally shaken and depleted. As the weeks passed and I recuperated from both the miscarriage and my Cuba trip, I delved head-on into projects outside of the job to take my mind off of things. I was on the board of directors of a Puerto Rican dance troupe. I was on the board of directors of an environmental group. I was involved with a progressive funding agency that gave money to grassroots organizations working for social justice. All of which meant that I was hardly at home, which was an effective way to keep my mind off me and my troubles.

I didn't speak to Ceci or Ro very much at all, and they weren't calling me much, either. I felt like such a failure. I mean, here I was wanting to show off my pregnancy to them, my hermanas and peers, but now with the miscarriage, I felt like such a loser. That's how I kept seeing myself and how, in my gringa-bred competitiveness, I assumed my friends saw me that way too. As a failure. My grief was coming between us. I was too empty and hurt and angry to reach out to them and they didn't know how to reach out to me.

During that November and December right after the miscarriage, my friend Sandy and I, on the other hand, were talking often. She was doing a lot of traveling to New York on business, and she would stay with us in the little second bedroom I had already begun to call the baby's room. It was good to see her. Because she was older than me I didn't have any of the competitive stuff with her that sometimes surfaced with Ceci or Ro. Instead, she was like my older sister, mentor mom, and best friend combined into one. We were like the odd couple, though. We would walk arm in arm down Broadway like schoolgirls, she standing just under six feet with dreadlocks past her waist, wearing a power business suit underneath a full-length African mudcloth coat. And I next to her (at only five feet), wearing bluejean overalls and cowboy boots with my wild curly hair shooting up to the sky in the autumn winds.

When Sandy and I met in the mid-eighties, I was just starting my career as a reporter, but by that time she had already been a reporter, an anchor, a news director, a senior editor, and an executive producer and was now a vice president. I used to call her Miss V. P. A. T.—Vice-President-All-That. She had been through it all in terms of her career, and unlike me, she was not afraid of facing up to power and authority and speaking her mind. She was my Amazon role model. "I want to be like you when I grow up," I would tease her.

Sandy worked at her job like a maniac, pulling all-nighters for days in a row. But she exuded an inner peace that I never imagined I could have. She would tease me by calling me Miss Drama Queen. With me, everything was always happening at ninety miles a minute. I was always in a

rush, and my emotions were on high all the time—whether I was jumping for joy in ecstasy or in tear-jerking tristeza. Sandy never let me forget about the time when I was initiated into my Drama Queen status. It
was years ago, before I had become a full-fledged reporter, and I was
trying to write the script for my first-ever half-hour documentary. It
was called "Silver or Lead," and it was based on several weeks of research into drug trafficking I had just completed on a visit to Colombia.
Just the thought of having to write a script that long made me uncon-
trollably nervous. I would look at the blank pages and shudder, "I can't
write this! I can't write at all." Even though I was a journalist I had an
internal disconnect and never saw myself as a *writer*. (People who grew
up speaking English were writers. Not someone like me.) So how could
I write this script? I was so nervous that night trying to write that documentary that I felt sick to my stomach. Sandy picked me up from the
studio where I was working and took me to three different restaurants
because I insisted that each one was making me nauseous. I left my trail
in each restroom and also on the side of Sandy's new black Volvo.

"Remember when you couldn't write a script without getting sick
first?" Sandy would say to me when faced with yet another one of my re-
current bouts with writer's doubt.

"Yes," I would say quietly.

"And now you write scripts with no problem. So get out of your
funk and believe in yourself, girlfriend!"

Sandy was not only my amiga, she was my elder. I respected her immensely.

On her visits to New York after my miscarriage, Sandy helped me get
out of my feeling-sorry-for-myself-way-beyond-the-necessary-time
doldrums. She would often stay over on the weekends and treat me to
manicures and pedicures, or something equally mindless like buying
shoes, which we both loved to do. Gérman called us Imeldita la Grande
and Imeldita la Pequeña.

As autumn moved into winter, and Manhattan brought down the
stars by lighting up the trees along every major avenue, I ever so slowly
moved beyond my loss. Sandy came up for another business trip and
stayed over for the weekend. I made us all a scrumptious meal of shrimp
taquitos, arroz Mexicano and my favorite salad of greens, hearts of
palm, and sesame-oil salad dressing. After the meal, we sat in the living

room and listened to the new Milton Nascimento CD. Gérman, who also calls Sandy his "seester," joined us with a pint of mango ice cream. He was working on a red-blue painting of a woman with huge wings and a strong face and forceful eyes but who had a small frown etched across her mouth.

"You did a great job of capturing Malu's face there, brother," Sandy said to Gérman.

I hadn't even realized that it was me in the painting.

"Yep, así es nuestra Malu. The sad angel. The woman who has everything in life but who is still triste," said Gérman, putting down the ice cream and picking up his paintbrush.

I didn't realize this was how Gérman and Sandy both saw me. I was quiet.

"I hate feeling this way, Sandy. I just want to be over the sadness already," I said.

"Sugar, the only way you're going to get over it is to make peace with what has happened. You need to give yourself permission to stop mourning. You need to allow yourself to move on. Otherwise you are going to stay stuck here and the more stuck you get the more difficult it will be to get unstuck."

"Well, how so do I get unstuck?"

"Malu, life deals you the cards that it knows only you can handle. Yeah, I was sad when I realized I couldn't have kids. But then I realized that I had to move on. And I looked at everything else that I had in my life, and I didn't need anything else. I had my life and my health. I understood I needed to stop asking for things and start giving thanks. Every single day. Every single morning and night. That's how I got unstuck."

I looked at her face. Sandy was beautiful. Her light brown skin was smooth and wrinkle-free. Her smile was as warm as a cup of hot chocolate. She radiated serenity. We *were* both alive and healthy. In that instant I realized what a gift that really was.

"You need to trust yourself more, sis. You need to know that when you are ready to have your children they will come. But not one day sooner. No matter how much you worry or pout about it. If they are yours they will come."

I kissed her on the cheek and sat down next to her, curled up like a cat, and she slowly rubbed my back. That night, before I went to bed, I told all the gods listening that I thanked them for bringing Sandy into my life. And then I said, I will learn patience if it's the last thing I do. I promise. I closed my eyes and fell into a deep winter's-night sleep.

The next morning Sandy and I went down to Chinatown before she took off for the airport. Often when she came to New York we made our ritual trip down to the Chinese gourmet grocery store, and we would stock up on dried mangos, spicy ginger candies, and green tea.

Sandy also needed to pop in for a quick visit to her Chinese acupuncture doctor. So after squeezing through the aisles at the grocery store and picking our way through the overcrowded streets where people were hawking everything from baby turtles to faux Chanel bags to live lobster by the pound, we entered an old building where her doctor had his office. Sandy got her medicine from her doctor who greeted her with a big hug even though he hardly spoke one word of English. "He treats all his patients by taking their pulse and looking at their eyes," she whispered to me. "He doesn't need words to communicate."

Back on the crowded streets, I gave Sandy a good-bye hug and she hopped into a cab. I decided to walk north and stop by Macondo, the Spanish-language bookstore on Fourteenth Street. I wanted to get the new Isabel Allende novel. Since the miscarriage I hadn't had the desire to read much. Time to move on, I said to myself. Light those candles and start speaking to the gods of "moving on"!

I was feeling good as I made my way uptown, past Little Italy and Washington Square Park. The blond-haired dreads were playing "No Woman No Cry" on beat-up guitars while the Jamaicans were at the other end of the park listening to some British ska. A group of cultural antiques—pseudo punk rockers with pink mohawks sprayed six inches above their head—was gathered under a tree, listening to the Sex Pistols and jumping up and down. I wondered, where do these guys go when it starts raining? A couple of drops of water must destroy their hairstyles. I thought about them wearing those little plastic Woolworth rain bonnets like the kind Mom used to wear a million years ago. Life is a trip, I smiled to myself.

I hit Fourteenth Street and before I realized it I found myself walking amongst dozens of Mexican families. What was going on? I took a deep breath and realized that it even smelled like Mexico City. But here I was in downtown Manhattan. I closed my eyes and let it all flow in. Oh, it smelled delicious! I was getting whiffs of tacos al carbón, tamales, churros and chocolate, cilantro, cebolla, limón and tortillas. I felt as if I was standing on any street corner in downtown Mexico City, the De-Efe, as Mexicanos call it, the Distrito Federal, the city where I was born. But when I opened my eyes, I was on a New York City street, staring at little boys wearing white campesino pants, white socks, and huaraches, straw cowboy hats and little mustaches painted on their faces, just above their full dark lips. The little girls were wearing satin rainbow rebozos, white peasant skirts, their hair in braids. Their parents had on Nike baseball caps, Gap jeans, Fayva shoes, Walkmans, and colorful winter jackets. Mariachis and racheras played on boom boxes and the familiar cantito of Mexican Spanish was being spoken and tossed among friends along the entire block. Suddenly I wasn't a New Yorker anymore. No, now I was a Mexicana en la Calle Catorce, a woman who could navigate through the sights, smells and memories of Mexico City—memories that had been transported to the skyscraper streets of lower Manhattan.

I had not realized it but it was December 12th, the day of La Virgen de Guadalupe, the patron saint of Mexicanos and one of the most important religious holidays for Mexicans. And on Fourteenth Street in Manhattan there is a small church that is named after the brown virgin who watches over immigrants who are far away from their homeland.

I stepped inside the packed church and made my way to one of the pews. My paisanos looked at me as if I didn't belong there, and I wondered what they thought. Do they think I am a lost gringa who has just come in off the street to see what all the commotion is about? Do they think I don't speak Spanish? Do they think I am an immigration official or an undercover police officer? Do they fear me or laugh at me? Unless they hear me speak, I am just one of "them," one of those people who they think must have been born and raised in this city, one of those people who walks New York streets as if she owns them, one of those people who speaks perfect English, una que puede defenderse en esta ciudad—one who can defend herself in this metropolis. I am one of "the others," someone who has money, a job, an office, a career, a nice apartment in a nice neighborhood, donde la pobreza no se ve—where poverty is out of sight. In their view, I am not one of them, not a Latina, not a Mexicana. I am one of the distant others, the gringos.

I felt them staring at me while I turned my eyes to la virgen and spoke to her in Spanish (though I called her by her Nahuatl name, Tonantzin) and asked her to give me strength so that I could rise up from my loss and learn to not fear life, my life. Paciencia, Virgencita, I whispered. Give me patience and peace of mind. I looked at La Virgen but I felt them staring at me. I felt like such an outsider but in so many ways this place could be one of the most familiar scenes from my life. I grew up surrounded by places like these, visiting church every day with my abuelita when I was in Mexico.

I stopped and looked around. We are in a church, but it is anything but silent. All you hear is the murmuring of women's voices praying and of children. The children. The children who call this New York church home. The children playing in the pews, crawling under the seats, squirming next to their mothers who are praying to La Virgen. The children. Everywhere. Los niños.

I study the women's faces that I am surrounded by. And the women I see in this church on Fourteenth Street do not look afraid. They are living in a foreign land, in a cold, harsh city, in a place where they do not understand the language. But these women do not look afraid. They do not look daunted by the task of living in this new city or by the love or the pain and the work that family brings, that bearing children brings. Children are a part of them and these women are a part of me. I have this—I have them—inside of me. Si ellas le hacen frente a la vida, yo también puedo. If they can take on this life, then so can I, I think to myself. Sitting in this church, I can feel I come from this tradition, a tradition where family is central, a tradition where women are strong, strong enough to keep families going, to bear children, even in the face of the worst possible circumstances. Certainly more difficult circumstances than the pain of one miscarriage.

For a few minutes I pray quietly again to Tonantzin. I don't think about who is watching me anymore. I am still, quiet, listening to the murmuring, of which my voice is now a part.

I am thinking about my grandmother and her five children, my great-grandmother and her ten, and my mother with us four. Todas estas mujeres le hicieron frente a la vida. Yo también puedo, I repeat to myself as I look around in quiet wonder. I remembered when I first came to New York and I used to have to take a half-hour subway ride to Fourteenth

Street just to get a dozen tortillas. And now look at this. México en la big apple! I never thought I would see this. But with patience, I say to myself, anything can happen. Cualquier cosa puede pasar.

A tiny hand taps me on the leg softly and I turn. It is a little boy with a crooked penciled mustache and a crumbled straw hat. He says to me, "Puede pasar me mi huarache? Se cayó debajo de sus pies." Can you pass me my huarache? It fell under your feet.

I reach under my seat and take the small brown sandal and put it in his hands. "Thanks," he says to me in perfect English. "Thanks a lot, nice lady," he says, and disappears under the pew again, giggling.

I think to myself, he looks like an angel. Delivered from Mexico straight to my heart via la Catorce, via Fourteenth Street.

*A*ll through that following winter, it felt like my body had closed up like a caterpillar in a cocoon. I was warm and affectionate with Gérman but I was also distant.

As far as I was concerned, why have sex if you can't try to make a baby? Wasn't that what it was all about? The doctor had told us that it might be good to wait at least four months before we tried again. Yes, we made love. But my heart wasn't really there. I wanted to make love to procreate.

With all my calculating I had figured that we could start trying again in the spring. I wanted to start off our new attempts at procreation with a big bang. But I wasn't sure how to make that happen without letting Gérman know, without making him feel like we were on a stage and the curtain was lifting and that it was time to *perform*.

Sex had become a mission for me. Gérman couldn't have been more turned off. He sensed that I was getting back into my life-schedule-operating mode again. Hadn't the miscarriage been enough to teach me that you can't calculate your life, that it doesn't always work the way you plan it? Obviously not. So as the months passed I started studying the calendar again.

Then one morning I heard Arthur Frommer talking on the TV about supercheap flights to Bali and I said to my husband, "Honey, what if we go to Bali? You know how much you have always wanted to go. And since Mom and Dad went a few years ago, they have always told us that it is one of the most romantic places in the world. Let's make reservations! Vámonos a Bali!" In the back of my mind I was thinking Bali would be the perfect place for us to try again for a baby. So exotic, so idyllic! Now if I could only get a plane reservation to get us there during the week that I would be ovulating.

I picked up the phone and called the travel agent.

"But why does it have to be those dates?" she said to me, frustrated when the dates and flights and price just didn't want to work out.

"Um, um, because there is a special festival in Bali that I want to see . . ." I answered, making it up as I went along.

"There is no festival in Bali during that week. I know about every single special event in Bali and there isn't one then," she pressed.

Jesus! Why did I have to get stuck with a Bali expert as a travel agent? "Well, it's some special event my mom told me about. I think it's only celebrated by this one family my parents met when they went to Bali. Yeah, that's it! We are being invited to stay with this family as they celebrate this ritual in their small town." Uh-huh.

"So does that mean you won't need the hotel for the seven nights? What is the name of the town where the family is from? Let me see if there is a hotel there I can get you into."

Ay Dios.

"Oh just do what you can to get me there as close to those days as possible!" I said and hung up the phone, feeling bad—lying about something so stupid. Why didn't I just tell her, "You see, this is my plan. If we get there on the tenth that means that having sex every other day, as the doctor recommended, then we will have exactly four nights to try to conceive because I will start ovulating on the morning of the eleventh, which should be about five P.M. Bali time, and so we can start doing the baby-production activity that evening followed by another interlude forty-eight hours later." Sure.

When I told my office mates I was going to Bali in two weeks they were stunned. This was the first time in my life that I had done something so extravagant and spontaneous.

Two weeks later we were on a plane ride that crossed the world and seemed to last forever. Once we got to Bali I realized I hadn't calculated time for our exhaustion from the twenty-six-hour flight and jet lag and the overall physical strangeness one feels after flying across the entire

planet. There was no way I was going to be able to seduce Gérman under these conditions. He would know exactly what was going on. And
for Gérman, if sex wasn't simply a spontaneous reaction to a wonderfully loving moment, then it just wasn't worth it.

Oh, I tried so hard to be Miss Sensuality in Bali. I really did. I wore
my sarong and Brazilian dental floss bathing suit. I put exotic flowers in
my loose hair. I made sure we ate lots of seafood and oysters. But our
body clocks were so out of whack that we would end up falling asleep
from exhaustion at eight o'clock at night and then wake up at four in the
morning, bleary eyed, just in time to catch *I Dream of Jeannie* reruns and
old Mexican soap operas dubbed with Indonesian dialects.

Yes, there was sensuality all around us on this exquisitely spiritual island, but it just wasn't happening in our tiny hotel room, no matter how
much I hoped it would. Finally, one morning just before we were going
to take off, Gérman and I did make love as a torrential rain shower came
down on the palm trees, as the bright red sun was coming up. Everything was quiet except for the sound of the rain falling softly through
the trees. It was beautiful and romantic and loving. But for all of the af-
terglow of sex that day I couldn't help feeling sad that it had come four
days too late. Patience, I told myself.

Back at home, the rest of the spring and summer I tried to be un-
premeditated about sex. But I would be suddenly spontaneous every
month at about the same time for exactly seven days—making sure the
spontaneity came and went every other day (following doctor's orders).

Gérman would do his best to play along with me. And I became truly
convinced that my man really did love me. Anybody else would have
slapped me upside the head. But Gérman would hug me and kiss me
and rub my head, from my forehead all the way down to the end of my
long hair. "Ay, mi Malu," he would say. "Tienes tanta prisa en esta vida.
You can't rush life, Mamita. Look at how much we have in our lives already. It's not good to be so demanding. You have to be truly happy with
what you have first, Mamita, before you can ask for more, as if you have
some kind of right to it. We have a right to be thankful for being alive
and for having each other. Can't you see that? And the children will
come when they are good and ready. Don't you understand that you
can't force it?"

I would nod my head yes but whisper no to myself: I've made things happen before, in my career, in school. I figured there was *something* I could do to make *this* happen.

Then I would turn to Gérman and say, "You're right, amor. I am going to try." And I would get up and walk to the calendar and check to see when my next ovulation was due to occur and start planning next month's spontaneous sex moment.

Six months went by like this. It was September already, almost one full year after my miscarriage. Every month that had passed there was the heightened expectation and then the predictable letdown. I was increasingly frustrated and now I was becoming angry with Gérman. (Obviously, getting angry with the person who you want to impregnate you was not a brilliant idea.)

Finally, on the morning of Halloween when I was three days late, I unwrapped the pregnancy test that had been sitting in the back of the closet gathering dust. Miraculously, the second line turned pink. I went back to bed to show Gérman with a great big smile on my face.

This time we were both happy but subdued. We told no one except for my parents. We decided to have no sonograms until the eighth week, when we could be sure to see a heartbeat.

It was a month of restrained excitement. In between covering stories and trying to act normal in the office, I would hear competing voices in my head. Something special had happened to us. Or maybe not. I was happy for a second but then something would tell me that this was going to be another letdown. But right after that another voice would tell me to think positive, that I had to fight against my tendency to be so negative. The little voices continued their constant jabbering until I would go to sleep and then they would start up again the minute I woke up and I looked at myself in the mirror. My body is changing—no it isn't—yes it is—no it isn't. I would touch my breasts all the time to see if they were getting bigger, rub my stomach every five minutes, try and figure out if I was nauseous from the pregnancy or just nauseous from my desperation. Day and night for a month. In silence. It's a wonder I didn't go crazy.

The day we finally went in for the sonogram there was a thunderstorm, the kind with lightening and thunder, the kind that are rare for New York City. I thought that was a bad sign. We arrived to discover that my regular doctor wasn't there so we had to see a new person. Oh-

oh. Up until that moment my husband kept on reassuring me. But when it turned out that we were going to have to do the sonogram in the very same room where the D & C had been performed the last time, even my husband lost his nerve.

By then we were expecting the worst and that, in fact, was what happened. Black and empty again, my womb was nurturing a mass of cells that was multiplying feverishly into nothing. Another blighted ovum. Another letdown.

The sadness was so immediate, so profound, so engrossing, that I felt as if I could have walked out in the middle of the street and not even realized that a car had run me over.

I didn't cry. The little voice inside of me kept saying, "Pendeja, why did you get your hopes up? You knew it wasn't going to happen. You dumb, stupid fool. How could you fall for this again?

My doctor scheduled me for a D & C, this time in the hospital a few days later and so I had no choice but to carry this false pregnancy until then. The day of the operation, the doctor was an hour and a half late. Every minute was an extension of this make-believe pregnancy. He finally arrived, and I was swearing at him under my breath, imagining that he had made me wait on purpose just to rub the pain in some more. I'll never forget when my usually unscattered and composed doctor came into the room, looking tired and disheveled and battling a bad cold. He said something that at the time sounded so curt and hurtful, but that later I would learn to understand. In a tone that sounded almost like "stop your pouting, Hinojosa," my doctor said: "You may not feel this way now, but you are actually one up on many of the women I see, Maria." Oh yeah, I said to myself. "How do you figure?" I asked sarcastically. "At least you *can* get pregnant. At least you've *been* pregnant. I have dozens of patients who wish they could get that far."

"Really?"

"Yes, really, Maria. Now let's get you up to the O.R."

Learn to give thanks for what you have, a voice said to me.

Before they put the anesthesia mask on me I did give thanks, to La Virgen de Guadalupe, Oshun, and Yemanya. I asked them to watch over the souls of these lost pregnancies and to protect them and me. And I gave thanks for what I did have. My husband, my family, my work, my friends, and the roof I had over my head. Gracias, I said. Muchas gracias. And then I was out.

Later I woke up in the recovery room, sad and groggy. I wanted to go home.

"Where are my glasses?" I whimpered. "Can someone please give me my glasses so I can see? I want to get out of here. Where is my husband?"

I thought I was speaking loudly but one of the nurses came over to my bed and said, in a thick Brooklyn accent, "Hi, honey. My name is Rock-saaane. Speak up, honey."

Roxanne looked and talked just like the TV character the Nanny.

"Ah, honey. Don't cry. I've been through this before. You're gonna be okay. You just gotta keep trying."

Trying? You've got to be kidding! I just had a miscarriage and surgery. I was dying inside and she's talking about trying again? I tried to smile at her. "I really would like to get out of here. Please," I mumbled.

"Listen, honey," Roxanne whispered getting even closer to my face. "There is somebody you need to meet. I have a friend who had nine miscarriages . . ."

Oh God no, not someone else telling me how good I have it because I have only had two. Why does this always happen to me? I was stuck. I couldn't move off of the stretcher even if I wanted to. Roxanne kept at it.

"My friend had nine miscarriages but now she has three kids. She saw this specialist. A group of doctors on Park Avenue who specialize in women who have had multiple miscarriages. I don't know what they do but all the women who go in to see them get pregnant. Give me your number and I'll call you and give you their names. My friend swears by them."

So I gave Roxanne my number and a week later she called and left me the names of the doctors on my machine. She sounded like a nice enough person. And it meant something that she had actually remembered and made the time to call me back. When I called to make an appointment with the specialists, they were so booked up I had to wait two months before they could squeeze me in. So much for getting my answers immediately. Patience, said the little voice.

I went back to work after just a weekend off after the operation. I knew that if I stayed at home I would only sink deeper into my sorrow, as I had with my first miscarriage. The morning I went back to the office I was riding the subway at rush hour being my typical New Yorker self, keeping my eyes down, staring at my feet, when all of a sudden, at the other end of the car, I heard an accordion. Just another subway musician, I thought. But then I recognized the tune. And then I heard a voice.

"Cucurucucuuuuuuu, palmomaaaaaa. Cucurucucuuuuu, amoressss."

It was the first stanza of a song from my childhood. My mom had sung it to me when I was a child. My cousins and I would sing it at picnics in the Mexican countryside. I used to sing it with my Chicano friends in college, when we would drink a couple of beers and get happy and reminisce. The song is so popular that it's like the Mexican national anthem. What was somebody doing singing it at nine in the morning on a New York City subway?

I sat up, but the subway car was so packed I couldn't see anything but men with briefcases and women in suits. But I kept hearing the accordion, the words, the voice, getting closer. I reached in my pocket and started fingering a quarter. I was smiling for the first time in days.

As the music got closer, the sardine-packed bodies began to part to let this person through. And then I saw him. An elderly man with gray hair and a potbelly with a huge accordion strapped around his chest and a little blue tin cup taped onto the side of his instrument. And then I saw a white cane hanging on a rope off his shoulder. He was blind but he was singing, and playing, and walking through a crowded, zooming subway, in perfect balance. Como si nada. As if it was nothing.

When he was standing right in front of me, I stood up and instead of the quarter, I put a dollar in the cup. I wanted to hug the man, press myself into his chest, like I did with my abuelito. Then the subway doors opened and in a minute I was pushed out by the crowd and I thought he was gone and I was thinking, he's gotten away, and there was something I wanted to say to this man. When the subway car zoomed off, and people had rushed to the stairways, there he was, standing right next to me.

"Hola," I said.

"Cómo le va, señorita? Usted quería hablar conmigo, verdad?" How are you? You wanted to speak to me, right? he said unhurried, as if he had known me for years.

Yes, I had wanted to speak to him. I thought he would make a great story, a wonderful sound piece for radio. I just wanted to meet him. But how did he know that?

He began to tell me his story as people rushed around us to get to work. His name was Don Pablo. He had come to this country two years ago to try to make money for his family. His wife and mother of his five children had come to the States first and worked in a chicken-packing plant in Georgia. He had gone there to meet her but after six months she had taken her children and left him all alone. He had no idea where they had gone. He had heard there were jobs in New York. So he walked and hitchhiked for days until he made it to Brooklyn, where he was living in one of the poorest neighborhoods. Someone had helped him rent a room. And everyday, for the past year, he would make his way to the subways and play from nine to five. He made just enough money to pay rent and buy food. Although he was from a small town, he had lived many years in Mexico City. There, too, he had played the accordion in the subways to survive.

"Señorita María," Don Pablo said in Spanish. "If I could play in the subways in Mexico City, I knew I could play in the subways in New York. Once you learn how to keep your balance in one moving subway car you can do it anywhere in the world."

I got to the office and I called my editor right away and told him how much I wanted to do this story. I was prepared to fight for it since more and more of my editors seemed uninterested in anything but hard news and analysis. I, on the other hand, wanted to tell stories. Something clicked though and he said to go ahead.

I followed Don Pablo around for a full day and met all of the friends he had made in New York. The subway token booth clerk in Brooklyn who helped him through the turnstiles, his neighbors who would walk him down the four flights of stairs, the guys from the diner up in Harlem. Everyone cared for Don Pablo. It was as if he had an angel walking next to him.

"Yo tengo un ángel, Señorita." I do have an angel, he said to me smiling.

While we ate fried chicken at the diner on 125th Street, I asked Don Pablo how he kept his spirits high. I told him I knew so many people who, if he excused me saying so, had so much more than him, who were wealthy, who had good jobs, nice apartments, and all five of their senses but who were unhappy or angry, unsatisfied or impatient with life. I didn't tell him, but I was also thinking about myself.

"You have to be happy with what God has given you. You have to find the joy in your life everyday. I have my music, I have my friends. I lost my family but I have an angel who protects me. I am content with life. I am at peace," said Don Pablo.

When my story ran on air people all over the country called to tell me how much they loved it.

It felt good to be doing my storytelling reporting again. After all these months of working without my heart in it, I felt as if I had found my voice as a writer once more.

But even though I loved putting personal stories on the air, I was the last one to share my own story with my colleagues. No one in my office (except for my editor in D.C.) knew what I had been going through. Even if I felt weak, I couldn't break out of my "professional" mode and let anyone here see it.

After the Don Pablo story ran, I spent a day cleaning up my desk and answering phone calls and opening mail. Someone had sent me a book about graffiti murals. What a great story, I thought. I read through the book. These weren't just graffiti pieces but were actual memorial walls that were painted for people who had been killed in violence or who had passed away, and whose family members wanted them memorialized. I picked up the phone and my editor again gave me the go-ahead. If only it was this easy all the time, I thought. Since he was the only one who knew about the miscarriages, maybe he was feeling sorry for me. And he was probably feeling even a bit guilty because his wife without planning it was now pregnant for the second time.

I hooked up with the guys from the TATS CRU in the Bronx, three sweet, young Puerto Rican graffiti-taggers-turned-memorial-muralists who had been featured in the book. These guys had spent their years in high school dodging the cops while they did their work on subways and now they were being hired as community artists. We made plans to meet that evening to take a tour of the dozens of walls they had painted.

For four hours the guys and I crisscrossed the Bronx, looking at paintings that were dedicated to the dead. One with a six-foot-tall vibrant red rose dedicated to six-year-old Jessica who had been killed in the crossfire of dueling drug dealers, another for a young man who was stabbed to death in a street brawl, another for a community organizer who died of a heart attack, another for a young man who had leukemia, another for a young man killed in a car accident.

Surrounded by all of this death, I couldn't help but think of my miscarriages. Of course I was sad. But hearing the stories about all of these people who had passed away gave me some perspective. People here had lost their children to stray bullets. I couldn't even imagine such grief.

By the end of the evening I was drained, but we still had one last mural to visit. A mural, the artists told me, they considered the most powerful one they had done.

We drove to a quiet tree-lined street that looked more like it belonged in a small New England town rather than in the heart of the South Bronx. On this pitch-black night in the middle of this street there was a house on the block that was shining. There were garden lights coming up from the ground and a light from the roof was beaming down on the front wall of the house. And on this front wall there was a huge painting of a child's face, an innocent smiling baby looking out to anyone who happened to drive by. I had never seen anything like this before. A mural of a baby's face painted on the wall of a house in the middle of the Bronx on a street where the steady silence was disturbed only by the distant sounds of sirens and trucks on a faraway highway.

We walked in the house and the guys introduced me to Rita. She was a pretty, young woman, but the dark circles under her eyes left her whole face tinged by a lingering sadness. Rita had lost her six-year-old son to heart failure just two weeks ago. The little boy had been born with several birth defects because Rita had been in labor too long. The doctor at the public hospital where she was giving birth hadn't responded in time when the baby had shown signs of distress. The baby lost oxygen and as a result, Rita told me, had been born deaf and blind, with a congenital heart defect, epilepsy, and cerebral palsy. Soon after he was born, Rita sued the hospital and with the money from the settlement she bought this house. The doctors had told her the baby would live only months, but he had survived until he was six.

"This is my baby's house," Rita said to me quietly, pacing her words. "Even though he is gone, this is his. And I wanted him to know that I will never forget him for as long as I live. That is why I wanted his face to be painted here. So that every time I walk in the door I think of him and keep his spirit alive," she said.

She asked me to sit with her on her couch. The plastic crinkled underneath the weight of our bodies. Rita continued. "At first my neighbors thought I was crazy. But when they heard the story about how I lost my son they understood why I wanted to have this mural painted here. Now when they walk by they bless themselves and say my son's name. He will not be forgotten. His spirit is with us all."

As we talked I realized that the day I lost my last pregnancy was the same date Rita's son had died. We got up and walked outside and I lit a candle in front of the mural. I told Rita about what had happened to me. As soon as the interview was over, I whispered it in her ear—yo también acabo de perder un bebé, un embarazo hace dos semanas—a secret shared between women, a loss shared by mothers, but I wasn't even a mother yet. She didn't say anything and instead just hugged me. I felt a lump in my throat and my eyes welling up. I decided these would be the last tears I'd shed for this.

Rita told me how she had learned to find strength from her son who was deaf and blind but who was still full of joy. She then whispered these words in my ear, "You've got to reach down into the deepest part of your soul and find the strength to continue. Just like my little boy taught me that I could."

That night when I got home it was past eleven. Gérman was just cleaning up from working on a painting. I dropped my heavy backpack with my tape recorder on a chair and threw my coat on the couch and then I walked up to Gérman, lifted up his paint-stained T-shirt and pressed my chilled face into the warmth of his bare chest. He put down his paintbrushes and turned to me and wrapped his arms around my small frame. His hands stroked my head and I turned my face up to him, stretching like a cat looking for affection. I gave him as tight a squeeze as I could and went to start the tub. I lit three candles and some incense and stepped into the warm water.

I whispered to myself that I was not going to be taken down by my own sadness. That even though there was something, some reason why

I was having to go through these miscarriages, I was not going to let this mourning win. I told myself I was going to fight this. And I said this out loud to whoever was listening. "I am not going to let you beat me! If you want me to have another miscarriage I will just try again. And again. And if I cannot get pregnant, I will adopt a child. I will be a mother. I am stronger than you. I have no place else to go but forward. I will become a warrior woman. I am going to survive."

I felt more than a little bit ridiculous, but this is exactly what I did, in my bathtub with my candles and my incense. As I dried myself off and then slowly massaged some lavender cream on my arms and legs, I realized that I felt better than I had in weeks.

Once you hit rock bottom there *is* no place to go but up. As Adaluz, my therapist had once said, go ahead and jump off the cliff of life. The furthest you will fall is the ground.

The next morning I called my brother Raul and told him that yes, Gérman and I would join him and my other brother in Mexico for Christmas. It was time to start rebuilding my spirit. What better place to start than in la madre patria.

La Limpia—The Cleansing

It had been two years since I had been back to la madre patria—the longest time I had ever spent away from Mexico. Just planning for the trip lifted my spirits, and now I was counting the days till my departure instead of counting the days that had passed since my pérdida. We flew to Mexico City and spent three days there and the first place we went was to have a big comida at my tía Gloria's house.

My five cousins were there with all of their kids, a total of sixteen grandchildren. Maritere, my cousin who was my same age and had a six-month-old daughter, talked openly about her baby blues (that strange enfermedad that she read about in those American baby books, my tía said) but I kept silent about my last miscarriage. Maritere wasn't ashamed to talk about the fact that because of her blues she had, at first, felt no love for her newborn, yet here I was feeling like my miscarriage somehow made me less of a woman, menos mujer.

Gérman, my brother Jorge, and I spent the first few days meeting with journalist friends of mine and painter friends of Gérman's and political activist friends of my brother's. Three days later we were on a plane to Cancún. I hadn't been to Cancún since I was twelve years old. As soon as we got off the plane and on the Yucatán highway I could immediately see all of the changes. Cancún had been transformed from an uninhabited track of land with white powder beaches to an imitation Miami Beach. There were Pizza Huts and dozens of tour buses and Mayan Indians dressed up in traditional outfits doing indigenous dances in the middle of sparkling new Dunkin' Donuts restaurants. The dirt road I had driven on when I was twelve had been paved over and a shiny new highway was in its place. I was going through culture shock. This wasn't the Mexico I was used to. This was the new Mexico.

Luckily for us we had made reservations at a quaint hotel in a small village, and we spent our time visiting the ruins and swimming in pristine lagoons that were hidden from the tour buses. We drove on the back roads through the Mayan villages that the new superhighways bypassed while we blasted Juan Luis Guerra singing merengue and Salif Keita with his melancholy guitar rhythms on the car cassette player. Just as Mom had done when we were little, I brought along two overstuffed suitcases of old clothing and at every stop we gave away items to families who humbly accepted our gifts. There were moments, during this trip, when I actually felt happy again. Just content at being surrounded by my family, by my history, by beauty, and by the bluest of waters.

In the capital city of Mérida, we stayed with my aunts and uncles and celebrated Christmas Eve by sitting around a table in their garden and telling jokes until four in the morning. My status-conscious tías wore their mink shawls even though it was seventy degrees outside. It is winter, they told me, and asked why I hadn't brought my own coat down from New York. Their teenage sons danced to American pop music from a huge jukebox they had rented for the occasion. But I was finally old enough to sit and listen to the sexy chistes colorados my uncles always told. I laughed until I cried, and for the first time in almost two years, my tears where laced with delight.

Gérman and I made love for no other reason than to please ourselves. Good-bye calculated love plans. Hello fun in paradise.

I also ate everything in sight.

For me, eating in Mexico has always been filled with meaning. As a little girl I remember hearing about "Montezuma's revenge." My American friends would always tease me when I would go back to Mexico, taunting me about drinking the water and "getting the runs." Even though we were just kids, their jokes were a way of letting me know that they thought I came from a country where things were dirty, a place where even the most basic necessity, water, was dangerous. In a word, I came from a country that was backward.

When we were children in Mexico, on the other hand, my cousins would tease my brothers and me because they said we had become like the gringos who ate como los perros, like dogs, with the whole meal served on one plate. In Mexico, my family ate every course separately. First the soup, then the rice, then the vegetables, followed by the main dish. They also claimed we were no longer real Mexicanos because we didn't eat chiles and picantes. My cousins ridiculed us because they knew we would occasionally eat fast foods (although in my household McDonald's or Burger King were rare treats because we couldn't afford to eat out that often). And my cousins knew that I, in particular, liked to eat the other quintessential American fare—canned foods like Campbell's chicken noodle or cream of chicken soup, or my superfavorite, SpaghettiOs with meat balls. My cousins called me a vendida, a sellout.

In response to these cross-border pressures, I always felt I had to prove something by what I ate in Mexico. As I got older I dealt with this by eating everything I could get my hands on. That way my cousins couldn't mock me about being a picky eater. And when I would get back to Chicago, I would tell my friends that I ate everything in Mexico and never got sick. I would tell them that because I had been *born* in Mexico I carried the antibodies that they, my gringo friends, would never have. I was a real Mexicana because I could go to Mexico and never be attacked by Montezuma's revenge. I, on the other hand, would be quietly gleeful when I would hear stories about people being victims of Montezuma. They deserved it for talking bad about my country, I would say as a child.

It was inevitable though, that eating this way would make me sick. Then my cousins had the last laugh. I would end up lying on the couch with a fever, throwing up, missing all of the fun. And worse yet, the one thing that I truly wanted when I was sick to my stomach was not té de manzanilla and homemade consomé de pollo (the Mexican home remedies), but instead that gringo of all gringo things—a bowl of Campbell's chicken noodle soup. Ay ay ay! My cousins were right! I was a sellout—a vendida—a pocha—a gringa. I was a disgrace to la patria and should never dare call myself Mexicana again, no matter how many chiles I ate.

Food and Mexico and me—it often felt like a losing battle. This visit to the Yucatán was no different. But for two weeks I was sailing. No canned soup, no revenge, no problems. Yet.

We were nearing the end of our trip after two weeks of driving through southern Mexico when we arrived late one afternoon in a small mountain town called Catemaco. The town wraps around a huge freshwater lake that sits, unbelievably, in the mouth of a volcano. Such a magical and majestic place is Catemaco that every year the annual brujo—witch doctor—convention is held there. The belief is that because of its location, this place allows for spirits to communicate with mediums and witches. The majority of tourists who visit Catemaco are Mexicanos, some who come to see the mountains, some who come to see a brujo, and some who come to eat the delicacies that exist no place else on this earth but in Lake Catemaco.

I, of course, had come for the food.

My *Lonely Planet* guidebook had information about snails, called tegogolos, which, they wrote, were not only delicious but also were aphrodisiacs. So the night we arrived, after telling several young tour guides that we were not interested in seeing the brujos, we found a great little restaurant and I ordered my first plate of tegogolos. They were exquisite, served in a ceviche with warm homemade corn tortillas. I was in heaven.

The aphrodisiac tegogolos worked, but the next morning the strange energy of Catemaco had seeped into all of us. My husband and I fought for the first time on this vacation, and then my brother argued with Gérman and with the tour guide, who was late to take us out on a tour of the lake.

By the time we got on the tiny fishing boat, none of us was talking to one another. Hoping that our moods would change, the tour guide decided to make our first stop at the shrine where La Virgen de la Caridad is said to have appeared centuries ago. There, a mysterious and shrouded old man was blessing the visiting tourists one by one, whispering something unintelligible in their ears as he made the sign of the cross in front of their face and then put his fingers in the shape of a cross on their lips so they could kiss them and say Amen. Before I knew it the old man was blessing me. Feeling sentimental, I told the viejito I wanted to make an offering to the virgin. I took off one of my favorite African beaded bracelets and gave it to him to lay beside her in the gated alcove where the statue stood surrounded by burning candles. The old man asked for some pesos for the virgin and I took some out and lay them next to my bracelet.

But then he asked for more money for himself and I felt a shiver as if all was not right, and when he tried to force himself on my husband to bless him against his will, I knew that it was time to go.

The three of us were still not speaking when our tour guide took us to brunch at a lakeside restaurant. Hoping to catch a positive aphrodisiac vibe once again, I ordered my second plate of tegologos. They tasted a little bit different than the night before, but because I didn't want to make any unnecessary waves, I ate them. Late that afternoon we drove to the port city of Veracruz, where the next day we would spend New Year's Eve.

The morning of December thirty-first, I woke up so ill I couldn't lift my head from my pillow. And despite taking some antibiotics, three hours later my fever was still climbing and had reached 103. Against my protests of "I'll be fine!" Gérman called the hotel doctor. When he arrived a half hour later, I was delirious and in so much pain that I could barely answer his questions about what I had eaten. I began making a long list of foods but when I got to the word *tegogolo,* the doctor interrupted and said "That's it! You have typhoid! Tegogolos carry typhoid!"

I opened up my eyes, looked at the doctor, and started crying. My whole life there was only one illness that I ever remember being afraid of and that was typhoid. I was sure it has to do with the fact that one of my cousins, who loved to eat as much as I did, had typhoid three times. Her mother, my tía Licha, would on a daily basis remind my cousin that if she was not careful and ate another one of those street-vendor helados (ice cream) or elotes (corn on the cob) or raspados (flavored shaved ices), and got typhoid just one more time, that she was going to die. No questions. Get typhoid and you die. I grew up worrying that every time I said good-bye to my cousin after our yearly visits that I was never going to see her again, all because of typhoid.

Needless to say, I thought I was going to die in that tiny hotel room in Veracruz on New Year's Eve.

Any physical pain I had been through paled in comparison to the typhoid symptoms. For eight hours I felt as though a huge gorilla was walking on my back and hitting me on my legs with a steel baseball bat.

My head weighed as much as a bowling ball, and when I moved it, I felt as though I was smashing it against a glass pane. Somehow, throughout this pain, I would have to get up every fifteen minutes to either puke or sit on the pot. And then I became delirious. In a deep and eerie voice, I told my husband that I had seen the devil, that the devil was every-where, that the old man by the lake was him.

And then, when the fever and hallucinations broke for a minute, I made a promesa to los santos, to God, and to anyone else who was lis-tening: "If you cure me, if you don't let me die, I will cleanse my body—I won't drink, I will take care of myself and eat well until the day that I give birth to a child. I promise. But please don't let me die. Just save me from this agony."

At about one in the morning after the New Year had been ushered in with firecrackers and a live band in the plaza right outside our hotel, the fever finally came down thanks to the drugs the doctor prescribed. I sat up in bed and gave Gérman a kiss and wished him a happy new year. He hugged me, relieved beyond belief that I was not only awake but alive. Then we turned on the TV set and watched *Saturday Night Fever* dubbed in Spanish. Everyone was dancing danzón, drinking tequila, and party-ing in the streets. But after my fever and hallucinations laying in bed, watching an old movie in this smelly hotel room was like paradise.

I came into the new year with nothing in one piece except my spirit. I had sweated, vomited, excreted everything I had inside of me. I came into the new year cleansed. I knew there was a reason why I had gotten sick and this was it. I had given myself my own limpia, my own ablution. I was emotionally, spiritually, and physically emptied and renewed. I was like a baby, a virgin, a new person.

I could start my life fresh. And whether or not any of this was true, it didn't matter. What mattered was that it was true for me. And now I was ready—for what exactly, I was still not sure. But I felt ready.

We returned to New York City and I went back to work immedi-ately. My first assignment had me sitting in a wood-paneled courtroom in downtown Manhattan, surrounded by federal agents car-rying semiautomatic weapons, frantic notepad-scribbling journalists, and the ten men who were accused of heading the conspiracy to bomb

the World Trade Center. It was the biggest terrorism trial in the history
of the United States. My assignment meant that I wasn't going to get a
chance to do my story-form reporting, but I was excited by the challenge of covering this major trial.

Unfortunately, not everyone else was as piqued as I was. All
they wanted to hear about was O.J., Marcia, Johnnie, and Judge Ito.
Aaarrrgggghhhhh! O.J. versus the biggest terrorism trial in this country's
history? There was no question which was the more important story.
But it didn't matter. O.J. was winning out. I would spend my days going
to the courtroom, riding the subway from way uptown all the way
down to City Hall, befriending smug lawyers, criminal investigators,
and Muslim family members, trying to get anybody to go on tape, piec-
ing together stories and then fighting to get them on the air.

During lunch breaks, after filing my short news spots and inhaling a
sandwich, I would check in with my journalist hermanas and complain.
Squeezed into an old wooden phone booth in the hallway of the court
building, I'd rant about the state of modern-day journalism with Ceci,
Sandy, and Ro. They would empathize with me, but there was nothing
they could do.

So I took advantage of my predictable courtroom day (the few times
in my life when I would work nine to five) and started doing things I
thought would feed my spirit. I started to really take care of myself, as
I said I would in my promesa.

In the evenings I began taking yoga class. I was a baby yogi compared
to the professional dancers who could stretch like Gumby and the
meditation experts who would Zen off in headstands while I kept
falling on the floor. But I forced myself to go at least once a week. I went
to get Rolfed for the first time in my life (a kind of intense massage) and
let the Rolfer dig her powerful fingertips deep into my back until I saw
the colors of the rainbow. At the end of our sessions, Kayte, the Rolfer,
would place her hands on my head and do energetic healing. Even
though I was a skeptic, I would lie there and swear that I had seen stars
rolling around in my head. I had another friend who was a macrobiotic
alternative healer, and she told me about what vitamins and teas to take
(red raspberry, to help make your woman side strong) and what to eat
(anything with seeds because you want to plant something inside of
you, and anything red to build up your blood—yeah, I thought it was a

little weird too but I did it). I went back to see Adaluz regularly and in therapy we would talk about life—not just pregnancy envy. In the mornings before work I had acupuncture treatments and then arrived floating into the courtroom. The last thing I tried out was a couple of sessions of light therapy, a form of guided meditation that works with one's inner light. I pooh-poohed it at first, but whether or not it really worked wasn't so much the issue for me. It just felt good to go and spend an hour doing a guided meditation moving light throughout my body.

I never thought I would see myself doing all of these things, opening myself up to all of these alternative experiences that not too long ago I had never given much thought to. Even though I loved my altars and my candles and my own form of praying, this stuff was new to me. I felt as if I was letting go of the cynic in me as I learned about new ways of feeling and healing.

At the end of January, after a two-month wait, I also finally got an appointment to see the specialists Roxanne the nurse had told me about. The doctor there reassured me that what I had gone through was not so entirely out of the norm. He told me he knew several women who had been through the same kind of situation—even worse—but who were now moms. In my new positive frame of mind, I chose to believe him.

Sure the ultimate goal was that all of these self-help, alternative efforts would help me get and stay pregnant, but after going through my typhoid experience, I felt like something had changed profoundly inside of me and as usual it was Gérman who helped me see what it was.

There had never been a time in my life when I had been close to death. And maybe I wasn't really going to die from typhoid, but I felt as if I had survived a brush with la pelona, death. Surviving something like that gives you perspective, which I finally realized I had lost over the past year.

One Saturday night in late January and a month into my healing adventures, Gérman and I climbed up the stairs to our loft bed and looked out the window at the crescent moon hovering over the city lights, brilliant against a clear, deep blue-black sky. I hugged Gérman from behind, my arms like a baby chimp's wrapped around its mother's back.

"Thanks for taking care of me in Veracruz, honey," I whispered in his ear and felt him take a deep breath. I wanted to thank him for not abandoning me, for being a mother to me as well as a husband. As I hugged him closer to my body, I thought about a night many years ago when an alcoholic ex-boyfriend of mine had left me alone in a small town in Puerto Rico when I was reeling with pain from a urinary tract infection. The cabrón had just up and left me there with my bladder slicing me in half so he could go out and drink with some friends. I had never felt so miserable. In pain, alone, with no one to help me, defenseless and weak. I never forgave that man for doing that to me, and it was months later that I left him for Gérman. But what had happened in Veracruz was so different and I realized that over the past year, in my eagerness to get pregnant, I had been taking Gérman for granted, seeing him less as my life partner, my honey, and my husband, and more like a sperm depositor.

Veracruz had been a sign and I was finally getting the message.

For the past five years, Gérman had chosen to be at my side no matter what happened to me. I trusted he would never leave me—even if I couldn't have his children. This man was going to be my partner, my compañero, forever, and making our life together meaningful and loving was what mattered most to him—not whether I could have his child. Gérman had been wonderful at taking care of me. Now I needed to learn to take care of him *and* me. I needed to walk away from my self-imposed baby deadline and learn what Gérman and Sandy and my parents and family and friends had been trying to teach me for so long. Paciencia.

I had pregnancy-planning overdosed. I had life-planning overdosed, too.

"Mamita, you have no idea how afraid I was that I was going to lose you," Gérman said that night as we stared at the moon. "There you were, delirious and burning up in my arms. I was so scared. You don't remember but I kept you up that whole afternoon and evening until the medicine kicked in because I was afraid to let you go to sleep. I thought you would never wake up. The most precious thing in my life lay in my arms limp and weak and losing you forever felt too real." Gérman took another deep breath and continued. I looked up at the moon and listened in a way I usually don't. With humility and without interruptions. "Nobody has loved me like you do, Malu, not even my mother. You want me to think about having a child, but I love you more than any baby. Can't you see that *you* are what matters most to me because even if we have a child, at some point that child leaves, and you and I will be together alone again. You and I are already a family, Mamita, can't you see that?"

Gérman turned around and hugged me, and I let myself relax into his arms. I ran my hands over his smooth muscles and wrapped my fingers in between his rough calloused painter's hands. I felt myself letting go. All of my rushing, all of my calculating, all of my pressures left my body, and for the first time in more than a year, I understood, *this* is what matters most. And though it's hard to believe, the little baby-calculating part of my brain shut down, like a shade over a window, and I let myself fall slowly into Gérman's calor.

Todo vendrá en su momento. All things will come in time, I told my-self that night.

The following weekend Gérman and I went with Victor and Graci to their cottage in Connecticut. The town of Bethlehem was like a pic-ture-perfect winter wonderland with everything covered in soft snow outside and a warm fire crackling indoors while Mercedes Sosa warmed us with her lush voice. It felt so Connecticut-Wasp slash Argentinean-porteño—apple pie and maté. One night for dinner I cooked Gérman's favorite seafood lasagna and the next morning made chilaquiles, eggs, and frijoles refritos for breakfast. At night Gérman and I lay in bed talk-ing about how blessed we were to have Victor and Graci in our lives. Everything they had they shared with their friends.

"I would love to have a little cottage out here someday," I said to Gér-man. "We could invite all of our friends, just like Victor and Graci do. We could have huge parties and get people to play the drums outdoors under the full moon. That would be a first for Bethlehem, I bet."

"Yeah, and the police would come and throw everyone in jail for dis-turbing the peace," Gérman said and laughed.

The next morning while we were cleaning up the dishes from break-fast one of Graci's neighbors came by with some fresh-baked chocolate chip cookies. We got to talking and somehow in the conversation I men-tioned that if she ever knew of a cottage for sale in the neighborhood I would love it if she would call me. As if we could ever afford it, I whis-pered to Gérman and poked his side.

"Well, you know, there is an abandoned house next door to mine.

You probably have never noticed it because the bushes and shrubs are so overgrown that you can't see it from the road. I have the key if you want to look at it."

I was almost trembling as I put on my boots. Could this be a dream come true? "You see? Be careful what you ask for," Gérman joked to me as we went outside, "because you might just get it."

We climbed over small mountains of snow and had to pry open the screen door to get inside the hidden cottage, which was old, crooked, and dingy. I took one look inside and then darted away immediately. The smell of musty raccoon droppings was sickening. I gulped some fresh air and then held my breath to take another peek. It was definitely abandoned, but I could tell by Gérman's face that he was envisioning a palace here.

The cottage had been owned by a Catholic priest who had died ten years earlier and since then no one had been to the place. We called the woman who was managing the estate and told her we would offer a tiny sum of money if she would sell it to us as is. Much to my surprise she said yes. Gérman and I looked at each other ecstatically but then our faces froze.

"What are we doing?" I said. "How are we going to be able to afford this?"

"Quién sabe," said Gérman. "But let's just imagine that it's all going to work out."

That night back in New York we started doing calculations and we figured if we couldn't afford to use it for ourselves that we could at least fix it up and rent it so that the cottage could pay for itself and we could use it in ten or twenty years. We borrowed money from a friend of my father's so we wouldn't have to go through another five-month-long mortgage application and we handed him over all of our savings. In less than six weeks we had our own little poop-filled cottage in Bethlehem, and we named it Boca Chica after a beach in the Dominican Republic. We spent every weekend with the Penchas at Rayuela, sleeping at their house at night and fixing up Boca Chica during the day. It would be several months before we could actually spend the night in our own cottage, but Gérman and I were embarking on our second Domini-Mex production. It was a Caribbean-style, Mexican-flavored cottage in the middle of Wasp-landia.

Those first several months in 1995 were exquisite. Gérman shifted into major production mode with Boca Chica. And after years of rushing to do everything (most recently to have a child), I was basking in my project of developing peace and patience.

I spent more time doing things for Gérman. I would make him his café con leche every morning and for dinner treat him to fish taquitos and pescado frito con quesadillas. Mom always told me nuestros hombres always felt loved when they were served well and even though I had fought against this because I didn't want to be that "typical servile Latina," I started being less of a pushy New Yorker and more of a good friend to my man.

February had been a great month on the job as well. I continued covering the trial and for *Latino USA,* the new radio show I was hosting, I interviewed the only group in existence of female santera drummers. They were beautiful Cuban women who by day dressed in sweatpants but by night wore all white and played the sacred batá drums that usually only men are allowed to play. They were hot. The day after one of their concerts, I felt inspired and so I decided to clean up the space on my dresser that I used as an altar to my ancestors. I had been careless in tending to it and weeks had passed since I had even poured fresh water in the goblet.

I decided to put the altar on the floor in the corner of the living room. I got a clean white lace tablecloth and laid it on the ground. I put Yemanya, Oshun, and La Guadalupe in the middle, a goblet of water on one side, and a white candle on the other. On one side I put all of the photos of our ancestors—Gérman's mom and dad, my grandparents, tías y tíos, and photos of friends. On the other side was a veritable United Nations of fertility gods that my mom had started buying for me on all of her trips. I had put them all away in a box in my closet but something told me it was time to let them out. There was a wooden statue with a nose ring and stringy hair from the jungles of Irian Java, a jade doll from Taiwan, a straw fertility statue from Thailand, an African goddess Sandy had bought in Ghana, and a Mayan sculpture I had picked up in Yucatán. I put fresh white tulips in a simple vase and right under the flowers I laid out three cowrie shells, one for me, one for Gérman, and one for the baby. I lit some incense and I put a silver baby milagro in the center of it all.

And then I forced myself to sit down and meditate. I stared at the Catholic saints, African deities, Chinese dolls, Indonesian statues, African sculptures, Mexican potions, bodega-bought candles and incense, feeling ridiculous sitting on the ground waiting for something to happen. So I decided that the best meditation was simply to be quiet. And soon it started to feel all right to be sitting there on the floor in silence, just me and my dreams.

Several days later I was at the office writing a news spot about the terrorism trial when the phone rang. I was being invited by a literary group to go back to Cuba to participate and document the first-ever American book fair in Havana. My boss, probably fearing that I would come back traumatized like I did the last time, was not happy about the invitation but finally he gave in. I wanted to see how things had changed since the government had enacted some "opening up" reforms. One person I had stayed close to who had been starving just months before told me she had now opened up an underground restaurant in her living room and that dozens of people had done the same thing. Farmer's markets were back she told me when I called to tell her the good news that I was going to visit. And now if you tried to leave on a makeshift raft she said, the police, who had not long ago turned a blind eye, would now be forced to arrest you.

Havana was misty and hot that first day we arrived, the heat closing in around us like a boa constrictor. I took a walk with some of the American booksellers down the malecón and couldn't believe how much Havana had recuperated. During the exodus the streets had been totally empty, the city was gray and depressed. The only people out were those who were jumping into the ocean on crippled rafts, a wildly crazy form of playing Russian roulette with the Caribbean Sea.

Now it felt like a different country. Havana was alive again. Music could be heard everywhere and people were back on the streets, finding a way to love their lives as they struggled to survive. The first man I saw crossing the street to the malecón murmured a totally Cuban, perfectly poetic, piropo to me.

"Ay, Mamita, if I was your husband, I would never let you walk the streets alone. You are too beautiful to be unaccompanied."

I translated to one of the American writers.

"How romantic," she oohed and I laughed.

I had brought the phone number of a Cuban santero, Horacio, with me from New York, and I was just waiting for a break in my busy schedule to call him. I had been told that Horacio was one of the oldest living babalawos (Yoruba priests) and spiritual readers in Havana. I was excited but a bit scared about seeing him. What was he going to tell me? That I would never have children? That I was going to get hit by a bus? That someone in my family was going to die? I wanted to hear only the good stuff. But that's the leap of faith you take when you go see a reader. If you're going to go, you've got to be willing to hear it all.

I finally called him. "I can see you in an hour," he said. So I snuck away from all the American authors selling their books and hopped into my friend's 1956 Opal, taking off for "my lectura." Of course, I had forgotten to tell Horacio that that's why I wanted to see him so when I walked into his small old flat in a working-class barrio of Havana he said to me, "What can I do for you, young lady?" I was silent. I must have had nervios written all over my face. I had had readings before. I didn't know why I was acting so strange. I guess it was because this was my first reading in Cuba and Horacio was one of the grand poo-bahs of the Yoruba religion. Would he scoff at me for not being an initiate and just a casual dabbler?

"Venga, siéntese aquí," he said and walked slowly over to a tattered old sofa. Horacio was not much taller than I. He was dark like Louis Armstrong and, in fact, looked like a perfect combination of Armstrong and my abuelito. It made me sad to see him wearing an old pair of tattered and dirty tan pants. I wondered if he had family who looked after him.

Before I knew it Horacio was giving me information he wanted me to take back to Armando, our mutual friend in New York City. And it wasn't just random information—it was the Lectura del Año, the reading for the year. Here I am, a little nobody, and he is trusting me, a Mexican noninitiate, with secret santero info? (Later I would learn that the reading is made public . . . boy, did I feel foolish!) The reporter in me kicked in and I took out a pen and paper. "Tell Armando that the reading for this year shows that people are going to have to be very careful and take precautions with their health. It will be a dangerous year for los viejitos. They should be very careful when they walk outside so they don't fall. The reading for this year shows that this is the year for Oshun.

Everyone must wear something yellow every day this year in order to honor Oshun." Horacio continued to talk, as if he were reciting this mass of information from memory, as if for a moment I was not even there. I felt like just a messenger. Nothing more, nothing less. I began to wonder what I was doing there when Horacio said, "And this year any woman who has been trying to get pregnant and has not been able to, will conceive a child. This will be the year for them."

I let out a gasp. I lifted up my head from my notes and looked at him, piercing him with my eyes. I gasped again.

"Is this something that concerns you?" he asked me quietly.

"Yes," I said, holding back my excitement. "I had my second pérdida in December."

"Would you like to have a child?" Horacio asked.

"Yes."

"Then you will have one," he said simply and almost in the same breath started rattling off more information, but this time it was meant for me. "You will have to make offerings to Oshun, the fertility goddess. You will need to wear five yellow scarves tied together and wrapped around your waist. You will need to burn yellow candles and make offerings of yellow fruits to her on your altar. When you return, lay seven fruits on your altar for seven days and then take them and put them in the ocean, one by one. You will need to think about what Oshun symbolizes and bring that into your life. If you do all this, you don't have to worry. You will have a child. Now if you would like a reading, let's go to the backroom and you can also salute the altar I have made for Oshun."

I stood obediently and followed him down a tiny dark corridor. I peered behind the door into the third and last bedroom and was overwhelmed by the beauty.

There stood a four-foot statue of Oshun, a black saint, with yellow scarves draped over her head and shoulders. She was wearing dozens of strands of yellow beads and on the floor there were oranges, melons, bananas, lemons, and other yellow fruits and vegetables. There was a huge bowl of honey, yellow candles, and goblets of water. The room smelled of wild yellow roses and the flickering candles made it seem as if the whole space was floating through the stars. Horacio quietly asked me to lie down in front of the statue and gave me a gold-plated bell.

I felt self-conscious again. I don't know how to do this, I thought. I couldn't quiet the voices inside. Horacio started talking again and the voice inside shut up, pa' quick!

"Ring this as you pray to Oshun, as you ask for her help in your life and as you tell her your wishes. Ring the bell so she will hear you and heed your prayers," Horacio said softly.

I was lying there, wondering how it was that I was on the floor in this stranger's home in front of a statue and suddenly holding a bell in my hand. I was watching myself from above, wondering if I was crazy. I had seen this in the movies but now it was me. I started to ring the bell, slowly, tentatively, and I began to whisper to Oshun, "Por favor, Oshun. Entrégame un hijo." Please Oshun, bless me with a child. I felt totally and utterly self-conscious, like a child walking up the long church aisle to take her First Communion. But then I focused and said these words: "You are the goddess of love and passion and sensuality. I promise you I will bring passion into my life. I will love my husband, I will love my life passionately. I promise to be sensual and attractive, erotic and enticing." I kept ringing and I felt like I never wanted to get up from there. Like I could stay there for hours, just ringing this bell, lying here at this santo's feet, humbled.

I got up from the altar, a little dizzy, and Horacio sat me down in front of a makeshift table, an old piece of wood balanced on two milk carts. He began to read the coconut shells and everything this man, who I had just met, said was true. He talked for what felt like hours. I felt the room spinning and my chair tipping over but nothing moved. I was like a rock on my chair and so was Horacio, who looked calm. I was locked with his gaze and his voice, mesmerized by the movements of his hands as he threw the shells over and over again on the table. He told me things I know, things I should know, things I must do to take care of myself.

The first thing Horacio said to me was, "You must learn to listen carefully to things that are being said to you. You must analyze what you are hearing." He paused, took a deep breath, closed his eyes, and lifted his face to the sky. Then he continued: "Good things will happen this year but you need to be aware of jealous people who try to get close to you. Try not to cry this year. Ever. And do not fight with anyone. Listen to your dreams. You also made a promise of some kind, didn't you?" Yes, I said to him, remembering the night of typhoid, the night when I made my promise. "You must keep this promesa. Be organized in your life. Complete the projects you set out for yourself. And, stay away from dogs."

"Maria," Horacio whispered, "you have to learn to ask for the things you want. You have to ask for them out loud, every day. Y necesitas mucha fé. You need more faith. You have a strong character and are a powerful spirit, but you don't believe in yourself."

And finally, the last thing Horacio said to me was "Maria, you came here from very far away to hear what you already know. You can trust yourself, if only you would listen to your own inner voice. Mi hija, listen when I tell you that you came here to hear what you already know."

I sat in Horacio's living room, waiting for him as he finished praying at the altar. I saw a TV set that was thirty years old, a wooden rocking chair that was missing an arm, a dusty couch, old magazines. I didn't know why, but I felt at home there and I made a promise to bring my child to Cuba, when (not if) he was born, so that Horacio could see the power of his words. Because now I knew that this child was near. Very near. Close enough that I could almost touch him.

My last day in Havana I drove out with my friends to the countryside. I had been trying to hook up with some teenagers who were living in one of the AIDS sanatoriums and they had finally agreed to meet with me for an interview. Javier and his wife, Mireya, were waiting at the entrance of the sanatorium for us. He was tall and so skinny that it looked as if his shoulders were the ends of a thin plank of wood. Mireya was petite and quiet. But they were both dressed like heavy-metal fans. He had on a black AC/DC T-shirt, ripped jeans, and a Nirvana baseball cap. She wore a KISS T-shirt and skimpy shorts outlined in black lace. They were teenagers and they were dying not because they had caught AIDS by accident but because a few years earlier they, along with several of their friends who had already died, had self-injected AIDS-tainted blood. Actually, Mireya corrects me when we start the interview: She hadn't self-injected but had purposefully had unprotected sex with Javier. She was too afraid of needles, she told me, in her child-like voice.

"Too afraid of needles but you weren't too afraid of getting AIDS," I said as our interview began.

"Yes," she whispered, lowering her head. "Now I wish I never would have done this."

We talked for two hours hidden under a tree in the middle of someone's farm. Javier was afraid that if the police saw him talking to a reporter he might be harassed. They had self-injected, they told me as I listened sadly, because they were tired of being hassled by the police for being "antisocial" rockeros. They explained that they had decided to get AIDS so they could get into the sanatoriums where they knew they would be allowed to dress how they wanted, listen to the music they wanted, and have air-conditioning and food seven days a week.

"We were sure that someone would find a cure for AIDS in five years," Javier told me. "We figured we could spend five years living high in the sanatoriums and then we would be cured and free."

I tried to keep my shock hidden. I wanted to slap them and hug them at the same time.

Afterward, I treated everyone to pollo asado. On the way out to the sanatorium from Havana my Cuban friend had told me she was afraid of touching anyone with AIDS. But here she was sharing a meal with Javier and Mireya. In the early evening we drove them back to the sanatorium. As we arrived, a friend of theirs was being driven away by the police. A month ago this friend had given some of his blood to another teenager who wanted to become infected. Now the police were taking him away for helping to infect a fourteen-year-old. We said our good-byes quickly and in sadness. We knew we might not ever see one another again.

We drove back to Havana and for the two hours of the trip we rode in silence. How could it be that young people would do this to themselves? That night I interviewed a Cuban psychologist and she told me that these teens were social misfits who came from broken homes. This wasn't about rebelling against socialism as an American journalist had already written. This was an act of adolescent rebellion. These teens were victims of utter ignorance, thinking that a cure for AIDS was only five years away.

I got back from Havana feeling as if I had been put through an emotional wringer. But I followed the santero's instructions. I went to a fabric store and bought some yellow satin and cut it into five pieces. I

tied them all together and wrapped them around my waist. I put seven
fruits on my altar and a week later I put them in a bag and had Gérman
drive me down to the tip of Manhattan. With the World Trade Center
towers behind me and the Statue of Liberty facing me in the distance I
opened up the grocery bag and one by one dropped the seven fruits into
the Hudson River. I was sure people who saw me thought I was una loca
but I was completing my mission. There was closure. As I watched the
fruit disappear, I hoped Horacio was right. Maybe this year would be my
year to carry a child.

That same evening I sat on my couch in silence, my head resting in
my hands for a time, and then I would take my hands and wind them
through my long hair. The street was noisy outside, I could hear the catcalls of the drug dealers and feel the rumbling of the buses as they
rushed to make the light. The television was off, the radio, too. I could
have easily gotten up and started cleaning the house, dusting the lamps,
folding the clothes lying in a pile on the dining room chair. I could have
done anything to distract myself but I didn't. I let my legs weigh me
down like lead and I started to listen to my breathing. I closed my eyes
and I created an image for myself, of myself, in my mind. I *am* this
mother that I yearn to be, I *am* this woman I envision, I am *not* fearful.
Soy yo. Soy mujer. Soy fuerte. Soy una mujer fuerte.

Before I went to sleep, I lit a yellow candle, kissed each of my fertility gods, and blessed myself with my holy water. And I said this to myself:

> *I am at peace with myself*
> *I am at peace with my earth*
> *I am centered*
> *I am whole*

I entered those same words into my journal and then I put my pen
down, closed my journal, turned over, and kissed Gérman good night.
That night I dreamt about giving birth to a little boy. It was not an idyllic dream filled with angels delivering a child from the heavens into my
arms as I sat in a fluffy bed surrounded by white lace pillows. No, in my
dream I gave birth to a little boy who looked like a black Al Franken
complete with horn-rimmed glasses and a head of tight black curls. And

the first thing this newborn said to me was, "Mamá, quiero mi teta ahora!" He was the cutest and most bossy baby I had ever seen!

When we went to the doctor's office later that morning, the specialist we had been seeing said that this month we could at last get rid of the birth control and start trying again. Bravo!

 EL MILAGRO

It was April in New York and everything was in bloom and posthibernation Manhattanites were out on the streets en masse and I was happy. It had been five months since my last miscarriage and we had finally gotten the go-ahead from all of the powers that be—doctors and healers, my family, and my sistahs. The procreation mode was in full swing once again.

So off to the store I went. Even though my doctor hadn't instructed me to do so, I took it upon myself to buy every possible kit you could imagine. An ovulation kit, a pregnancy test kit, a basal body temperature kit. When the woman at the pharmacy register said to me, "Honey, it don't matter. You know this child is gonna come when he is good and ready." Of course, I already knew she was right. But just to satisfy myself, I was going to invest in a bit of science. And it was a way for me to exert some control over the process. (So much for the spiritual make-over.)

For the past month I had been going to the specialist's office regularly where they would draw blood and make me pee in a cup in order to determine my exact ovulation schedule. Now I was in control. I wanted to pee in my own ovulation kit, damn it!

The next visit to the doctor he informed us that he had an assignment for us. "This coming Thursday, I want you to make a 9:30 A.M. appointment to come and see me. But you will need to make love that same morning at 6:30. No condoms. And please don't be late. And don't forget to set your alarm."

What? This was one of the strangest doctor's orders I had ever heard. But I was willing to do just about anything at this point.

So that Thursday we had unprotected sex for the first time in five months—at dawn. It was the sleepiest, fastest, most unromantic, homework-assignment quickie in our history together. Sitting in the exam room later that morning, I couldn't help but blush. The doctor told me to lie back and he suctioned out some of what had been left inside of me and slipped it under the microscope.

And then he started reciting a list of words, like an excited little boy looking under a microscope for the very first time. "Moving, twitching, good motility, squirming, more with good motility, excellent motility, twitching . . . This is great!" He explained to us that he was looking to see how well my husband's sperm floated and survived in my uterine fluid. He let Gérman and me take a peek as well. There they were. A bunch of egg-hunting little sperm worms, squirming all over, searching for a base to land on.

Later that morning Gérman drove me to work from the doctor's office. I pulled out some little yellow Post-its and drew little sperms with faces, smiles, mustaches, and horn-rimmed glasses, worms with little tails and hats and scarves, and stuck them on the dashboard. We named them all—Juanita, Pepito, Ismaelito, Susanita. Gérman kissed me good-bye and I ran into the office, giddy with happiness.

According to the doctor's calculations of my body temperature and ovulation cycle and my husband's sperm count and motility, the doctor said since there was nothing wrong with either one of us that we should make love the next night and every other night for seven days. "Have a good time and think positive!" he said, giving us each a spontaneous hug. Doctor's orders, I remember thinking. Have sex. I tried to focus on everything I had learned over the past several months. Even if we didn't make a baby, I was going to make exquisite, passionate, hopeful, and unprotected love with my husband for a week. Period.

That next afternoon after work, Gérman came by and picked me up from the office. Fortuitously, I thought, this was to be the very first weekend we were going to be able to stay at Boca Chica, our cottage in Connecticut. The full-scale integration of Bethlehem had begun and if we were lucky the Latino population was going to grow by one more in nine months!

Our first night in Boca Chica would have been special in and of itself, but here we were, under strict physician's orders: *Make love!*

Our desire that night was whole, hungry, and full. It was unspoken and yet I had so many words flowing across my body. *Passion, entrega, amor, consuming, security, delicious, softness, warmth, belleza, esposo, cariño, husband, father, mulatto, mi hombre.* I was going to give myself to my husband and to my own pasión. And I called on Oshun to help me laugh and giggle, to love myself and my body. I asked her to fill this bed with her yellow flowers and honey, to make my head fall back in joy, to consummate this moment, not with a child necessarily, but with serenity and ecstasy. With security and pleasure. With sheer celebration. I opened my eyes and looked at the moon, with its roundness and fullness and said, me entrego. Soy tuya. I am yours. Luna, Oshun, Noche, Madre, Moon, Night, Mother. I am yours. . . .

Later, I opened the door that led to our back porch and boldly stepped outside naked. The neighbors were nowhere to be seen through the trees. My husband followed and hugged me. Looking up to the sky, I gazed intently at this brilliant circle of power, mesmerized by the moon's perfection, strength, and permanence. We stood there for a long, long time, in silence, breathing. And then suddenly, off to the right side there was a flash, a storm of shooting stars. One second and it was gone.

"Amor," I said to my husband with a deep slow breath, "did you see that?"

"Yes, cariño. I saw it. You didn't make it up. I saw it."

Gracias, I said, gracias a la vida por darme este momento. Thank you, life, for giving me this moment.

When I woke I couldn't believe I had slept the whole night in the same position I had fallen asleep in holding on to Gérman. I couldn't believe Gérman hadn't let me go. He always complained about me taking up the whole bed and never leaving him enough room to sleep, that even though I was a chaparra, a shorty, that I was like a giant in bed, spreading myself out like a spider doing a stretch.

"I tried to let you go, varias veces, last night," Gérman told me as he slipped out of bed, "but every time I would inch away from you, you would grab my arms and wrap them tighter around you. So I just gave up."

"Ay, mi amor!" I said. "How sweet."

"Sweet? Baby, yo te adoro but my back is a wreck. I'm going to take a hot shower and see if I can get the kink out of my spine. Nobody would believe me if I told them that you are mandona even when you sleep. You would think you would stop trying to control things once you close your eyes, but not mi Maria! Everything has got to be the way you want it all of the time. Dios mío! Not even a break in bed!"

So much for a romantic morning after our first love escapade in our new cottage. I made Gérman a café con leche and told him to take a hot bath instead of a shower and said I wouldn't disturb him for the next hour. I lit an incense and made a bubble bath for him. An hour to kill, I thought to myself, as I started making the bed and picking up our clothes, strewn all over the bedroom. That's when I looked outside and saw our neighbors for the first time. A little girl with hair the color of whipped butter was collecting flowers, her father had a small baby in a back carrier, and her mother was sipping coffee on their deck. It was a picture-perfect scene of family. Would this ever be us?

I finished making the bed and then picked up the phone and called Mom, one of my regular weekend cosas-que-hacer.

"Buenos Días, Ma," I said. "I'm calling you from Boca Chica. We just spent our first night here. It's so beautiful, Mami. I can't wait for you and Dad to see this place. It's our island paradise in the middle of country estates.

"Felicidades, mi'jita," she said in her sweet and unrushed Saturday-morning tone. Mom was so busy with her work now that the weekends had become the only time for us to talk without a million interruptions. She had become one of Chicago's most well-known and trusted counselors for Latinas who were victims of domestic violence. In addition to counseling victims, she gave workshops and held instructional training sessions.

I told her the good news about the visit to the doctor and the sperm dances. And then out of the blue she said to me:

"Sabes qué, mi'jita? I never have told you the full story about how you were conceived. And it really is such a beautiful story . . ."

"Pues, okay, Ma. If you want to share it I am all ears."

She took me back to the years before I was even conceived. They had just returned from an extended stay in Switzerland, where my father had been given a grant to work in a hospital there. It had been a very good year for him. But Mom had spent much of her time in Europe feeling sick and lonely and cold. She was pregnant with my older brother and all she wanted to do was sleep.

"I used to wake up, give your brother and sister their breakfast, and then tell them it was time for a nap. Then I would wake up and make them lunch and tell them it was time for another nap. I missed Mexico so much. I would look at your brother and sister and worry that they had no one to play with and meanwhile I would be thinking about la bola de primos, all of their cousins back in Mexico, playing in the streets of the capital, going to the store to buy dulces de mazapán and Carlos Quinto chocolates. I was counting the days so I could go home and have my baby and be taken care of by your tías and abuelita. I realize now that I was depressed during that time in Switzerland, deeply depressed. But you know, back then, I don't even think I knew the word *depression*. It was just life.

"The boat ride back from Europe was horrible," she continued. "I spent most of the days leaning over the side of the ship, holding my panza, praying that I wouldn't lose the baby. When we finally arrived in Mexico City, we had no money and so we all had to move back into the house where I had grown up, en la Calle Pitágoras, Pythagoras Street. Your brother was born and the five of us were living in the big bedroom that your aunt and I had shared as children. Pero mi vida, even though we were cramped, I was happy because I was home and I was surrounded by women who loved me and who helped me care for your brothers and sister. If they ever saw me get frustrated with the kids, your aunts, grandmother, or the nana would push me out of the house and say, 'Vete de aquí! Go away. Go walk around the block, do anything but leave the children here hasta que te calmes.' There was always someone I could turn to for help.

"Your brother had just turned a year old, it was September, and we had been back from Europe for a year. Mexico was clean and crisp and green and from our street we could see the snow-capped tip of the Popocatépetl Mountain. Your father and I were celebrating our seventh anniversary. That day we had all made an outing to the country. We must have been at least thirty people just between your aunts and uncles and cousins. A typical Sunday outing with carne asada and kids running like little loquitos everywhere.

"That afternoon, your father and I left early from the outing, told your tía Gloria to watch over the kids and we drove the old Volkswagen back to la Calle Pitágoras. It had been seven years earlier that we had gotten married and eight years since we had first met. The house was empty when we came home that Sunday. We unlocked the stained-glass front door and pretended like it was the first day your father had kissed me. Ay ay ay! He grabbed me from the waist and brought me up close to his chin. I smelled his hombría, his manliness, just as I had eight years before, when I was just a sixteen-year-old kid. Now I was a woman, a mother to three children, and a wife. I was happy with my life, fulfilled. And then your father picked me up and carried me, imagínate! He carried me up those tiled steps to the bedroom where as a teenager I used to sleep, dreaming of him at night, when I was still a virgin. I told him how he was such a good man, such a caring father, such a strong husband. Eres mi macho, I whispered in his ear. Te quiero, viejito."

"Ay Ma! I can't believe you are telling me this!" I shrieked. I was feeling as if I had invaded a private space, a space I was led to believe never existed between my parents. They were always very affectionate around me, kissing and hugging. But sex was an unspoken and untouched tema de conversación.

"Mi'jita, you are a grown woman. It's beautiful that I can finally share this story with you."

"Si, Mamá. Don't stop then! Tell me what happened next."

"Your father and I made love that evening and I can tell you it was one of the most passionate nights of our lives. Había algo en el aire. There was something in the air. Maybe it was that it was our anniversary, maybe it was being in my old bedroom, my sudden memories of being a virgin, maybe it was the empty house, maybe it was the mountains or the ceviche we had eaten. Maybe it was because there was a full moon."

"There was a full moon?" I asked anxiously.

"Not only that, mi'jita. Your dad and I gave ourselves to each other as we always did. Con mucho amor y cariño y seguridad. With love and affection and security. And we hugged each other for a long time that

night, lying close together in the soft double bed, looking at the shad-
ows of the full moon on the pink walls of my old bedroom. But then the
most incredible thing happened. When your father and I got up and
looked out the window, what we saw reflected on the moon sent shiv-
ers up our spines. On the moon we saw the face of a baby. Just for a split
second, a baby's face, made by a flash of shooting stars. I couldn't believe it but even before I could ask your father if he had seen it he said
yes, Berta, I did see it. And you know your father, the scientist, never
believes in any of those things. But that night, for the first and only time
in his life, he saw something that science could not explain away. And
what was even more beautiful, and what made me fall in love with him
all over again that night, was that he didn't even doubt what he had
seen. He knew something magical had happened and he accepted it.
That's why one month later when I told him I was pregnant, I wasn't the
only one that was crying. So was your father. We knew this was a baby
that was meant to be and so we gave thanks for being blessed and that
was how you were made. You don't ask for children, I remember your
father saying to me, they are sent to you, como un sueño, like a dream."

"Ay, Ma. That is the most beautiful story. Thank you for telling it to
me. I hope the night I conceive my firstborn is as special as that was."

"Of course it will be, mi vida. You will know. You will remember,
just as I do, I am sure. And then when your child is grown up just like
you, you can tell them the story of the night they were made from love."

"Ojalá, Mami. Ojalá. I hope so," I said and then thought about the
moon—the full moon Gérman and I had seen last night, the full moon
Mom and Dad saw the night I was made, the full moon abuelita saw the
night Mom was conceived. I hung up the phone and walked into the
bathroom and slid into the bathtub with Gérman.

"That moon last night was incredible," he said out of the blue.

I just smiled and said. "Yeah, papito, it sure was."

I told Gérman the story Mom had just told me.

"Qué linda historia," he said. "It's so different from the story of your
own mom's conception. That was the wildest story of a pregnancy I
have ever heard."

Yes, the story of my grandmother's pregnancy with my mom was a
strange one: Long before my mother was born, my grandfather had already left my grandmother. Most men in Mexico who had lovers rarely

left the women they had married. They would just keep what's known as la casa chica—the mistress's house—on the side. But they would continue to live in la casa grande, the big house.

Not my grandfather.

He moved out of la casa grande to stay with his mistress in la casa chica, but every day he would eat supper with my grandmother and his four children with her, my aunt being the youngest at that time.

Everyone blamed my grandmother for this situation. All of the tías and tíos criticized my abuelita. Oh, she was such a nag, she was so infeliz, such a pain in the neck, what with her ataques de nervios, her depression, her constant complaining. She would have driven any man away, was what the family would say. Abuelita at least could resign herself to the fact that she and her children had my grandfather's name and that he, at least en la sociedad, had to act as her husband and had to father and protect his children by her.

One day, the rumors got back to my abuelita that the other woman was going around la sociedad saying that she was my grandfather's *real* woman. In the code of those days, this woman was saying that my grandfather cared so little for my grandmother that he didn't even have sex with her anymore. My abuela was devastated and angry beyond words so she decided to prove her nemesis wrong, the only way that such a thing could be proven. She decided she was going to get pregnant.

One Mexico City summer night when the full moon was shining over the valley, my grandmother seduced my grandfather. She had asked him to stay late for a special dinner and she made him his favorite Yucatec meal, cochinita pibil, shredded pork with achiote and orange spices. She made an escabeche with fresh white onions, vinegar, and oregano, and spent hours making tortillas by hand. And in the white rice she put a potion a local curandero had given her. It was a tasteless dust packet called "Atame a Ti" or "Tie me to you." A month and a half later, she invited him over for another late dinner and then announced to him that she was pregnant. And she made sure that word got back to his lover.

"You will not have this child," abuelito told my grandmother. "Mark my words, Manuela, you will not give birth to this child."

Even though it was the 1930s, my grandfather and his mother (who despised my grandmother because she was such a nag) began to investigate how such a "problem" could be taken care of. They found a young doctor who was willing to perform an abortion. My grandmother's sisters did their own investigating and found out who the doctor was that was going to perform the surgery. The day before abuelito was going to take my grandmother to the doctor's private clinic, my great-aunts waited for the doctor outside his office on a palm-tree lined street in la Colonia Santa Maria. As he nonchalantly left his office that day, my aunts cornered the young doctor and told him they knew what he was going to do and that if he did this surgery, they were going to call everyone, from the police to the local senator. And if you think we won't do this, they threatened, just try us. We will destroy your life and your career forever. Para siempre. You will never forget us, they snarled and slipped away.

The next day, my grandfather and his mother went to get my grandmother. She screamed and fought and kicked and yelled, but they pulled her out of the living room, a fuerzas. "You can not force me to father another one of your children," he said to her as they drove to the clinic, "my life with you is over, Manuela. Se acabó. Me oiste? Did you hear me? SE ACABÓ!"

When they got to the clinic the doctor opened the door and let them in. But right there in his lobby he told them that he would not perform the procedure. They should leave right away and never come back to his office ever again. Ever.

My mother's life was saved, thanks to my aunts and to the fear they put in the young doctor. And my grandmother gave birth to my mother at her house while my tía looked up into the sky for the stork from Paris (which is where my aunt was told babies came from). My grandfather stayed at la casa chica, showing utter disinterest in the birth of my mother.

Mom was six months old before my grandfather ever touched her. He would still come to la casa grande every day and eat la comida, but he never even looked at the newborn baby girl. One day, though, when my grandmother was cooking and holding the baby at the same time, and my grandfather was distracted reading the newspaper, she turned to him and said, "Ay Hermilo. Cárgala por un segundo. Carry her for one second. Take Bertita and just hold her while I finish with these tortillas. Just for one second. Un segundito por favor."

Without thinking too much about it, my grandfather reached out his arms to take the baby, the same way he would have done if my grandmother had handed him a dozen tortillas. Apparently, it was so quick and appeared so innocent that my grandfather fell for it. Little did he know that abuela had been waiting for six months for this precise moment—the moment when he would be in a good mood and distraído, his mind somewhere else. But from the moment he first carried my mother that day when she was six months old, my mom became the love of my grandfather's life. He had never loved any of his children— whether from my grandmother or his lover—the way he loved her. He doted on her and spoiled her, hugged her and showered her with presents. From that moment on, all he wanted to do was be with her. He would come to take her out every Sunday to the park or to the zoo or for a ride on the trolley. He adored her forever. And my mother, who to this day defends her father, loved him back, con las mismas ganas.

My mother didn't cry as I did when I first heard this story. And I was the one who told her what had happened after my aunt confided the story to me. She simply listened and looked out the front window of her apartment. That was two years ago. At the end of the story she said, "Your abuelito loved me and all of you very much," as she looked straight ahead. "Don't doubt that for one minute. When you are young you do foolish things. All we can do is to learn from the mistakes of the past. Lo que pasó, ya pasó. What's passed is past."

And we all moved on and rarely talked about my grandmother's pregnancy.

Three weeks after that first night in the Connecticut countryside, I realized that I was late, by three days. Early in the morning, I went to the closet to pluck out one of my pregnancy tests. Just as I had in the past, I peed all over everything, but luckily managed to drench the little test area. I put the test strip on top of a shelf out of my view and walked away. I stood in front of my altar and waited for three minutes to pass.

Back in the bathroom I slowly pulled the test down from the shelf. It's pink in both places! But I worried it wasn't dark enough, so I did another test. And another just to be sure. The same! I was pregnant! I jumped in bed and hugged Gérman. He was still groggy but I was talking and feeling as if my life were going a mile a minute. I wanted to tell someone but that was exactly what we had agreed we wouldn't do. This

time no one was going to know. That way we wouldn't jinx it. I realize
it sounds absolutely childish, but at this point we would try anything to
make sure it worked.

After much debate, Gérman and I decided I should make one excep-
tion and tell my boss. We had agreed it might be good for me to slow
down a little. I was so nervous about telling him that when I picked up the
phone to call him I was shaking. He said to me, "Go home, do nothing,
and forget about reporting for the next month. I want this pregnancy to
work for you and even though your doctor says that your miscarriages
had nothing to do with stress, I want you home and relaxed. Nothing is
more important than this moment in your life," he responded after I
told him the news. I felt like a huge weight was off my shoulder and the
next day we packed our bags and took off for Boca Chica, returning to
the city every week to have my progesterone level checked.

Everything seemed to be going just fine. I was consumed with excitement. But I couldn't talk about this most important moment in my
life with anyone who really mattered. I ended up telling people who I
knew I would never see again in my life, like a gas station attendant and
the waitress at the local diner, just so I felt like I was spreading the news
to someone, just so I could share my joy with a human being. It felt
pretty ridiculous. Here I was about to become a mother (maybe) and
yet I felt like a giddy thirteen-year-old who wanted to tell total strangers
about the boy she kissed last night. More than anything I just wanted
someone to say, This is it. It is for real. But of course, no one could. I
was on my own on this incredibly lonely and fragile third-pregnancy
limb.

Finally, the seventh week passed and it was time for my sonogram. I
had been feeling exhausted, though not very nauseous. I had been
touching my breasts every minute, everyday, to see if they remained
huge and sensitive. This was the only physical manifestation of my pregnancy. But I had felt this before so who was to say it wasn't a false start?
The night before we were going to go in for the sonogram, suddenly my
breasts felt normal. They had gone down in size, they weren't sensitive.
I went inside the bathroom, turned on the shower so Gérman couldn't
hear me, and began to sob. I knew it was over. This was just another
failed dream. I started getting myself ready for the worst. Another
D&C, another recovery room, another loss.

Gérman barged into the bathroom, scolded me for getting back into my old ways, for always being Miss Negativity, and for rushing for answers. "Paciencia, mi amor," he said to me over and over. "It's going to be fine if it's meant to be." I began to feel even worse.

At the doctor's office that next morning, it was all eerily and wretchedly familiar. "Lie back on the table, cover yourself with the paper gown, put your legs up, and try to relax." I was prepared for emptiness, for a black hole, for an empty womb, for another letdown.

There was silence as the doctor and nurse prepared the machine. I felt as if this body was not mine, as if this body that had been through so much was just a mass of meat, a body that was once again going to be prodded with some strange machine, a body that was so tired of being touched and provoked into sadness. I was trying to make myself numb. I turned my face away from the sonogram machine and stared at the wall. I held on to Gérman's hand tightly and closed my eyes. Why had I gotten my hopes up again? Why had I allowed myself to think that I could actually do this? I was never going to be able to have a child. I squeezed my eyes tight and took a deep breath.

"There it is! Do you see it?" the nurse was speaking.

"Oh, yeah! I see it!" I heard my husband say.

"There it is Maria! There is your heartbeat! We have a good one here. And this little one is strong!" the doctor said.

"No, no. There is nothing there," I said as I turned my face and looked into the monitor that looked black to me. "There is nothing there. I don't see anything. There is nothing there. No, no, no. There is nothing . . ."

"Maria, look at this. Don't you see that? There is the heartbeat. It is really there! Why would I lie to you! Look at the monitor . . ." the doctor was telling me. But all I could say was no. *No, no, no, no, no . . .*

I was trying to focus, trying to understand why everybody else was smiling and I was just crying, when I saw this faint little star, flashing on and off like a . . . like the heart of a seven-week-old embryo. Nothing else looks like this. Nothing in this world except the heart of a seven-week-old embryo in the dark womb of his mother who now was sobbing and saying, *Sí, sí, sí, sí, sí, sí! Es un milagro! Es un milagro! This is a miracle! This is a miracle! Oh God, thank you. Thank you, thank you! Gracias! Por fin, gracias!*

I spent the next four weeks hanging out at Boca Chica, watching Gérman work like an unstoppable machine, transforming our cottage into
an island-colored paradise. I would lie in bed and watch him dart back
and forth, unloading supplies, weeding through the garden, painting the
kitchen, and all I wanted to do was sleep. For the first time in two years
my body was in no-go mode. I would wake up late, read in bed for a
while, take a long shower, and then I'd need a nap after my overexer-
tion. Besides being exhausted, though, I actually felt quite normal. In
fact, I was worried that I felt *too* normal and hoped, yes hoped, for at
least some morning sickness. Dios mío—then one morning when I had
just reached nine weeks, I woke up, opened my eyes, and then instinctively, sprinted off to the toilet, kneeled down, and heaved. Then I felt
fine and went to sit at the kitchen table for a minute and then again,
without even thinking about it, my legs just buckled under me and led
me straight to the john. And that became the way of my world for the
next several weeks.

How was this baby-to-be going to get nutrition when I couldn't hold
anything down except for cold popcorn with greasy imitation butter?
(My sister had told me that movies helped calm her morning sickness so
we were at the Cineplex every day.) Gérman tried to help by rattling off
all kinds of food to see if anything sounded appetizing to me.

"Yeah, yeah, that's what I want! A grilled cheese with tomato and
barbecue potato chips! That's it! Please, papito, please, can you go buy
me the chips?!"

So Gérman would run to the store, buy all the ingredients, make me the sandwich, and bring it to me on a gorgeous platter.

I would take one look at it and feel sick.

"It's too late, honey," I would say to him. "I wish I wanted it but I just don't anymore. But did you happen to pick up some ice cream while you were out? Oooohhh, yes! Baskin-Robbins jamoca almond fudge. That's what I want! Por favor, honey!"

So poor Gérman would run out and buy me what I wanted and if we were lucky he would bring it to me before my craving died. (Gérman did his best to get me all of my antojos because an old wive's tale from the Dominican Republic said if you don't get a pregnant woman what she wants to eat, then her baby will be born with manchas, "wanting" spots, all over his skin.) We were exhausted from trying to figure out what I could eat, when to eat it, and how to get it. And that was without factoring in my wonderfully amplified emotional state. When we went to see *My Family / Mi Familia,* I was bawling like a baby during the opening credits.

At night, when I would lie in bed, after the waves of nausea would subside, I would rub my hands over my puffy stomach and tingling breasts and a wide smile would slip over my face. I would think about how joyous I was. Then all of a sudden I would start weeping so I'd dash out of bed so as not to wake Gérman and I'd go sit on the old linoleum floor in the other furnitureless bedroom and look out at the stars that I never had a chance to see in the city. It was the pregnancy hormones. Worse than any PMS I had been through.

On one of those nights I remembered that not long ago I had been told I was going to have a boy and now I knew it was true.

It happened at the National Association of Hispanic Journalists Conference that took place in Albuquerque a few years earlier. Some colleagues and I had made a commitment to help young idealistic future radio reporters, so we designed the first radio-training project for students who wanted to attend the conference. We worked our tails off, pulling several all-nighters, but we had a wonderful time.

Franc, one of my cotrainers, was a transplanted Chicano from Iowa who had been living in Albuquerque for five years. He had told Mandalit (another colleague in the program) and me that he had planned a surprise celebration for us at the end of the conference: a visit to a sweat lodge.

"You mean like the real thing?" I asked, my eyes widening. "We'll be in the middle of the mountains sweating and everyone else from the convention is going to be dancing to rancheras in a hotel ballroom? This is going to be great."

"Yeah," he said, smiling warmly. "I have a Chicana friend who's a curandera who's married to a guy who grew up on the reservation. They have a house not far from here and they do sweats in their backyard. I'll pick you guys up in front of the hotel at eight."

In their backyard, I thought to myself? How mystical could that be?

Later that evening, Mandalit and I were riding down the hotel elevator to meet Franc, running our mouths like muchachita chatterboxes, all excited about going to the sweat. Out of the blue we heard someone in the elevator say, "Can we come with you?" We looked up and saw two other reporter friends—one who worked for a major news magazine, the other a writer from New Jersey. We said yes, thinking it would be cool to have some other New Yorkers join us for the experience.

So at eight o'clock that night, we drove off in Franc's beat-up VW bug, leaving the glittering four-star hotel off in the distance as we made our way into the suburban sprawl under the New Mexico moon and mountains.

I expected to find a simple house with incense burning, and soft drumming music. Instead, we pulled up to a plain-looking suburban row house with a couple of plastic tricycles on the front lawn. Inside I heard the Rolling Stones playing on an old tape deck, the television was on, and there was a Michael Jackson poster visible from one of the kid's rooms. There were lots of people milling about and I could have sworn we had made a mistake.

This was where the sweat lodge was going to take place? This was where a centuries-old tradition was being resuscitated?

We stepped out to the small backyard where there was more low-key mingling. There was a deep pit in the middle of the yard and there were several big rocks scorching on the huge wooden fire. The husband (the man from the res) had a long ponytail and he was wearing loose khaki shorts. He was kneeling near the pit, turning the massive rocks from one side to another, slowly, methodically, as he mumbled and chanted to himself. The rocks were bright orange, almost white, and had been on the fire for about twenty-four hours. Every time he moved them, bright sparks the color of lightning bugs flew up from the fire and disappeared into the black sky.

I felt a hand on my back and I was quietly led away into a small out-houselike closet. Angela, the curandera, whispered to me to take off my clothes and wrap myself in one of the towels dangling on the wall.

"Everything?" I said, lifting my eyebrows. The thought of being naked in the middle of a stranger's backyard was not entirely enticing. And with my luck, if someone's towel was going to fall off it would probably be mine. "Yes, mamita. Everything—but if you must, you can leave on your calzones." Angela smiled at me and rubbed my back with the kind of warmth I had felt only from my mother's or abuelita's hand. I wanted her to just stay there and rub me some more, but in an instant she was gone and I was left alone looking at a row of raggedy towels on the makeshift closet wall.

I walked out to the backyard holding on to the towel tightly with one hand and saw that everyone was now standing around the fire pit, and Angela's husband was kneeling down and praying. Over the brick wall that enclosed the backyard I could see the moon rising. And then I looked around the circle. There were ten of us, ten of the most disparate-looking people standing around this pit getting ready to take part in this sacred tradition. My cynic's voice took over.

What am I doing here with these imitation hippies and New York Luppies (Latino yuppies)? How sacred can this be? We're all trying hard to get back to our roots but this feels so ridiculous—doing a sweat in the middle of the suburbs with people who have never met each other, who have no connection to each other. With the sound of the Rolling Stones "Satisfaction" humming in the background? Give me a break!

Tomás, Angela's husband, stood up and started to speak as the music died down. "Welcome to our home," he started quietly. "Welcome to our friends and neighbors and to our visiting guests. For those of you who are new to this, let me explain that this is something that our an-cestors have been doing for centuries. This is a sacred cleansing of our systems and in keeping to this tradition there are certain rules we need to follow."

I stood up straight like a child listening to her second-grade teacher. He continued.

"We will all go into the sweat together and we will all come out together. No one can break this circle. We will go in and open the door to the sweat only seven times until we are done. Each time we open the door we will bring in another rock from the fire pit. And on top of that rock we will pour water to make steam. It is going to be very, very hot. But nothing is going to happen to you. You are going to sweat all of the toxins out of your system. But this sweat is also a test of your will. You may feel very uncomfortable but know that nothing bad is going to happen to you. This circle of power and strength cannot be broken."

One of the guys who had joined us cleared his throat and said, "What if you need to get out? What if you think you can't make it?" in his thick accent.

Oh God, I thought. The wimp had to be from our New York contingent.

"You must believe that you can make it. That is all part of the test. If you can't respect this, then, we respectfully ask you to please not join us."

Silence. Tomás started chanting and beating a small drum. The strangers in the circle all held hands. I looked up at the stars and down at the burning white rocks and then I followed the circle around the fire and walked into the sweat. It looked like a wooden igloo made out of branches with cowhides thrown on top. Inside it was pitch black and we squeezed in together sitting cross-legged in a small circle around a little dug-out pit in the center. My towel hadn't fallen off and I was relieved, although I felt stupid that I was concerning myself with something so unimportant just as I was about to take part in this sacred rite. Once we were all situated the assistant put one of the seething white rocks in the pit at the center of our small manmade cave. Then the last piece of cowhide was swung across the opening and we were in darkness. Tomás started chanting and drumming and I was feeling good. This was going to be a piece of cake. Why had he spoken about the difficulty, the challenge, the heat? This was no problem. But then Tomás poured the bucket of water on the rock and all of a sudden I couldn't breathe and I felt like my body was being scalded in boiling water. I closed my eyes and breathed in slowly and thought about Tomás's words. I can handle this, I told myself, feeling as if getting air through my nostrils was suddenly almost impossible. After several minutes the opening parted, we got a quick breath of fresh air, another rock was placed in the pit, the opening was closed, and more water on the rock created more intense steam.

I started chanting along with everyone else in the circle and I began to relax, to breathe, to feel the pores of my skin opening to the size of small craters. I swear I could feel the toxins oozing out, burning my back as they dripped out of me. Either that or I was just in a trance. Tomás asked us to chant the names of our ancestors, to pray out loud for the things we wanted.

I felt a little self-conscious but I said to myself, Go with it. I whispered the names of my abuelita and abuelito and tíos and tías and then did some low-pitched humming. I was just beginning to feel as if I had quieted all of the little voices in my brain when someone started yelling.

"Please, please . . . Let me out. I have got to get out!"

It was someone from our group, the same guy who had asked the question before. It had to be one of us, I thought, tough urbanites who can make it anywhere—anywhere but here.

"You cannot get out. Be calm. Take a few breaths. You will be okay. We are all going to help you. Let us help you. Relax. You are just nervous—"

"I can't make it. I can't."

This back and forth went on for a while, disrupting the mood, the circle, our collective will. I think we all sympathized but we also understood that we had promised to follow this tradition. Besides, couldn't he see that the more time that passed the easier it got, physically? The real challenge was in your mind, in getting over your claustrophobia, in quieting the internal chatter that said you weren't going to make it.

Our friend was quiet for a moment, finally, and we thought the episode was over. Everyone got back to their own little trancelike states, humming and breathing deeply. But then, in an instant, the same guy got up and trampled over all of us, including Tomás, and ripped the cowhide off the opening that was the little pathway to the outside, to fresh, cool air, to the night, the moon, and the stars, and to the security of the known. "He has disrespected our ways," Tomás said slowly, controlling his words. "Let it not disturb this circle."

For a minute it was hard for all of us to feel holy and mystic while we called this guy a jerk under our breaths.

The rest of us stayed inside for four more rocks, four more turns of chanting and heat and sweat and steam.

When it was all over and everybody was dressed and showered, we hung out in the house together and ate some wonderful food that was waiting for us. There was music, everything from rock to rancheras, and lots of smiles and laughter. I imagined this is what people must feel after they have climbed a mountain. The unspoken bond that comes from facing a challenge and meeting it, together.

When I was getting ready to leave at about two in the morning, Angela, the curandera, asked if she could speak to me for a minute.

"Are you pregnant?" she asked me, pulling me aside into the small pink kitchen, looking deeply into my eyes.

"No," I laughed. "I'm not even trying."

"Hmmmm," she said, and cocked her head to one side. "Well, I have to tell you that I saw the spirit of a child next to you. It was a little boy. He is very close to you. He follows you everywhere. This little boy loves you very much. He will come here to take care of you and protect you. His spirit is just waiting to arrive on this earth. But he is already with you. Your firstborn will be a little boy and know that he already loves you." She took my hands and squeezed them tightly for a few seconds. And then she smiled and turned around and left.

As I finished getting my things together I wondered why Angela had said these things to me. I brushed it off as a special way to end what had been a wonderfully special day. But that night, I couldn't sleep. I felt as if electricity was running through my body and my brain was racing with images of me back at work and in the New York City subways. When I did finally close my eyes, I had wild, rushing anxiety dreams—me trying to file a story and missing my deadline—which left me exhausted.

The next day when Franc picked me up to take me to the airport, I mentioned what Angela had said, laughing as I told him.

"Maria," he said to me seriously, "you're not going to believe this but I have heard stories about women who come from all over the state to see Angela because she can always predict what a woman will have . . . a boy or a girl. In the twenty years that she has been practicing, I've been told she has never made a mistake. Not once. So, I guess you're going to have a boy."

"But Franc, I'm not even pregnant."

"Well, now you know you have something to look forward to," he said in a hushed voice as he drove me into the mountains. "A boy," he hummed. "A little hijito. A baby Hinojosa to carry on your traditions."

I put my chin in my hand and looked out at the mountains. Suddenly, I turned to Franc and blurted out, "I'm going to name him Raul."

We both laughed nervously.

The weird thing was that I couldn't ever remember thinking that I would name my child after my father (who was named after my grandfather). It was as if the weight of tradition (in my family every firstborn son had been named after the father or grandfather) just consumed me so that I couldn't even contemplate thinking about giving a future son any other name.

And so here I was many years later, pregnant and sitting on the old linoleum floor in Boca Chica, and I thought to myself, "I'm going to have a boy. And I'm going to name him Raul."

But with my conviction also came reservations. I had grown up hearing the name a hundred and one times a day with my mother calling out for my dad or my brother. I had a wonderfully complex envy-love-competitive-reverential relationship with my brother Raul and had had a loving if distant relationship with my abuelito Raul—a businessman, farmer, and Mason from Tampico. And I loved my stern father but he was so different than I was. But my gut told me that this was a special gift I was going to give to him, perhaps as a way to close the circle on my family's arrival to the United States, which happened because of my father's decision to come here.

Papi was always questioning whether or not he had made the right choice by bringing us to the States. If only he had kept us in México, he'd lament, us kids would have turned out to be more like my primos, my cousins—all of whom were obedient, respectful, and straight as arrows. Growing up in this country, with the unpredictable mix of being Mexican and American, my sister and brothers and I were always pushing the limits in ways my cousins in Mexico never did with their parents. In the sixties, my sister, Bertha Elena, wanted to wear hip-hugger bell bottoms and listen to the Beatles while our Mexican cousins were listening to sappy love songs and wearing long skirts with nylons. In the seventies, my brother Raul became a wild hippy with long hair and a beard who dressed like a campesino and became a political organizer while my boy cousins his age in Mexico were fascinated with cars. My brother Jorge, in high school, did become fascinated with cars but only because they fit with his party-animal personality and his pseudo-therapist side—he would counsel his friends (who were doing too many drugs) in the front seat of his Datsun 280Z as he drove them home from late-night high school parties. And me? Well, I had eight different boyfriends in the time my primas had one steady beau with whom they inevitably became engaged. And I had this dream about becoming an actress—unlike my cousins who wanted to become magna cum laude mothers and wives.

If only we had stayed in Mexico—Papi would say to himself and to us, at least once a week—if only we had stayed, everything would have been so much easier, so much more predictable. Growing up we all respected and tried to honor him, but I never thought I would go so far as to name my son after him. I had been the little revolutionary and iconoclast who, as the youngest, always stood up to my father, telling him once that I would never even get married. (Qué cosa!) My girlfriends from my Latina sistahs journalist group (we got together every month to eat and bochinchear) teased me that I would name my firstborn Ché! But here I was being the most traditional of Latina daughters, choosing to name her firstborn after a Mexican male legacy of three generations of Rauls.

But this little Raul was going to be born in gringo-landia, I said to myself as I got up from the floor in the bedroom in Boca Chica and went to peek inside the refrigerator. As I scanned the shelves I thought to myself, this will be the little Raul who will stand for the survival of our Mexicanidad in the face of gringo-ness. This can be my way of saying to Papi that even though he brought us here, what he stood for and where he came from was going to withstand and endure. This was my way of reaching out to my father without words, to show him how much I loved and respected who he was and the roots he had given us. This was my silent apology for having tormented him with all of my high school boyfriends and for staying out late and for all those times when I wore my skirts too short. This was my way of saying Papi, I am more Mexicana than you think, I thought closing the refrigerator and moving on to the freshly painted kitchen cupboards. Deciding there was nothing to

eat and that it was way too late to be up anyway, I got in bed and Gérman peeked out from under the covers.

"Honey?" I said, upping the sweetness quotient in my voice.

"Uh-huh, mi amor," mumbled Gérman.

"I think we're going to have a boy," I said, and snuggled him close.

"Anything, amor, as long as it's healthy," he said.

Should I? I thought to myself. Why not?

"Baby, I think I have a name, too."

"Ya sé lo que es," he said and opened his eyes.

"You do?"

"You want to name him Raul. And so do I. So now you can go to
sleep," he said, and pulled the covers over me.

"How—how did you know that, honey?" I asked, my mouth wide
open.

"Porque te conozco, honey, because I know you. Now, duérmete, my
little gordita. And while you're sleeping why don't you make a list of all
the food you want to eat tomorrow. First thing in the morning we'll go
shopping," he said, and closed his eyes and dozed off.

La Vida Te Quita y Te Da

The week of July Fourth, my parents, my sister and her two kids, and my brother Jorge all came to spend the week with us so they could see our new little Caribbean-Connecticut cottage. I milked my "estado" as much as I could. I knew this would be the last time that I could be the baby in the family. The morning sickness was beginning to subside, so I would tell Mom all of my antojos and she would spend hours in the morning cooking away. She made me cochinita pibil, shrimps with garlic, taquitos de pollo, guacamole, flan, huevos rancheros, quesadillas, and bisteck encebollado. Bertha Elena made carne asada on the grill and baked me brownies and chocolate cake. And just as we had done when we would visit my cousins in Mexico, we laid out all of the mattresses on the living room floor and had one big slumber party. These were my last days off before finally going back to work.

My life felt so full. I was surrounded by love and was basking in it. The sadness and the loss that I had dealt with felt far away. There were times during their stay when I realized how much I had grown up in the last two years. I think I finally understood that this was, in fact, the right time for me to be pregnant. I knew that the fullness I felt meant so much more in the aftermath of the emptiness I had lived through.

But if I was full of life and love and familia and baby and so many regalos de la vida, did that mean that emptiness would soon return again? I kept my thoughts to myself and in the quiet of the dark nights when I could hear three generations of Hinojosas softly snoring I would give thanks to los santos for having brought them close to me. But I couldn't get this one refrain out of my head: la vida te quita y te da—life gives and takes away from you.

After our days in the country we drove back into the city and Bertha Elena went shopping for maternity clothes for me. I was just beginning to sprout a tiny little pouch and I could have gotten away with another month or two of wearing my own loose clothes, but I just had to buy something with a tag that said "mommy & me" or "pea-in-the-pod" on it.

My first day back to work, wearing a much too big maternity jump-suit, I was riding along on the subway and I started noticing all of these other pregnant women (but, of course, their clothes fit them). I was gushing with pride, knowing that I, too, was now one of the chosen ones.

Women are incredible, I thought to myself, as I sat in the rumbling subway. We bring life into the world. I was smiling at every woman on the car with this revelation at hand but they of course looked at me and then quickly turned away thinking I must be a looney.

It's the hormones, I thought to myself and then quickly wiped the smile off my face and buried myself in my newspaper. And then when I got into work I had a call waiting for me. My new boss for the local television show that I had hosted for three years was on the phone. She had called to tell me she was firing me. A woman, a Latina, a *sister,* was firing me from my first job ever. So much for my romantic image of women.

I was angry and hurt but I couldn't even focus on it. I let the job go and figured it was a blessing in disguise. Who wants to be pregnant and working sixteen-hour days doing a bunch of different gigs?

July and August went by smoothly. The nausea was gone and that energy spurt that I had been reading about in the pregnancy books hit me at just the right moment. I had decided I wasn't going to do any aerobics during the pregnancy—just to be safe—but Gérman had found a perfectly fine stationary bike at the Connecticut dumpster. So in the evenings, I would come home from work and put on some merengue and ride for a short while before eating an enormous dinner.

We had been advised by our doctor and by Victor (who is a pediatric geneticist) to have the amnio because of my age (thirty-four) and my miscarriages. So four months in, I sat in the hospital with my bladder exploding as the nurse slid the cold sonogram drumstick over my small belly. The nurse told us it was a boy but we weren't surprised by that.

And then one of the doctors told me I had placenta previa and that even though it was five months away, that I should prepare myself for having a C-section. My placenta was low and blocking the exit canal. I could hemorrhage to death if I tried to deliver. So much for the natural thing. There were moments during my fits of pregnancy-hormone overdose that I would cry about it.

Soon after that, in late August, the little spirit inside of me started squirming and I began to wish I could be five months pregnant forever. I was full of energy and bloom. Intimacy took on a whole other meaning. I had an internal dialogue going with my own body—I could talk to myself and know that I wasn't crazy because I knew I was talking to my son. I would feel a little tap on my side and know that this was his secret communication with me. I wanted to feel this organic joy every day for the rest of my life.

And now that I was showing, I loved people's reactions to me. On the subway, it was mostly women who would get up and give me their seat (men in suits would scan me and then bury their faces deeper into their laps). But in my neighborhood, it was mostly men who would smile and say "felicidades" when they would see my belly. In my office building, most everyone seemed to ignore the fact that I was pregnant. And at my job, people tried to treat me no differently than before, which I both liked and disliked. Like the time one of my bosses called to say they needed me to go out and cover the fires that were consuming Long Island.

"You want *me* to go?" I said, for the first time questioning an assignment. "Why?"

"Well, you're the only one in the bureau who has a car," he said matter-of-factly.

And just like that I said, "Yes, and I'm the only one here who is also pregnant."

A month later, when Puerto Rico was a few days away from being at the center of a hurricane another boss called me up. "I just wanted to know how you would feel if we wanted to send you down to Puerto Rico to wait for the hurricane and do some follow-up reporting. It could be pretty treacherous—no water or light for a few days. You want to go down?"

I was in shock. "Uh, let me think about it," I said, and wondered why he was putting me on the spot of having to turn down an assignment. I told Gérman.

"How dare he! How could he even think of asking you!" Gérman fumed.

"But honey, when I told one of my reporter friends about it she said that maybe my boss was actually being respectful of me by asking if I wanted to go. A lot of pregnant reporters get angry with their bosses because they no longer assign them to big breaking stories. My friend said maybe this guy was just being considerate. Maybe he was."

"Ni considerate ni que madres! How dare he ask my wife to do such a thing! Just let me call him on the phone, just give me two minutes with him!"

That evening I called back my boss and said no. I expected the worst. But nothing happened. I discovered that saying no to the boss wasn't the end of the world.

I was learning poco a poco to say no, learning to take a pause before jumping on every new assignment. I knew I was doing the right thing, but I wondered if this meant I was changing as a reporter. I had been fearless up until now. What did this mean for my work and my future? I prayed to the news gods that there would be no more natural disasters while I was carrying this child in my panza. I wanted to avoid having to say no anymore.

At home, Gérman and I continued to document my growth. Every couple of weeks I would get out of the shower, throw on some underwear, and stand next to one of Gérman's new paintings and he would snap pictures of me. I then compared the photos to see exactly how much I was growing and where. The thighs and calves were filling up and my torso was swelling slowly like the rounded part of a pear. My small tetas were finally big enough to fill an A cup (a miracle!) and my shoulders and the top of my arms were filling out and looking more like the arms of my tía and my mom. Perfectly squeezable. And I was finally getting what I thought was the sexiest part of the pregnancy. The natural black line tattoo up my belly to my belly button. How earthy, how primitive, how unscientific and natural, I thought.

I was standing there in the middle of our living room in too tight underwear modeling for Gérman when the phone rang that Saturday morning. It was Mom.

"Mi'jita, cómo estás?"

"Okay, Ma. What's up? Is everything okay?" Just a little alteration in the tone of her voice was enough to let me know that something was going on. She was edgy.

"Ay, mi'jita, something strange has happened. I just got off the phone with my best friend in Mexico, Emiliana. You know, from the old neighborhood, la Colonia Narvarte."

Emiliana and my mom had grown up together. She was like family to us. She had four kids just like us, and we were all the same ages. They were like cousins to us. In fact, we called them primos when we were kids.

"Anyway," Mom continued to tell me, "while we were catching up on neighborhood gossip on the phone, I heard someone coughing horribly in the background, and she told me it was her son, Miguelito. Emiliana said it was no big deal but Miguelito sounded really bad. Pues, I called your tío Pépe who lives next door to them right away and asked him what he knew. He said he had seen him about three weeks ago and that Miguelito looked extremely pale. He told your tío Pépe that he spent most of the day locked in his room. I can't figure out what's going on but something isn't right."

I got one of Gérman's turtlenecks out from one of his drawers and threw it over myself and went to sit down on the sofa. Miguelito was just a few years older than I, in his late thirties, but he was still living at his parents' house. The memories of our childhood together zoomed through my head as I leaned back and started rubbing my belly like a Buddha.

Miguelito had always been shy and quiet and as he got older we had lost touch. But he was special to me because even though I called him a primo I had always had a crush on him. I used to say that he was my first Mexican novio. He had beautiful toasted brown skin and clear green eyes, eyes that later, I found out, had made women fall head over heels in love with him. The latest I had heard about Miguelito was that he was a real party animal. "Le gustan mucho las mujeres," my tío Pépe had told me about him. He liked lots of women. "Pero no tiene los pies en la tierra," he said. But he doesn't have his feet on the ground. He doesn't have any direction in life.

"You know, Malulis," Mom said quietly on the phone. "There is one more thing."

"What is it, Mami?"

"Pues, tío Pépe said Miguelito had lost a lot of weight in just a month or two."

I lifted my head up and stared into nowhere and then I heard that "word" echoing in my memory. I could hear it clearly, that haunting, teasing word—a word that was the worst word for a Mexican boy to hear, a word that Miguelito had had to endure hearing from all of the neighborhood kids as a child. "Maricón, maricón, Miguelito es un maricón!" Sissy, sissy, Miguelito is a sissy!

I closed my eyes and my head fell back. I took a deep breath. "Oh, Ma, this is bad. This is really bad."

"Malulis, you don't think—"

"Yes, Mami. I do think. I can't believe I hadn't figured this out before. Oh my God, this is horrible. What did my Emiliana say to you that Miguel had?"

"A lung infection . . ."

I had heard that one dozens of times before when I had reported about AIDS and the Latino community. All of these young men and women mysteriously dying from lung infections—anything but AIDS.

"Mom, maybe Miguel has AIDS. Oh my God, poor Miguelito. I can't believe this is happening—he's like our own family. Someone we love may be dying of AIDS but people are lying about it. I've got to talk to Miguel. I should call him. But it's been at least fifteen years since I have spoken to him."

"No se lo vayas a mencionar a Emiliana o a tu tío, Maria de Lourdes," my mother said sternly. "Don't you dare do something crazy! You have no right!" I could tell Mom was scared.

The next week my mother called Emiliana to check up on Miguelito. He was in the hospital. Still Emiliana insisted, it was nothing serious. Just pneumonia.

I was convinced my friend was dying. And I was worried he was dying in shame and silence, locked in his room, kept away from la sociedad, so that nobody would start the rumor mill that could destroy Emiliana, who ran her life by la sociedad's rules.

I wanted so much to call Miguelito and tell him that if he needed a
place to stay he could come here to New York. I didn't know how to tell
him what I suspected. I just wanted him to know that he was okay with
me. That I had friends who were gay, friends who were living with this
illness, that I might be able to help him get some treatments, that in my
house he didn't have to keep any secrets, that there was no shame, that
I loved him for who he was. But it had been so many years since he and
I had spoken. How could I call him up out of the blue about something
so personal?

For days I tried to put together the words that I would say to him if I
called him. But then I would start doubting myself. What if he didn't
have AIDS? What if I insulted him? What if he wasn't gay? Or what if he
wanted to keep his homosexuality in the closet? What if he had never
fully accepted he was gay? What if he hung up on me? My mother told
me that I had no right to make such a phone call, to be so presumptu-
ous. I kept going back and forth and the days passed and I didn't make
the call. But I couldn't get the image of my friend alone in his bedroom
out of my mind. Was anyone going to visit him? Was anyone holding
him? Were they still calling him "maricón"?

Two weekends passed and I had let one more Sunday go by without
making the call. It was Monday morning when my mother rang me at
my office.

"Malulis, algo ha pasado . . ." she said, leaving a long pause so that I
would have time to gather up my strength.

"Con Miguel? Mami? Qué pasó? Qué pasó? Tell me! Tell me! What
happened?" I said feeling an empty pit in the same belly where I was carrying my son. My palms began to sweat.

"Mi'jita. Please don't get upset. Quédate tranquila. I didn't want to
tell you this because of your estado," she said slowly.

"Mami, I'm just pregnant! That's my estado! It doesn't mean I have
to stop hearing about the world around me. Please, Ma." I stood up and
closed my office door.

"Okay, pero cálmate. Stay calm. Miguelito died last night at ten
o'clock. . . ."

I started crying. No, no, no. I slammed my fists onto my desk. Why
hadn't I made the call? He had died alone! And I couldn't even make

myself pick up the damned phone. I was a weak piece of shit. I let my friend go and he never knew I could understand.

"What are they saying? What did my tío Pépe say?" I asked through the tears.

"Your uncle said the same thing everyone is saying. That Miguelito died from a lung infection. Es todo."

They buried him just hours after he died. There was no wake, no open casket the way it was accustomed for my extended family in Mexico. And he was cremated—a rarity, according to my mother. He was dead and buried and gone within a matter of hours. A midnight funeral with three people to watch his ashes lowered deep into the ground. The chapter on his life was closed. Miguel had died in silence. And this was his legacy. Silence

"So do you think Miguelito was gay?" my mother said she had asked my uncle tentatively.

"Oh, no, of course not! He may have had AIDS but he wasn't a joto, a maricón, or a faggot! Not Miguelito! He just liked to party," my tío Pépe said angrily.

Anything but gay. The worst possible curse for a Mexican man. To be gay. To be a maricón and be proud.

This was the first of many deaths I would experience during my pregnancy. It seemed the losses I feared would come were now arriving. First Miguelito. Then our friend Alex's lover, who also died of AIDS. Then Meg from Miami who died from bone cancer. Then tío Hector, an old family friend from Chicago. I had grown up calling him "Tío." His was one of the first Mexican families we became friends with soon after we had arrived in Chicago. Tío Hector had worked in the frozen meat department of a supermarket back in the early sixties. He had to change jobs when one day at work his hands turned blue because of the cold. He was always in the freezer, chopping meat, seven days a week. He died of cancer when I was six months pregnant.

Then there was Jerry, my abuelito who spoke English. When I was seven months pregnant, I went home to Chicago for Thanksgiving. That was the last time I saw Jerry. Everybody always thought he would live until he was one hundred. When we first met him back when I was six years old, he was fifty-five and used to water ski several hours a day, depending on how rough the Lake Michigan waves were. Jerry Morgan and his large family became our family's best friends. We would spend the summers up at their house on Lake Michigan. They went to Mexico several times to meet us during our yearly tours across the country. Jerry loved Mexico so much he ended up buying a house in Cuernavaca. During the summers in Michigan, the kids would go down to the beach, make bonfires, and dance to Motown—the Jackson Five, the Supremes, Marvin Gaye. And on the weekends we would eat eggs, grits, and corn-bread for breakfast; fried chicken, baked ham, sweet potatoes, collard greens, and macaroni and cheese for dinner. The Morgans taught my parents about the civil rights movement and my parents taught them Spanish. It sounds like a made-for-TV-movie but it was true.

We kids called Jerry "Pa," just as his own grandchildren did. He taught us about discipline, about having dreams and working to make them come true. On rainy summer days when we couldn't play outside, he would give us slide shows and screen the movies he made on his vis-its to Africa where he told us his ancestors came from. Pa talked to us about growing up in the South and about his days when he was a teacher in Harlem. He was always making jokes, but we knew never to cross Pa. His temper was as large as he was tall.

When I saw him that day after Thanksgiving, the cancer had gotten into Pa's brain. The six-feet-four man who had towered over me had become a limp body covered under layers of white sheets. His hands, twice the size of mine, didn't move or twitch when I held them in mine. I knew he wanted to talk but he couldn't. And I imagined he knew I wanted to cry but I didn't dare in front of him.

"I'm pregnant, Pa. I'm not a little girl anymore, Pa. Can you believe it?" I whispered to him, holding back my tears. I took his huge hand and placed it on my belly. But his hand felt cold and clammy and I felt strange and a little bit sick all of a sudden. I couldn't bring myself to kiss him because I felt like death was too close, so I whispered I loved him, that I had hoped some of him stayed with my future son, and then I left the room.

Pa died two weeks later. Another phone call at the office, this time from my father, to give me the news. Papi was crying when he called, because it wasn't just my Pa who had died, but my father had just lost his friend, his only best friend in the United States.

And finally, there was Ilka, an old friend of mine and Gérman's.

When Ilka had announced three years earlier that she was HIV-positive it was big news. There was a press conference, TV interviews, magazine articles that talked about how this telenovela actress turned immigrant-rights lawyer was now moving on to be a spokeswoman for the Latino HIV-positive community. I remember when she made the public announcement—just days after my first miscarriage. She stood at the podium surrounded by her family, reporters, photographers, lights, and cameras. She stood like a statuesque angel, composed, sure of herself while people around her lost their composure and burst into tears. I watched it on television, frozen in my chair.

The last time we had seen each other was in April when I had just found out I was pregnant but still wasn't telling anyone. She looked stunning and as always, radiant, her six-feet frame elegant and playfully sensual, her toasted cinnamon brown skin, her clear hazel eyes, her movie star smile always exuding the contagious Caribbean warmth she carried with her even though she had left the Dominican Republic decades before. She told me that her sisters in the Dominican Republic no longer wanted anything to do with her.

La vida te quita y te da. Now I knew why I had been hearing that refrain that summer day many months ago when my belly was still small. Life gave me these friends and family. And it took them away from me as well. But la vida also gave me this blessing of my unborn son. Why did it always seem that for me life was full of yins and yangs when for others they seemed to "get" in life without having to give? Así es la vida? Así es *mi* vida, I was beginning to understand.

Naming Raul

As I got bigger and bigger I lined up all of the monthly, fresh-out-of-the-shower Polaroids that Gérman had been taking of me and stared at them to marvel at my body. Finally there was a moment in my life when I could look in the mirror and believe that I looked beautiful. My tetas had become full and round (I had cleavage for the first time); my nipples, dark brown like my mom's; my thighs, thick like Iris Chacón's; and my hair, wild and wavy like Sonia Braga's.

I was working every day even though my high energy was now slowly slipping back into second gear. There were days when I would be sitting at my desk trying to write a script and I couldn't seem to make my brain function through the fog. And now I had all of these strange physical ailments. Suddenly I found myself actually listening to those TV commercials about heartburn remedies and hemorrhoid creams. The sweet little taps of my son had become rolling somersaults and tae-kwon-do kicks, and I couldn't go out anymore without knowing that a bathroom was strategically locatable within minutes.

I read about the nesting instinct but I never felt it. I just knew I had all sorts of deadlines that I had to meet. Deadlines for my stories, deadlines for writing a project proposal, deadlines for the radio show, *Latino USA,* I hosted, deadlines for mailing the shower invitations, deadlines for filing my hospital admission papers, and the big deadline of birthing this child.

I wished I could nest but it was impossible. Instead, people would see me out on the street covering a demonstration and have pity on me, but

I would just waddle away and trudge into the subway to get back to the office to file my story in time to meet my deadline.

Those last months I would vacilate from feeling completely vulnerable to feeling like the fiercest mujer on the planet. I would get weepy if someone would give me their seat on the subway but then there were times when I felt like I could slash someone with my words if they crossed me. I had never felt that way before. Even though people who heard me on the radio or saw me on television thought I was some kind of powerhouse (they all said I had the voice of a tall woman), I never did feel that way about myself. I still feared and respected authority the way I had been taught by Dad. On the other hand, I knew there was a determined, ambitious part of me that wasn't afraid to keep quiet in the middle of a news conference or debate politics with anyone—from politicians to my brother. But my image of myself often seemed out of sync with the public perception of who I was. So that day when I was about seven months pregnant and feeling exquisitely feminine, I was shocked when someone I considered a friend said to me:

"You look so funny."

And without skipping a beat, I surprised even myself when I flew back with: "Funny? I don't look funny. I look fabulous!"

And then I turned away and smiled at myself. Wow. Maybe this baby was going to turn me into a powerhouse after all. Maybe I would become like one of those wild animals that will kill to defend her child. Maybe I won't allow anyone to disrespect me so that I can pass down this warrior-self to my child.

It was an exciting proposition. I won't only become a mother; I am going to become a woman now. A real woman. I'm going to become that woman everyone thinks I am.

I was learning how to protect myself. Finally.

Or so I thought.

A week later I was at an event to commemorate Manuel de Dios Unanue, the former editor in chief of *El Diario,* New York's Spanish newspaper, who had been murdered by someone in one of the drug cartels. Unanue had been pointing too many fingers and they killed him, just like they've killed dozens of journalists in Latin America, to keep them silent, for good. My good friend Ro, who now ran *El Diario,* was there working the crowd. Ro knew everyone, it seemed, from the mayor on down. I loved watching her in action because she never looked like she was second-guessing herself. She had no qualms telling a big city official he was full of caca, but she was a dove to the shoe-shine guy or a busboy. She had two babies at home but she never appeared to feel guilty if she wasn't around them 24/7. This woman was in control. I wanted to be like Ro when I grew up, I would tell myself, and would stand close to her, letting her largesse encompass me like a rainbow. Ro was a big woman who seemed proud of her size. She always looked impressive no matter what she was wearing. Even with her thick Bronx accent and the bilingual swear words that rolled off her tongue (Ese hijo de la gran puta! That man is an asshole!), Ro still exuded an elegant sense of power and poise.

If it hadn't been for Manuel de Dios Unanue, Ro and I never would have met. Years before, he made her the metro editor at the paper, taking her under his wing and transforming her from a cub reporter to a power broker, the first woman ever to have a position of power at *El Diario.* I met her when I was just starting out as a freelance reporter (filing my first stories for Spanish-language NPR by day and by night waiting tables at the local Tex-Mex restaurant), and I did a story about how *El Diario* was publishing daily photos of open-air drug deals in all of the barrios around New York City. Under the photos the captions would say, "Mayor Koch, why aren't you doing something about this?" No other paper was challenging the mayor as much as *El Diario,* and Ro was making it happen. I interviewed her and she and I became instant admirers of each other and friends.

That day at the event for Manuel de Dios, people were swarming around Ro because she had been one of Manuel's closest friends. So I politely slipped away and went to rest my swollen feet, waiting for her to finish so we could go home together. As I'm walking through the crowds an elderly man comes up to me and says, "Are you that Maria person who works for NPR?"

I figured he was going to give me a compliment so I puffed up my chest like a proud eagle, ready to receive a word of praise. People had stopped around us. I puffed up even more. "Yes, I'm Maria Hinojosa. I'm the reporter here in New York—"

The elderly man started shaking his head and frowning and suddenly his finger was pointing at my face and I realized I wasn't alone anymore. A bunch of people were now standing around us. "Well, I just wanted to know how come you have to say your name the way you do on the air? It bothers me everytime I hear it! Why don't you Americanize it?" he snarled.

I withered and the strong Amazon woman who I thought I had become just a week earlier was now dumbfounded. All I could manage to eke out was, "I'm sorry but I can't do that. I just can't." I said excuse me and walked away, my trembling hand wiping away the sweat from my forehead. How embarrassing.

The man could have no idea how much my name had been an issue for me. When I was growing up I hated my name, especially my full name—Maria de Lourdes Hinojosa Ojeda. Maria was okay, I guess, but what was this "de Lourdes" thing and the two last names? There were times when I would think of my name and I would say yuck right afterward. It sounded disgusting, expecially when you compared it to my friends' names. Liza Tym. Randee Kallish. Suzie Goldstein. How come I couldn't be Jessica, or Elizabeth, or Becky, or Linda? *Randeeeee. Suzieeeee.* Those names sounded sweet and light. Pleasant to hear and to say.

Not *Mah-ree-ah.* In English it sounded deep and tough, anything but nice and girlish.

As a kid, I would secretly practice writing my friends' names on paper, over and over again, practice making a slew of *e*'s, with just enough curviness to look really cool. I fantasized about changing my name when I got old enough. I named my two Barbies Liza and Randee. Everything about those names reeked of privilege, of Americanness, of fitting in.

If I needed proof that Maria was a terrible name, I needed only to visit Walgreen's. I would make my way down the Maybelline aisle and turn up the candy aisle catching a whiff of the chocolates, turn down the school-supply aisle, wishing I could buy a new three-section notebook (the one with the sunflowers on it), and then finally hit the round key-chain display. I would wait until no one was standing nearby and I would slowly turn the display, making myself crazy with anticipation— maybe this week they finally got one, maybe this time it'll be there— and I would finally get to the *M*'s. There they were, all of the clear

Plexiglas rectangular key chains with letters elevated and painted in gold. Oh, these key chains were to die for! How I wanted one. I would slowly look through the *M*'s wishing the key chain gods would finally make my dream come true.

But no.

Right after *Marie,* there was *Mary.* Time after time after time. Not once did I ever find a *Maria.*

And I searched the entire country, too. Every year when we would drive from Chicago to Mexico, through Illinois, Missouri, Oklahoma, and Texas, I would get off at every gas station and check in every pit stop, but there never was a Maria key chain.

I'd stop thinking about this when I would get to Mexico and there my family would call me the sweetest of names—reina (queen), chaparrita (petite one), mi cielo (my sky), mi vida (my life), tesoro (my treasure). And everyone called me by my nickname—Malulis—a delicious combination of Maria and that god-awful Lourdes.

But as soon as we crossed the border back into the United States, my name-hating madness would begin all over again. I would run to the first gas station we hit in McAllen, Texas, and start spinning the key chain display. Nothing. I became invisible again.

Luckily, all that changed when I was ten years old. It was 1971 and the movie *West Side Story* was going to be shown on television for the first time. I got special permission to go watch the movie with my older sister at her friend Betsy's house. There were going to be teenage boys there and I was in heaven—hanging out with my big sister, having gotten permission from my father (this did not come easily) to watch a risqué movie like *West Side Story.* I was so cool-o-mulo.

Once the movie began, I didn't really understand what it was all about. I could see it took place in New York City, which I had heard about but never visited. The guys who spoke with an accent sounded like Mom and Dad but were mean and angry. I was afraid of them. The guys who didn't speak with an accent were just stupid. And there was this girl, who looked a little like me, who had my same name. After the first half hour of the film I realized it was a love story and that I could understand. So I was all googley-eyed watching this love story when all of a sudden Tony starts belting out a song and it is about me. Maria!

Finally, there was somebody in this country who shared my name! I was shining. I existed in this country. But I still kept searching for the key chains, to no avail.

As a teenager, I didn't worry about my name as much as I did about fitting in. I was a Mexican inside my house with my family, but as soon as I walked out the door my friends considered me an American. But it was never as smooth as that. I had strict curfews and a jealous father whose stern demeanor frightened all of my boyfriends. I wanted so much to be like everyone else. In fact, my first real boyfriend was the son of a banker who came from a long line of men from the Ivy League. But I always doubted this boy could really love me. He wanted me to stop calling myself a Mexican, but how could I? I figured what he really wanted was a Randee or a Suzie or a Liza, and that just wasn't me.

My first year in college, I decided to major in Latin American studies. And I spent my summers doing volunteer work in the barrio Mexicano in Chicago. And the more I read and the more involved I became, I began to define my own particular sense of cultural identity, and studying and perfecting my mother tongue was a big part of it for me. I began to own my Spanish name and began to pronounce it as such. I fell in love with my name as I grew into my Latina-ness and I was so relieved to be able to be Maria with the sensuous rolling r's and the poetic longing of it when it was pronounced just right. And after so many years of hating this part of me, it was liberating to just say who I was and feel fine about it.

As a journalist and a writer, I assumed my name publicly because this is who I had become. I did it for myself but my personal decision now was a point of public debate. Some people would tell me how glad they were that I said my name in Spanish—assuming I had done it only to make some kind of statement. But then there were the nasty old men who would stop me and challenge me, or the pro-and-con letters I would get about the Hinojosa-name-pronunciation debate. And there were some days I wished I could sign off with my full name—"This is Maria de Lourdes Hinojosa Ojeda reporting from New York." And see what everyone had to say about that one!

As the countdown for the due date approached, Gérman and I hadn't thought a lot more about the other big name issue we were facing. Besides Raul, what else would this little guy be named?

Things just kept popping up that needed to be taken care of and we kept putting off discussing it. We had to see the doctor every two weeks, transform our second little bedroom from Gérman's art storage room into a baby's room, and plan the baby shower.

Graci and Victor had volunteered to host the baby shower and Gérman designed a multicolored bilingual invitation with an umbrella on it. Forty people came and I felt like all of my friends were as in love with this baby as we were. They gave us beautiful gifts—a down comforter, a kente cloth blanket and matching bib and hat, a CD of international lullabies, a stuffed Babar elephant, a Native American wool blanket, and much more. This was more fun than opening my own birthday gifts. I just sat in a big chair with my legs open (I couldn't squeeze them shut, as hard as I tried) and my belly hanging down and held my pregnant-woman's court.

The day after the shower with just over a month to go, we went to see the doctor. Jenya, the nurse, always gave me a big hug as she shuffled seamlessly between me and the Hasidic couples. My doctor would patiently answer my long list of questions and tell me about his own wife (a former delivery room nurse who had had three C-sections). For that particular appointment, I had written up my birth plan in detail, hoping that maybe my placenta had moved during the last months and that I would be able to have a regular delivery. Ro had inspired me in my birth plan—she did it all on her own, saying she wanted to feel the same thing her abuelita did when she birthed in el campo de Puerto Rico, and if Ro could do it, so could I, I told myself. I wanted an all-natural delivery, no intervention if possible, no IV's, no drugs.

The doctor said he would do a late-term sonogram to check on the position of the baby and the placenta to see if it had moved. It hadn't. If my placenta was still blocking my cervix, the doctor told me, and I was to try to push this baby out, we could both die from a hemorrhage.

He said we would need to schedule a cesarean. I began to cry and cry.

I felt so much like an un-natural mama. Everybody else's baby arrived when the baby was good and ready, but I had to choose a date and a time for this child to be born. It felt entirely sacrilegious. This was not how babies were supposed to be born, I could hear abuelita saying in the background. She never forgave my mother for allowing herself to be induced with my sister because her doctor was going to be on vacation the week of her due date.

"Eso no se hace! You are playing with God's will. He will punish you for interfering with nature!" my mom told me that abuelita yelled at her when she left for the hospital to be induced.

Abuelita must be watching from above and shaking her head. "Qué ha pasado con el mundo moderno? There is no respeto for Dios y la naturaleza anymore."

Unfortunately, if I let la naturaleza have its way, I would end up dying if I tried to birth this baby.

On the drive back from the doctor's office, Gérman did his best to console me, but he told me he could understand my fear of major surgery. He put the lullaby recording we received as a gift on the CD player and then surprised me with a copy of a book two friends of ours had just published called *100 Hispanic Baby Names.*

"Ay, honey. That's so sweet," I said and reached over to kiss him. But in the back of my mind I was thinking that baby name books were written for totally and thoroughly unimaginative and uncreative minds.

We still had a few more weeks to decide our son's middle name. We knew he was going to have at least two names, and Gérman and I joked that wouldn't it be fun if we gave him sixteen names to choose from. But we hadn't even been able to come up with a second name, so who were we fooling that we could come up with a long list of names to follow after Raul.

I took the book and opening it absent-mindedly, my eyes fell on the name Ariel. *Ariel,* it said, *angel of light.*

Raul Ariel. I was amazed. It worked beautifully and since this baby was created by the light of the moon it even had meaning.

"Honey!" I said, "Qué te parece Raul Ariel? It flows, doesn't it?"

"Beautiful, baby. Me encanta," he said, happy that my mind had been taken off the news of the C-section.

The CD with the lullabies stayed in the car and for the last two weeks of work Gérman would drive me to the office every day and we would listen to it as we made our way through the morning traffic. There was one song that we both loved and that just by chance was sung by Tish Hinojosa, a singer with whom I had become friendly.

This is how the song goes:

> *A na nanita na na, nanita na na nanita eh ah . . .*
> *Mi Jesús tiene sueño,*
> *bendito sea, bendito sea.*
> *Fuentecita de luna clara y sonora . . .*

On one ride, my husband started to sing, but instead of Jesús, he put in Raul. I started crying (and then Gérman did, too) in that way that first-time mothers cry at the drop of a hat when they think of the littlest thing in relation to the new baby. I looked around to see some truck drivers staring at us. What a sight we must have been. Big man Gérman in tears and me with mascara running down my cheeks.

I loved that part of Gérman—he was really sharing this pregnancy with me. We would see a commercial for diapers and we would just tear up. Finally Gérman and I both had PMS at the same time.

"What if we named this little guy Jesús?" I said to Gérman, as I tried to put some lipstick on, thinking that bright red lips might distract from my smudged black owl eyes. "He would probably never forgive us."

"Yeah, and then he would be nicknamed Chuy or el Chu, as they say in the Dominican Republic. And then we could sing him that merengue about the Chupacabras. . . . El Chu-pa-quí, el Chu-pa-cá. It would be just too much. El Chu. Imagínate!"

That night when I got home from work Gérman said he had been thinking about the whole Jesús thing and he said he thought this baby "tenía un Jesús cruzado por alguna parte." He felt like this baby had a Jesús that was aching to be part of his name.

"What do you mean?" I asked, wondering if I would actually have the nerve to go through with this and name our child Jesús. I could just hear what my primos in Mexico would say: "Ay, esa Maria tan loca. She doesn't even go to church on Sundays but she names her child Jesús. Pobrecita. She must be looking to make up to Him for being so far from religion for so many years." In the back of my mind I was thinking that I would tell my cousins that Jesús had always defended the poor and the downtrodden. "He was one of the first revolutionaries!" I would say to them as they looked at me and shook their heads. "Ay esta prima gringa. They have the craziest ideas in gringo-landia!"

But Gérman was serious.

"Look, I've been thinking about this. And this is what came to me to-day as I was painting," my husband said. "We conceived this baby in the town of Bethlehem. You are Maria like la Virgen Maria and in our house in Bethlehem, I am a carpenter, rebuilding this little cottage. Don't you get it? I'm a carpenter just like José!"

I started laughing. He couldn't be serious but it looked like he was. "It sounds like it fits, amor, but somehow I just can't see it. Anyway, it would have to be something like Jesús de todos los Santos, because he is not going to have only the Catholic Jesus as part of his name. We would have to say Jesus of all the saints because he has so many santos that are watching over him. Ay, but this is too much. If I blamed my parents un-til I was eighteen, this guy will probably not forgive us until he turns thirty-three. The age of Cristo. Forget it, amor. If we want him to have sixteen names let's find other ones."

We chuckled about it, but a part of me thought that there were too many strange coincidences—Bethlehem, the Tish Hinojosa song, my being Maria, my husband the carpenter like Joseph in Bethlehem. It was strange and funny but it kind of had a ring to it and it sounded just like I wanted it to sound. It was ornate, baroque, and old-fashioned to the point of being kitsch. I could see it now. My son would become the de-fender-of-people-with-nine-names. He would start a trend, a fashion statement. Soon everyone would want to have nine names just like him. I was throwing all of this up for consideration, half serious, half not, when something happened, and then we knew we had no choice.

The doctor asked that we choose a date anytime between December 30 and January 7 for our son's birth. We both liked the Second of Janu-ary since I was also born on the Second of another month. And so, just like that, we made the thoroughly unnatural decision about the day our child was to be born, and it was scheduled in our calendars as if we were making a lunch date.

Later that evening, I pulled out Raul Ariel's baby book. It wasn't one of those typical specialized baby books with all of the pictures and say-ings and little envelopes for locks of hair. No, our baby book was a gift from an artist friend of ours who found it in an artbook store. It was a paperback datebook printed in San Francisco with wonderful pho-tographs of knickknacks of popular culture in Mexico. It had pictures of the candies I loved to eat as a child, it had photos of la lotería (Mexican bingo), it had photos of the sculpted wooden utensils you use in the kitchen, and photos of old movie posters with María Félix and Cantin-flas. And in the tradition of Mexican calendars each day was dedicated to a saint, and in this agenda the names of those santos were written un-der each date.

When I opened the agenda to January Second to see what Santo Raul Ariel was going to have, this is what it said:

January 2nd—Día Santo de Jesus.

Raul Ariel Jesús de todos los Santos Perez-Hinojosa!

Raul—because you were named after your grandfather, great-grand-father, and uncle. *Ariel*—because you are an angel of light. *Jesús*—be-cause you were conceived in the town of Bethlehem; and, *de todos los Santos*—because you are blessed by many, many saints. This is what I will say to my son when he asks me why.

I still check the key chain displays in stores across the country and I almost always find Maria now. And it so happens that the first store I checked after my son was born was when I was in a town in Kansas where I had gone to give a lecture when Raul Ariel was just a few months old. And there it was. A key chain with palm trees that said in big black letters *R-A-U-L*. Made in the U.S.A., bought in Garden City, Kansas, his little key chain awaits him in a wrapped box on a shelf in his room.

OTHERNESS AND OTHER LOCURAS

The second week of December I filed my last story and said good-bye to my office mates. I loved my job, but I didn't feel I was going to miss being there. I had been working in that office for six years and it felt like a good time to take a break. I was also very ready to take a break from office politics. I had this naive notion that as a reporter, all that mattered were the stories I had to tell. But I found myself getting sucked deeper into workplace discussions about whether or not the network was still interested in long feature stories, like the ones I did, or was ready to focus instead on hard news. During my first years as a reporter, I had been able to get those long stories on the air with no problem. Now it felt as though I had to fight for every minute. I was tired of having grandiose debates over the future of American public radio journalism. I just wanted to be at home having small thoughts about when my nesting instinct was going to kick in.

This would be the first time since I was fourteen that I wasn't going to be working in some kind of job. I had started working in a jewelry store when I was in high school and then had been a waitress for all of my years in college and when I started off as a freelance journalist. This would be a time for me to focus on my own projects and my family.

It had been ten years since I had started my career as a radio journalist in 1985 and for the first time in all of those years I actually felt secure enough in my work to ask for time off. So I requested a full year—half of it for my maternity leave and half of it to work on my first big writing project—and all of it unpaid. (If there was ever a time in my

life when I could try my hand at being a writer this would be it.) We had
a little bit of money saved up and Gérman's work had been selling more
and more and he had some major exhibits at galleries planned for next
year. I was still going to be hosting *Latino USA,* which gave us some survival money, but any way we looked at it, this was going to be a year of
living frugally (and for Raul Ariel making do with hand-me-downs).

Gérman was wonderfully supportive of all of this. He always complained that I was a workaholic and that I needed to slow down, and
frankly, I knew he was ready to take a break from hearing my constant
complaints about the office. He would always say to me, "I send you off
to work beautiful and happy every day but you come home angry and
throwing chispas. A job isn't supposed to do that to you." So in many
ways this time off was a gift for him as well. He was going to be able to
see more of his wife than he had seen in all of the years since we had
been together.

Mom and Dad arrived in New York from their winter vacation in
Mexico three days before my predestined due date. After we caught up
on all of the recent gossip (we're such a tight-knit family but what fun
would it be if we didn't have chismes?), Mom began to unpack her
presents for the baby. In Tampico, the small town where Papi was raised
and where his mother and sister and several of my cousins still live,
Mom went shopping for her little nietecito. The first gift she pulled out
of her suitcase was a red-and-white crocheted pants suit with suspenders and a matching superfly-style hat.

"Where in Tampico did you find such a wild outfit?" I asked laughing.

"Allí, cerca de la plaza del centro, in that baby clothing store that has
been downtown for over fifty years. You know, it's the kind of place that
has each baby suit wrapped in plastic on a separate hanger. I had always
wanted to get something from there. When you kids were born we
couldn't afford to."

I looked more closely at the hat. It actually was a combination of a su-
perfly and Rasta cap. A Rasta hat bought in downtown Tampico! Quién
se lo iba a imaginar?

"Your aunt and grandmother couldn't believe I was going to give you
this! 'No seas ridícula, Berta,' they said! 'How are you going to put that
outfit on a little boy?' Well, you don't know Malulis and Gérman, I told
them. They are artists. They like things like this."

Sometimes I thought Mom enjoyed the fact that she had such a non-traditional daughter. It let her show off how nontraditional she could be, too. There are times when I think she wants to be even hipper than we are just to let us know she's cool beyond her years.

We ordered from the local Chinese place and over dinner Mom told me about a conversation she had with a phone operator the day before she left for Mexico. She was calling my tía to let her know what flight they were arriving on.

I could imagine Mami with her wonderfully thick accent as she called AT&T and asked to be connected to Mexico under the Reach Out America plan. When they said no she asked the operator to let her speak to a manager. "Sir, I just have to tell you that if your ad is correct, that I can call anywhere in America for ten cents a minute, then I would like you to please connect me to Mexico and charge me that same rate."

"I am sorry, ma'am. I can't do that. Mexico is not part of our plan," said the man, calmly at first.

"I don't understand. Mexico is part of America, just like Chile or Colombia or California is. America is a continent, not a country. Your promotion is deceiving and you should correct it."

"Mom! You didn't!" I said laughing, my belly wiggling just like an old man's.

"Ah, si, mi'jita! Claro que sí! And then I told him to look up America in any dictionary and you will see that it says America encompasses the entire Western Hemisphere and the continents of South and North America!"

As Mom cleared the dishes I, so full and exhausted I could barely move, shook my head and smiled. Here I am, finally trying to feel comfortable with calling myself an American, something I never did until just recently, and here is Mom fighting it. I became a citizen almost a decade ago after years of soul searching, but I had only recently started using the term *American* for myself as a way of making my American experience my own. But every time I do say I'm an American, Mom interrupts me and says, "Not American, mi'jita. United States person. You were an American before you became a citizen." I love her for her determination, but I wonder what she will call herself after she takes the citizenship exam and gets that navy blue passport that exudes privilege just by its color.

After dinner, while Gérman and Dad watched some TV, Mom called up my sister, Bertha Elena, to find out if she had mailed in their citizenship application. They had decided to apply together, like a little pact (*I'll* do it if *you'll* do it . . .). I got on the phone, too.

"So why did you finally decide to do it?" I asked my sister as I boiled water for ginger tea.

Mom had told me she wanted to become a citizen because she was angry over the California proposition that was voted in to deny immigrants benefits. ("I'm going to get back at that governor," she had told me.) But I wanted to know why my sister, who lives what is stereotypically regarded as the quintessential American life—a house in the suburbs, two kids, two cars—had suddenly decided it was time to take the oath for the U.S.A.

"It's not a big deal," she began, "the issue of becoming a citizen had just never come up before."

"Right," I said.

I didn't think it was as easy as that for her. I knew that changing your nationality went to your gut. It was a simple process but it made you rethink everything about your identity. Why you choose to hold on to certain things over others.

"What do you say to your kids about it?" I asked her.

"Nothing. They just know that Mommy comes from Mexico. That is my history but it isn't theirs. They will have their own history to make as citizens of this country," she said.

"But I don't understand. You are saying that maintaining your Mexican citizenship for all this time was something you did without thinking much about? You didn't hold on to it as some kind of symbol? It didn't mean anything special to you? If it didn't, then why did you keep it for so long?" I kept pressing her. I knew there had to be more to it because we were raised in the same household; we knew we were supposed to be proud of our Mexican heritage and nationality. We heard what my uncles and aunts said to my father when he became an American citizen thirty something years ago. They jokingly called him a gringo, a pocho, a vendido—a sellout. Those words stick with you when you hear them as a child and that's exactly why I was so concerned about my own soon-to-be-born-American child and his future identity muck.

Finally my sister blurted out, "You know what it is, Malulis? I kept my

Mexican citizenship because I am glad that I am a Mexican living this lifestyle, here in the middle of suburban middle America in the middle of everything that is so middle of the road and mainstream. And yet I am *not* an American citizen. I kept it because when people find out where I am from they can't believe it. 'What? You're Mexican?' they say to me, and I say, Yes, I am. And I am your neighbor, and I am teaching your kids, and I speak perfect English, and I am right here next to you. I am living right here on your territory. I am a part of this American life, I am a part of you and yet *I am not.* I am a foreigner in your land. And even though I am not politically active, the fact that I maintained my Mexican citizenship for so long was a way for me to educate people around me to accept difference. If you can see me and accept me then you can learn how to let other people who are different into your life and your community, too. It was my way of saying we are here. It was my way of saying, don't fear difference because it is everywhere."

I knew there was a reason.

Of everyone in our family, my sister has been the one who has had to face the identity question most intensely. She was the eldest and so she was the first one of us to crash head-on into any limits. Twenty years ago, when she got married, it was not easy for either family to accept the other. From our side we saw her fiancé as a guy raised in the suburbs, who rode a motorcycle, who served in the navy, who was a Republican, who was white and spoke no Spanish. A gringo. From their side they saw our family as Mexicans. Period.

The two families came to know and like one another in those months before my sister's wedding and the awkwardness of the first meetings gave way to hugs and kisses and invitations for dinner. But one day, just before her wedding, my sister's future mother-in-law made a comment to my mother that stopped her in her tracks.

"Berta," she said, "you know they sold the house next to ours to a Mexican family. I'm a little worried. Don't most Mexicans have lots of kids and play loud music?" she asked my mom, genuinely concerned.

"Well, Helen, we are Mexicans, too. I am sure they will be fine people. Just like we are, and we're your family now."

Helen apologized and nothing more was said about the conversation ever again.

Mom and I finished cleaning up from dinner and I lay on the couch sipping my tea while Mom used her manos sobadoras to get the kinks out of my ballooning feet. That night I slept sitting up, propped with pillows everywhere because I couldn't bear the pain in my right hip and because sitting up was the only way that the heartburn wouldn't keep me up. The next morning, in the grogginess of the first shades of day-light, I had this thought.

I am going to give birth to an American baby but I realize I don't know how I am going to teach him to "own" his American-ness. Nobody ever taught me. Mom and Dad never thought of themselves as Ameri-cans. We were Mexicans living in the United States. Temporarily. (But forever . . .)

Teaching him to own his Latino-ness will be easy, I think as I stuff some pillows under my hip. He will see it everywhere around him. But I need to know how I will teach him that his Latino-ness doesn't make him any less American. Will he understand that? I don't want my son to feel the otherness that comes when you realize you are different. I don't want him to feel that isolation.

Gérman woke up and I told him what I was thinking.

"Honey, it's too early to be having this discussion. Can't you at least wait until I have my café?"

But my hormones had gotten the best of me and when I got out of bed I started telling Gérman about a time when I was six years old back in Chicago. It was 1968 and I was walking home from school with my best friend, Linda. We were talking about this man named George Wal-lace who we had seen on television. He might become the new presi-dent and we were scared. It was a warm autumn day in Chicago and our first-grade teacher, Mrs. Turner, was wearing my favorite sweater. It was the dark rusty orange button-down sweater she wore for our class photo and I loved the way it looked. Mrs. Turner was warmth and hugs and understanding. I loved her and I knew she loved me back because she wrote it in a little note with her red felt tip pen at the top of my homework assignments. That day in school we read some more about Dick and Jane and their dog Spot. Dick and Jane always looked so happy, I thought as I looked at the pictures of their peach-colored faces. They were always smiling. I wondered where they lived.

That day in class we did one of my favorite things. We tracked another day in the voyage of Thor Heyerdal. He was going around the world in a canoe that was made out of wood and straw and in our first-grade class we were keeping track of how his trip was going. We all wanted him to make it although we didn't really know why he was doing it. Something about how he wanted to prove that Indians from down there by Mexico and Chinese people had met on boats like this hundreds of years ago, way before Christopher Columbus arrived.

Anyway, Linda and I were walking home holding hands. I was wearing my red plaid skirt (the one that has a little gold pin holding it together in front) and my favorite red turtleneck that Mami let me pick out of the thick Sears catalog. I wanted to look just like one of the girls from the catalog but those girls always have long blond hair. More than anything in the world, that was what I wanted. Long, straight hair the color of butter. Today, Linda was wearing a dress and some pants underneath. We were still not allowed to wear pants to school unless we wore them under a dress. Only boys can wear pants. I liked wearing skirts and dresses because then I could show off my shoes. Mom bought them for me in Mexico at a big shoe store called Canada. I loved wearing my Mexican shoes, the brown leather ones with the big buckles, because I knew no one else in school would have this same pair except for me.

Linda and I knew that we had to stick together and find a place to hide because we had heard that an election was going to happen soon and we had also overheard some adults talking about what was going to happen if this man named George Wallace won. He had said horrible things. We heard he had even said he was going to kill people like us. That was why we had to find a place to hide. In case he won the election, we had to be prepared.

Linda and I were different. I knew she was something called Jewish. And I knew I was born in Mexico. But we both knew that these things were different. So we figured we had to make a plan. The first part of the plan was finding our hiding spot—one that would be big enough for all eleven of us to hide in—six from my family plus Linda, her sister, her grandmother who lived with them and had a silver streak in the middle of her teased black hair, and her parents.

When we got to the front of my building, Linda said it might be better if we thought about hiding in her building because it had an elevator that took us down to the basement and her family had a room there where they kept her banana-seat Schwinn bicycle locked up.

We took the elevator down to the basement and walked into the wooden locker room where her bike was. We stood next to each other for a while in silence. I imagined my mom and dad and my sister and brothers lined up around the room. I figured we could all fit in as long as we put the bikes outside. But it was cold and dark and I started to get scared and almost felt like I was going to start crying. We swore that this would be our secret hiding place and that we would come here as soon as we heard if George Wallace had become president.

And then I said, "Linda, how long are we going to have to stay here?"

"I don't know. I guess until someone comes to rescue us."

"Oh," I said and was quiet for a few seconds. I thought about Martin Luther King, Jr. My mom said he was a good man. I bet he would save us, I thought to myself.

"I want to go home now," Linda said quietly.

"Me too," I said. "I want to go home, too."

By now, as I was telling this story, Gérman and I had moved into the shower. He was scrubbing my back while I washed my hair. And then he told me, "Mamita, that is a very special story but honestly I have to tell you that I'm more concerned about your surgery tomorrow than about little Raul Ariel's identity issues fifteen years from now."

But I wouldn't stop.

"Honey, I just can't imagine when it is going to happen to our son. Somebody is going to make him feel like he is different, an outsider. I don't mind him recognizing he is different but I don't want him to be told that his difference is something bad. My God, what if he comes home and says he never wants to hear me *speaking* Spanish in public, the same way I asked Mom and Dad one day when I was just eight years old? Thank God, they just told me que dejara de hablar tonterías, that I should stop saying dumb things like that. But things are more complicated now. What if I end up talking about this stuff so much that our son shuts me out? Do I tell him about racism or wait until he comes home with a horror story. Honey! What are we going to do?" It wasn't that I hadn't thought about these issues before. It was that now, twenty-four hours away from being a new mom, I felt suddenly overwhelmed by them.

Gérman wrapped the towel around me as far as it would go and rubbed my shoulders. "Mamita, everything is going to be just fine. He is going to love who he is because we are going to teach him that. He is going to love being Mexican and Dominican and being a New Yorker and being an American. He is going to love all of those things just the way we do. And that is how he is going to learn it. From us. So you don't have to worry about it."

There were times when the strength in Gérman's voice was enough to make me stop. Thank God, this was one of those times. I left him in the bathroom and went to the kitchen to make him his café that I promised him an hour ago. Mom was just waking up and she walked by the dining room table where we left her unpacked bags and she mindlessly started folding all of the funky Tampico baby clothes and putting away the canned chile chipotle she brought me back from Mexico. And then I suddenly got this craving. A craving I hadn't had for months.

"Ma?" I said, sounding like a little girl.

"Sí, mi'jita?" she answered all warm and giving.

"Can you go out and get me some McDonald's for breakfast? Por please!"

Él Nacimiento

It was six o'clock in the morning on Tuesday, the Big Day, January Second, 1996, and I was staring at myself in the mirror wondering why I cut off all of my hair. Yesterday I told my honey to drop me off at one of the local $9.99 haircut places. "I'm going to get a trim, papito. I'll be home in half an hour." Then I sat in the chair and told the woman to take off six inches. "Are you sure, ma'am?" she asked over and over again until I almost yelled at her, "Yes, I'm sure. I'm pregnant, not crazy. Cut it off." And so she did. When I came back home that afternoon Gérman looked at me with horror. Instead of consoling me on my rash prebirth-locura decision he said to me, "The next time you cut off all of your hair I am going to do the same thing!" I lost it and started to cry. I was so ready to deliver this baby already!

Everything had a surreal feel to it that morning, like I was in some sort of slow-motion bubble. There I was in the shower looking down at my huge belly, but in just a matter of hours I was going to have a baby in my arms and be a mother. How could that be? Careful not to slip in the shower, I got my razor and in preparation for my body's being stared at by numerous strangers, I started shaving everything everywhere. And then I was overwhelmed by a visit from the spirit of my ultravain tía Patricia, the one who would have her daughters put on her makeup when she was sick in bed just so she would still look pretty even though she felt like death. I stepped out of the shower and plucked my makeup bag out of the cabinet and started putting on layers and layers of guck. I drew in my eyebrows so they looked nice and dark and I put on a red lipstick that had been sitting in my cabinet for a year without ever being opened. I smeared on pink blush and then used my favorite makeup tool of all—my eyelash curler. For almost a year I'd been wearing my five yellow Oshun scarves tied around my belly (the way the Cuban santero Horacio told me to) but today I untied them and wrapped them around my wrist. I looked in the mirror. Something was wrong with this picture. I just couldn't figure out what it was. Gérman took the last pregnancy Polaroid of me and it was only then that I realized what the problem was.

I looked like a total, absolute geek.

My curly hair was now so short that it stood up on the ends and made me look like Bozo the Clown. The blotches of pink and red makeup on my face made me look like my ninety-four-year-old abuelita from Tampico. My belly was so huge that I looked like I swallowed a basketball. I was surely radiant, not from joy, but from all of the goop I had on. It was too late to change anything though. We had to be at the hospital by 7:30. Scheduled delivery time was 9:30 A.M. sharp.

Oh yes, Miss Natural Earth Mama plastered in makeup was ready to bring this child into the world. And all I had to do was lie back on a table. Not even one little push.

By eight o'clock in the morning I was wearing my hospital gown, I had a fetal monitor contraption stuck to my belly, and the most painful thing, a catheter, had been clamped on to something somewhere down there that felt as if it were squeezing the life out of me. I spent two hours like that while we waited for the operating room to be unoccupied. My parents were nowhere in sight. "They came all this way to be late to my delivery?" I grumbled to myself as Gérman held my hand. Finally, just as they were wheeling me into the operating room, Mom and Dad showed up in the hallway and told me they loved me. And then I overheard Mom say to the doctor, "Take care of our daughter" and I felt like *I* was the baby as the little-girl tears welled up in my eyes. How could *I* be the baby? I was supposed to be a grown woman. I was about to give birth, for God's sake!

The operating room radio was tuned to an oldies station and I heard my fifth-grade idol, Michael Jackson, singing, "Never Can Say Goodbye." As they began to prep me, I distracted myself and remembered the letter I wrote to Michael Jackson when I was ten years old: "Dear

Michael: Even though you are black and I am not, I am a lot closer to you than you think. I am Mexican. Would you think about going out on a date with me? I love you very much and Jermaine, too. You can come over to my house and I will make tacos for you. Your (girl) friend, Maria." (Of course, he never wrote back.)

I looked around the operating room and surveyed the scene. My doctor, who lived on Long Island (and vacationed in Puerto Rico with his family), would deliver my baby. The anesthesiologist was Asian. The doctor's medical assistant was a Puerto Rican woman. The nurses were Jamaican, African American, and Filipino. Our gay pediatrician was waiting outside. Victor, our Argentinean surrogate father, was with us in the O.R. (he worked in the same hospital) and was ready with the camera. And my husband, his dark, curly hair swept back in a ponytail under a green hospital cap, was at my side, trying to look calm but I could read the anxiety in his eyes.

Marvin Gaye's "Sexual Healing" was on the radio. The whole O.R. was singing along (except for Germán and Victor). I was terrified and yet I was humming along myself. I closed my eyes and it calmed me.

In a matter of minutes, I was numb from my neck down. I was only supposed to be numb from the waist down but the anesthesiologist pumped too much of the drug into my system by mistake. I felt some slight tugging, as if my belly were a washing machine and then I heard the delicious sound of my baby's voice, his screaming lungs saying Vida! Vida! I am alive! I am alive! I saw two little arms flailing about and his screams were now causing me the pain I now knew was a mother's pain. "Ven, mi'jito. Ven aquí. Te quiero abrazar, apretar, y besar. Ya no llores, mi hijo. Ya no llores. Tu mamá está aquí y no se va para ninguna parte." Don't suffer my son, don't suffer. Your mami is here and I am not going anywhere. Come my son! This was where I thought maybe I could rescue the earth mama in me after all. At least I would be able to hold my child now that he was born and he would feel that all-important mother's warmth. That was what the books said you were supposed to do, right? Hold your baby the second he was born and he was guaranteed to be centered for the rest of his life, right?

But I couldn't do any of this because I was tied to this table, my arms strapped down and stretched out as if I were on a crucifix. I could not move. I could not see him. I could only hear his screams. My husband left my side and I heard him singing "A na nanita nana, nanita na na, nanita eeh-aah. Mi Raul tiene sueño, bendito sea, bendito sea." And in a matter of seconds our son was quiet and as he was dried and measured by all of the different nurses, he turned his head to his father's voice and listened quietly.

Earth papá.

In a matter of seconds I started to feel woozy and dizzy and then nauseated from the pitosin they had just shot through my body to help my uterus begin to contract. I tried to focus but I could barely see what my baby looked like when my husband finally brought him over to my face. I was so sick I couldn't even kiss him. The doctor told me everything went fine. I was intact. But I felt horrible. As I was rolled into the recovery room, I tried to throw up every thirty seconds, but I had no muscle sensations so I couldn't. All I did was gag over and over again as if I was some kind of pathetic animal. I felt like this must be the worst thing I had ever gone through in my life.

My parents met me in the recovery room and my husband followed carrying our baby. "Don Raul," my husband said to my father as he extended our son from his arms toward my father's, "Aquí está su nuevo nieto. Se llama Raul." No one knew what his name was going to be until now.

I heard my father start weeping softly and from the corner of my eyes, lying in my bed, I could see my father take my son in his hands. "Tocayo," he said cradling him softly in his arms. Namesake. "Qué tocayo más lindo me han dado." What a beautiful namesake you have given me, he said. The strict, stern, serious, scientist, the Mexican macho, the hombre that was my father, broke down and tears slowly rolled down his face. We were all crying.

I was complete. The circle was closed. The next generation had arrived.

But I still couldn't hold my son. I was in so much pain they called the nurses and the anesthesiologist in to see me. They gave me morphine and Motrin. I wanted to throw up but I couldn't. And for the next five hours, I lay in this bed, writhing, clamoring for drugs, demanding anything to help with the pain.

I had thought because I was having a C-section that I was going to be deprived of that most womanly of sensations—a contraction. I felt like

I was a lesser woman, a cop-out because I would never experience them. But I was wrong. Thanks to the overdose of pitosin I was given, I had one long contraction that lasted for five hours. And so during that time all I could do was moan and groan and twist my head from side to side à la Linda Blair. But I didn't want an exorcism. I wanted more drugs!

"If I give you any more dear, you're going to die of an overdose," was all the nurse could say.

Gérman stayed by my side and every twenty minutes would run up-stairs and look through the glass window in the nursery to see how our baby was doing. "He is sound asleep. All of the other newborns are screaming their heads off but Raul Ariel is sleeping like an angel," he would say to me.

My God, I thought. This baby is so wonderful and understanding that he is letting me recuperate in peace. The curandera was right. This baby is here to protect me and to love me. Gracias a los Dioses.

Finally, at 5 o'clock P.M. the interminable contraction stopped and I was taken up to my room. I was able to hold Raul Ariel in my arms, al-most a full eight hours after he was born. He had a head full of black hair and a softly sculpted angelic face. Round full lips like his father, a small nose like his mother, and dark eyes like the both of us. He weighed just six pounds but he was long and supple and his hands and feet were wide and extending, as if he already wanted to touch the world around him.

In our hospital room, Gérman set up the two dolls we brought from home that were made especially for this day. One of them was dressed in blue and had dark curly braids wrapped like a crown around her head. Yemanya. The other was wearing a yellow dress and had brown curls falling over her shoulders. Oshun. The Goddess of the Ocean and the Goddess of the Rivers looked down on us from a shelf next to the hanging television set. A goblet of water was next to them and so was a small statue of La Virgen de Guadalupe, Tonantzin. The nurses walked in and stared. Some smiled. Others looked and quickly turned away.

Raul Ariel was "rooming in" with me and was so small that he could barely get his mouth over my nipple. He sucked for just a little while and went to sleep. So did I. Four hours later, in the middle of the night, loud nurses woke me and took him away for his bath. They sponge bathed me and when they brought me back my baby he was crying desperately.

"Why didn't you wake the baby up? This baby is hungry. Didn't anyone tell you that you can't let newborn babies sleep so long without eating? You have to wake him up. Don't let that happen again," I was told by a nurse. First experience with motherhood was being scolded by a stranger. Great. Welcome to the land of guilt and inadequacy and feeling as if you would never be able to do the right thing.

Early the next morning, I called Ceci (who was now four months pregnant herself) and the two of us started bawling on the phone. I called Bertha Elena and she told me to be strong. Victor and Graciela stopped by my hospital room and told me they loved me. Ro sent me a bouquet of white flowers. I called Sandy, my friend from Washington, but by this time I was high on the postsurgery drugs again.

"Sandy," I whispered into the phone, "I'm doing it. I'm really doing it. I'm a mom."

"I knew you could, sweetie pie. I'm so proud of you."

"Yeah, it's unbelievable but it's true. He's snuggling to my breast, he's sucking so well. I feel like an earth mama after all."

"Yes, you are sugar. I've always told you that you were a natural. Now your time has come."

By the second day, my moods were regulated by this volatile mixture of Percoset pills and hormones. I never knew how I'd be feeling from one minute to the next. My mom was upset that every five minutes a nurse or someone else was barging into my room so she took a chair and planted herself outside my door like a security guard. No one would be allowed in to see me unless she gave her approval.

"My daughter must sleep!" she barked as she gave the evil eye to the nurses.

I closed my eyes and as I dozed I started to remember the first time I saw a woman breast-feeding. I was five years old and we were driving through the mountains of southern Mexico. The mist that had been hanging over the hilltops had turned into a jungle rainstorm and we had no choice but to stop. There was a little village off the two-lane road and Papi maneuvered our green station wagon up the unpaved streets of the town until we found a safe place to park. Everyone in the pueblito stopped what they were doing to see who was going to come out of this long green overstuffed car. Even though we were "home," we were always being stared at and studied by people all throughout Mexico. It was strange being considered a tourist in my homeland, but that's what I was.

We all filed out of the station wagon and made our way over to a little open-air shack where many of the locals had their wares spread out on the floor. I was enjoying the visual feast of colors—pink mangoes, radiant red cactus fruits, bright yellow baby bananas, and a rainbow of different-colored candies that I never saw at home in Chicago—everything stacked into neat little piles or carefully arranged into triangles on the floor. Then I saw something familiar. I started to smile but after a second I realized that I wasn't supposed to be looking and I turned away. I looked around to see whether or not my mother had caught me but she was several feet away and had her back turned to me. So I twisted around again and let my eyes set on this woman who had her big round breasts out in the open, a shiny blue rebozo draped over her shoulder holding her baby who was looking up at me, a drop of milk easing slowly down his chin.

I was five years old and shocked. This woman had her dark brown breasts and even darker nipples exposed, right there in the middle of the day, right there in front of my father and brothers, in front of all of the men and children who were milling about the stall where she was selling dulces, fruits, nuts, Chiclets, and pink coconut pastries. And nobody seemed to notice except for me.

I had never seen tetas before. I mean, I had seen them in the *Playboy* magazines at our downstairs neighbor's house when my brother and I would go there specifically to sneak a magazine into the bathroom and take a quick peak at the women in the pictures who always had their mouths open for some reason.

In my house, tetas were always covered. Especially my mother's. It was unspoken but I sensed there was something bad about breasts. As far as I could tell, tetas were not only mysterious but were supposed to be hidden. They were something I didn't have yet, but when I did, would certainly be covered up, too.

But that day, how I saw tetas, my own and everybody else's, changed for the rest of my life.

My mother, who made a point of holding her pajama top pressed to her chest with her hand anytime she bent over when she was making beds (which was the only time I would ever get close to catching a peek at hers), was also as calm as everybody else on that day that I first saw the woman with the bare breasts. I didn't understand what was happening. Was I the only one who had seen this woman? Impossible! Everyone was walking right in front of her. So why wasn't anyone going up to her and telling her to cover herself up?

I decided I had to tell my mom. She would say something to this woman, I was sure. My mom wasn't afraid to talk to anyone about anything. I pulled her aside and whispered into her ear. "Mami, por qué esa señora tiene sus tetas así al aire libre? Why is that woman half naked? Isn't she ashamed? Why doesn't she cover herself? Can't she see all the men plus my dad and brothers are looking at her?"

"Ay, mi amorcito! Nadie la está mirando! Eso es lo más natural del mundo. Esa señora le está dando el pecho a su bebé." My love, my mother said, no one is looking at her! That is the most natural thing in the world. She is nursing her baby.

The look of amazement must have been etched onto my tiny face because my mother stopped what she was doing and knelt down by my side.

"Mi'jita, you shouldn't be so ashamed. You know, I did the same thing for you. And your grandmother did it for me. And all of your tías have done it for your primos. And you will probably do it for your children. This is one of the things that makes being a girl, a woman, and a mother, so special."

It took a second for this to all settle in and just as I had thought, my mother decided we should talk to this woman so that I could see for myself that neither she nor my mother was ashamed to speak about this. She took me by the hand and I walked just behind Mami, close enough to feel her pink polka-dotted dress waving in the wind and brushing against my face. The woman was sitting on a straw and wood stool. Her baby was nuzzled against her chest, sucking on one of her tetas taking long, deep gulps. I could hear him swallowing and I wondered what the milk tasted like. He seemed to be enjoying it so much he looked like he was about to doze off into the sweetest of dreams.

Mom started talking to the woman who was smiling broadly now. As this woman spread her lips and smiled I saw her two top teeth were outlined in gold. Mami had told me when people did that it meant they were rich. I didn't like the way it looked, though. No one in my neighborhood back in Chicago had gold front teeth. Many of the older kids had silver braces, though. I didn't want either.

My mom started talking to the woman, explaining that I had never seen anybody nursing a baby before. The woman giggled and I wondered why she thought this was funny. Then the baby startled and he pulled his face away from her nipple and looked straight at me. She was bare again and I couldn't help but stare. It felt so good to look at her and not feel bad. It felt good to look at her while I was holding my mother's hand, knowing I was safe, knowing there was nothing wrong with me marveling at this woman's tetas. I was in awe. They were brown and round and full and her nipples were the color of dark chocolate, stiff and pointed. We stayed there for quite a while, while my mom continued to talk to her, asking her where she lived, how business was, how many children she had. I just stared and smiled and laughed with the baby who was playing with his mother's breasts now, running his small hands softly over them, gently twisting her nipples as if they were doorknobs.

From that day on I knew I was going to nurse my own baby and I started looking forward to the experience that I knew was decades away.

Two weeks before Raul Ariel was scheduled to arrive, Gérman and I were sitting in the auditorium of a hospital with about forty other expectant moms and couples from all over the city preparing for a lecture and slide show about breast-feeding. I was glad that I was sitting close to the front so that no one could see me. There was something about these parenting seminars and birthing classes that made me feel like I was in first grade again. I know I should have felt solidarity with the women around me but I felt like we were all adults now—we didn't have to be lectured about everything regarding babies. I mean, women all over the world had babies every single minute and they didn't have to go to seminars about diaper changing, baby bathing, and nursing. These classes made me feel like a dunce. It didn't help that I had excruciating heartburn that day or the fact that my left hip socket felt as if it had been unbolted from the rest of my body and was carrying the forty pounds I had gained all by itself.

What on earth was I doing here? Why had I agreed to come? I couldn't wait to get home and eat some Chinese food, I thought to myself. The lecture hadn't even started yet and already there was all of this lovey-dovey bonding going on between some of the mothers and one of the teachers. Yuck.

The presenter seemed nice enough but I imagined she was from La Leche League, one of those dogmatic mothers who goes around making nursing her raison d'être, as if nothing else could be more important. I mean, I supported breast-feeding wholeheartedly and when I was in college I boycotted Nestlés because of their policy of giving third-world women free formula, but in truth, I felt there were many more important causes for women to be fighting for. Now all of a sudden, since nursing had made a comeback in this country, these women had suddenly become nursing guerrillas. I just couldn't imaging making something as natural as nursing into a political movement. I mean, my mother didn't have a nursing support group and she survived.

"Ay, estas gringas locas," I said to myself, "who could ever need *help* breast-feeding?" It was the most natural thing in the world. But here in this country you have to have organizations, newsletters, websites, books, support groups, self-help videos. Modern American women are the only ones who could ever have any problems or issues around breast-feeding, I remember thinking to myself, my own thoughts drowning out the lecture. But, hey, not *me*. This stuff is in my blood! This is part of my culture, my history. I knew I was going to breast-feed, I knew it was the natural, motherly thing to do, I knew *I* wasn't going to have any problems. So what was I doing in this lecture hall, anyway?

During the presentation I felt too embarrassed to raise my hand and ask a question about nursing and C-sections, so I waited until it was over and I spoke to the lecturer directly, after everyone else had left. She was very sweet and got down on the floor and pretended to be in a hospital bed and used a doll to show me all of the positions I could use as I recuperated from the surgery. And because she was so nice I also confided to her that I was worried I had flat nipples and that this might make it harder for me. She took me into the bathroom, had me pull up my shirt, and she peered at my nipples. Then she washed her hands and started massaging them and I began to get antsy. She gave me some little plastic cones (à la Madonna) to help them get into shape and she wished me the best of luck. "Don't hesitate to call when you are in the hospital if you need any help," she said.

"Thanks, but I am sure I am going to be just fine," I said and almost threw away her number. Instead I stuffed it into the pocket of the dress I was wearing. It turned out that was the dress I wore to the hospital on the day I delivered. Todo pasa por una razón. Everything happens for a reason.

On the evening of the third night in Raul Ariel's short life, in that horrible hospital room, just after Mom had left her guard post at my door, Jenny, the nursing guerrilla lecturer, was making her rounds and stopped by unexpectedly. She asked how everything was going and I said really well.

"Has your milk come down yet?" she asked.

"I don't think so," I said, and once again she asked if she could look at my breasts. She started touching them all over as if she was squeezing melons at the grocery store. I looked straight ahead as if what was going on was the most normal thing in the world.

"It looks like it might happen tonight. Just make sure you get him latched on and that he nurses very well every couple of hours or so you don't get engorged." She had a little bit of a worried look on her face, but since I couldn't feel anything and was still drunk on the post-op drugs, I didn't think much of it.

That night Raul Ariel slept from midnight until five in the morning. When I woke up my tetas had turned into two huge cement mountains. My skin was stretched so tight I felt like I was being ripped open at the seams, and my nipples were flat as a sheet of ice. I had no idea what to do, it was too early to call my mom, the nurses were all apparently busy, and Raul Ariel had just woken up, screaming. When I put him to my breast he couldn't get my flat nipple into his tiny mouth. He continued to wail. I called a nurse and she told me I needed to use a breast pump to soften up my nipple. I never thought I was going to have to use this mechanical, artificial, contraption, but there I was pumping away. Forty-five minutes later another nurse walked in and told me a patient needed the pump.

"How long have you been pumping?" she asked, looking at my exasperated face.

"Half an hour," I mumbled, exhausted.

"What! Didn't anyone tell you that you only need to pump ten minutes on each breast? And what are you doing putting on those hot compresses? You should be using cold compresses! Just sit tight and I'll be back as soon as I can," she said and left.

I started crying. Gérman, who had been sleeping on a mattress on the floor, didn't know what to do. Raul Ariel was hungry and upset and still couldn't get his mouth around my now pump-abused nipples.

Feeling desperate, I remembered that Jenny's phone number was in my dress pocket and I called her at home in a state of panic. So there I was, little Miss Natural Mama calling on the nursing guerrilla to help save my shattered image of myself as the perfect Latina-lactating mother.

Jenny showed up within the hour at my hospital room and by now the once embarrassing sensation of her pinching and prodding my tetas had become commonplace. She stood over my side and stuffed pillows under my arms and settled my baby into the perfect position so he could suck the milk that was filling me up like a balloon. As long as she was there to help, he would suck fine. But as soon as she left me alone with him I couldn't get him into a position where he could latch on. I felt like a total loser. I had failed my son, my husband, and my mother, not to mention feeling like I had failed my culture. My image of my mothering self was crumbling right before my eyes.

I had painted myself into a corner. I felt like I couldn't talk to any of my sistahs about what was happening to me. It was bad enough that my mother image was being destroyed for me—but my ego couldn't bear letting my friends find out as well.

So there I was, in my little high-horse corner, in distress, all alone with my two cement tetas with nobody to talk to.

Except for the gung-ho nursing guerrilla who was able to see beyond all my layers of sadness, anguish, confusion, and humiliation. Of all of my sistahs and familia, she was the only one who came close to me, wrapped her arms around me, and whispered into my ear, "Do you feel like you are a failure?"

And when all I could do was nod my head slowly like a little girl and hold back the lump in my throat that was about to explode, she just said, "Maria, it's okay to cry. If you want to cry, it's okay to let it out. I am here for you. I have been here before and I've been on the other side when things are better. And they are going to get better. I am sure. But if you want to cry, I am here . . . "

And so I did. And while I cried, my mother held my son, and she cried. And my father, who was not ashamed to be looking at my cement tetas, cried with us. And so did Gérman. And so did my gringa-guerrilla-nursing nurse, as she held me and rocked me, never imagining how much she and I had just become sistahs.

HOME SOLITA

They finally let me go home from the hospital after I proved to all of the nurses and doctors that I could pass gas, pee, poop, and burp. It was raining ice the afternoon we left the hospital. Mom and Dad had gone and rented an industrial-size professional breast pump and it was clunking along in the backseat. I was holding on to the handles above the car windows, making sure my colita did not touch the seat for the entire ride up the FDR Drive. I cursed everyone in New York City who might be responsible for the hundreds of potholes that Gérman was now trying to dodge. Inevitably, he hit a few and with each bump I felt like my staples (I had been stapled together, not stitched) were going to pop open and all of my life was going to be poured into the backseat of this car.

Once we pulled up to our building, the shock of living in a five-floor walk-up sunk in. It took me about a half hour to go up the stairs, but I finally made it. And as soon as I arrived, Raul Ariel wanted to eat. The question was—would I be able to feed him myself without the assistance of my nursing assistant and life saver?

The answer was no.

No matter what I did, no matter how many pillows I used, no matter if I was sitting up, lying down, upside down, or in a yoga position, my son could not latch on. We lugged out the breast pump, opened it up, and plugged me in. It looked like a small time-activated device and I imagined barking, bomb-sniffing dogs showing up at our door. I had to admit, though, it was capable of getting the milk out of my cement tetas and for that I was grateful.

This sure didn't fit my image of nursing—the miracle of life—this felt like being professionally milked.

Help was on the way. In the middle of what had now become a snow-storm, I had called a lactation consultant who made home visits. She arrived and after her hands had warmed up, assumed the position that had now become perfunctory. My teta was out, my baby was propped up around me with dozens of pillows, my arms were at my sides while somebody else's hands were maneuvering my breasts and my baby, trying to find a way to get this child to do what he was supposed to do naturally.

I couldn't stop thinking about how lucky other mothers were. Mothers who didn't have C-sections, mothers who nursed with no problem, mothers who could walk around without gripping their gut. I couldn't focus on how lucky I was to be seeing my milagro baby alive and by my side. Unfortunately, my hormones were starting to get the best of me and the complainer part of my personality seemed to be taking over.

No matter what we tried, Raul Ariel could not open his mouth wide enough for my nipple. I was so ready to give up. I was so ready to get that bottle of formula and put it into his mouth—both for his sake and mine. I wanted him to be fed and healthy. And I was getting tired of feeling like such a failure.

We decided that for the time being, my husband would finger-feed Raul Ariel. I would pump milk into a little bottle and Gérman would attach a long skinny tube from the bottle to his pinky finger, and out of his finger-tube would come my sweet-tasting milk that Raul Ariel loved. He had no problem latching on to his father's finger. *Why couldn't he do this for me?*

I was jealous of the bond forming between Gérman and Raul Ariel while I was bonding with this lookalike bomb-machine suction pump!

Mami could see how distressed I was. She would come and sobarme la espalda, exuding all of that love that mothers can with just their touch, and I would think about how much I wanted to be close to my son and do the same thing. Yet I felt so inadequate, so unmaternal.

I knew, I was convinced, it was irrevocably true, that no mother ever in the history of time had had it as bad as I was having it. The pain of motherhood began and ended right here, with me and the story of my son. I was convinced of this.

My second day at home, Mom came and sat by my side after the lactation consultant had come and gone and still Raul Ariel was unable to take my teta out of his own free will.

She picked up my feet and tucked me into the couch, just as if I were a child again, home sick from school. Then she lifted up her shirt and took one of her own tetas into her hand.

"You see these marks here on my nipple? she pointed. "Your brother gave me those. He sucked so hard and so crooked that he drew blood. And all I could do was feed him and cry because I was in so much pain. And I never told you the stories of your sister? When she was born, her mouth was so small she couldn't grab on to my nipple, either. She used to cry and cry and cry, screaming at the top of her lungs because she was starving and yet she couldn't eat. And all my mother would say to me was 'Don't give up. Don't get frustrated. Just keep trying. Just keep putting your teta in her face and you will see that one day she is going to take it." And I would sit there and cry because your sister would cry and I couldn't do anything about it. Mi amor, that is frustration. To see your child hungry and know you have milk and not be able to give it to her. At least you have this fabulous pump. Imagine if I had a pump! At least you know your son is being fed, he is growing, and he is getting your milk. Bendito sea esa pompa mugrosa. God bless that ugly pump. It is saving your child."

"But Ma, didn't you feel like you were a failure and the worst mother on earth?"

"I just knew I had no choice but to seguir adelante, to keep going ahead. I may have been too young, too much of an inocente, to realize all of the feelings I was having. I knew I was sad and frustrated, but I never took it so personally. Mi'jita, don't be so hard on yourself. Give yourself some time. You are a wonderful mother. You are doing a great job. Look at everything you are sacrificing for your child. So many other women would have given up already, but here you are pumping on that machine every three hours. That is a beautiful gift you are giving your child and you are doing it because you want him to be nurtured with the best food there is, la leche materna."

"I don't know, Ma. Maybe this breast-feeding thing is just so *I* can experience it. It's not about my baby but all about me and what I want to feel. I am so frustrated now that I find it hard to justify not giving him formula. Maybe that is better for him. Maybe I am being incredibly self-ish by trying to breast-feed."

"Mi reina, you have every right in the world to want to nurse him. Don't feel bad about that," she said, and paused for a second. "Why is it that everything you say you find a way to criticize yourself? Estas mujeres modernas! You are so hard on yourselves. I don't envy you. You have so much information about everything that it makes it hard for you just to feel things without analyzing them a million times. So you want to breast-feed. And you want to do it because you want that experience. Pues, qué lindo! Qué sacrificio! And how noble!"

"You think so?"

"I know so, mi vida."

It was the first time that anyone (besides Gérman) had said I was doing something right. The first time someone had said I was a good mother. And then there was that keyword. *Sacrifice. Sacrificio.*

Los hijos son sacrificios, was what Mom had always said. Children are sacrifice. I had heard that a million times in Mexico and now it was being said about me. It was like now I was part of the Mexicana Madres Club. The one that said that you are only a good mother if you put your child's needs before yours—every day. I wasn't sure I was ready or even wanted to be part of that club. But Mom had used that laden term for me. I couldn't help but feel proud—and conflicted.

The pumping and finger-feeding went on for several days, but I stopped feeling like I was in a competition for something—whether it was to bond with my son, or to get him to nurse without any help or to prove anything to anyone. I watched Gérman as he fed Raul Ariel, delicately taping the tube in place, his huge hands manipulating the baby and his finger and the tubes with the nimbleness of a surgeon and the gracefulness of a dancer. I saw how comfortable he looked holding our son while he sucked from his dad's pinky, as if this was the most normal of fatherhood experiences. Nothing to prove to anyone nor to themselves, just hanging out there, finger-feeding. Just a father loving his son and a son being given a chance to love his father in a special way.

Seven days later, at three in the morning, after I had finished pumping and Gérman was done feeding the baby and he was asleep in his bassinet, and my husband was watching an old Cantinflas movie on television trying to get drowsy and I was under the covers and warm, I started to cry. No, I wasn't just crying, I was heaving, I was sobbing. "What is it?" my husband asked, startled, thinking I might have hurt myself.

"Ay, nada mi amor. I am just so, so, so happy," I managed to say between sobs. "Estoy feliz. Verdaderamente feliz. Entirely happy." I cried.

"You're happy?" Gérman said to me. "So why are you crying?"

"I don't know," I said, and blew my nose and turned over and closed my eyes and fell asleep just like that.

You've just got to love those postpartum hormones.

I stopped calling the lactation consultants as soon as I made the commitment to myself and to my son to stick with this breast-feeding no matter how long it took. And all I had to do was think about my mother and her nipple scars and it gave me the strength to continue. After not speaking to anyone for several days, I finally called my sister on the phone. Although she hadn't had any problems breast-feeding her children, she gave me some good pointers about positioning myself. I told her I had been trying to do it just like the lactation consultant said I should. But when she asked me if it felt comfortable, I said no, that there were other positions that seemed to work better for me.

"Then why are you doing it the way they told you to?" she asked.

"Because I'm good at following orders, I guess," I said.

"Motherhood is about listening to other people," she said matter-of-factly. "But it's also about following your own voice and intuition. In the end nothing else matters. It's about you and your child y punto."

I had been a mother for ten days now. And I was learning so much. Not only about babies, but about me. So I started trying to nurse the way it felt right for me and even though Raul Ariel didn't latch on completely, at least I felt a little bit more in control. Even after everything I had been through, I was still addicted to this very potent need to feel in control. How long would it be?

One night before we went to sleep I asked my husband why he thought things were happening the way they were. Why did he think I was going through this whole battle over the nursing?

He threw the question back at me. I was quiet. I really hated it when he would do this to me. I mean, if he knew the answer why didn't he just tell me already?

"What are the first words that come to mind when you think about what you have had to learn over the past week?" he asked me.

I thought for a minute and then said, "Paciencia. Que no puedo controlarlo todo." Patience. That I can't control everything.

"There is the lesson. Children are not little machines that you program. You can teach them certain things, but they have their own rhythm in life. Tu siempre vas tan rápido, mi amor. You always are going so fast. And even though we love you, we may not need to go as fast as you. Let us go at our own pace, too. I think that is the message Raul Ariel is giving you. He will do this when he is ready."

I went to sleep thinking about all of the patience I had had to learn ever since the moment that Raul Ariel came into existence, not as a baby, but three years ago when he was just a dream. I had learned that I had to wait until it was the right time for him to arrive. I just hoped his learning to nurse wouldn't take three years, too.

At three o'clock in the morning I woke up and got myself ready to pump. I had overslept for an hour and so my tetas were beginning to feel engorged. After doing this for more than a week, I could literally do this in my sleep. But when I put the suction cup over my nipple and slipped the switch to on, nothing happened. My eyes popped open. I tried again and again, but there was something wrong with the pump. I was dying. How was I going to make it through the night? I was going to explode. I started thinking of where I might be able to get a working breast pump in the middle of the night. This was New York. Someone had to have one. I was getting into a panic when Gérman said, "Why don't you just put Raul Ariel to your breast? You never know."

And so I took several deep breaths while Gérman massaged my shoulders and I felt the milk starting to rush down, like a faucet being turned on behind my shoulders. I lifted Raul Ariel, this tiny angel with jet black hair and fingers that were reaching to the sky and nuzzled him close to me, where he could smell the natural perfume of mother—of mamá who had just woken up, of mamá whose skin was warm and luscious, of mamá who always smelled fresh even though it was the middle of the night, of mamá who smelled like leche, leche not from a tube or from his father's finger, but from a full, round teta. I nestled him close to me and I said, "Okay, Raul Ariel. I really need your help now, amorcito. So do your thing."

And I held him and watched his mouth open just the right size as he turned his head instinctively toward me and stuck his tongue out and rubbed his nose on my nipple and then, with the greatest of care and just a shred of I-know-what-I-am-doing, took my nipple into his mouth and let the power of hunger work this miracle of wonder as he sucked us both into the peacefullness of sleep. It had been a long ten days, but with patience, the both of us had made it.

The day after Raul Ariel latched on, Mom started amenazando that she was going to have to leave and go back to Chicago. (Dad had left when Raul Ariel was less than a week old. I expected that from him. But my mom?) I panicked. How could my mother leave me now? She was the only one who could transform a shrieking Raul Ariel into a quiet newborn in less than a minute.

And even though Mom had been working ever since I was nine years old (first as a clothing saleswoman and now as a social worker), I felt as if I was confronting head-on what it felt like to be the daughter of a working mother.

How could her job take precedence over her newborn grandson?

I begged her to stay and she did for another four days but I could tell she was getting stir crazy. Not only was it freezing and snowy outside but our block had, in the past six months, taken a real turn for the worse. The dealers were out on the corners all day and night, squawking and whistling their secret codes warning drug buyers and sellers of impending police cars. Apartments just around the corner from ours had long lines of people outside in the early morning to buy their fixes of heroin and crack. The addicts and prostitutes rushed along our streets in double-speed as if they owned them and the police were nowhere to be seen. Mom couldn't believe it. The sadness and anger about the state of our community that I was reluctantly learning to live with had Mom disgustada and worried about our safety.

"Do you think any babysitter is ever going to want to work here?" she asked me one morning? She knew that I was set on hiring someone early on to help me (even if we could afford just a few hours a week), so they'd really know Raul Ariel by the time I returned to work.

I was just beginning to settle into my two-week-old role as a new mother. Now I was going to be someone's boss as well. Too many new roles in too little time, I thought.

Through a friend of a friend's nanny I had been told about a young Mexican woman named Paty who was looking for part-time work and so I called her and asked if she would like to come by and meet me. She would come the next day at one o'clock. I had no idea what to expect nor what to do in my first-ever interview as an employer. Mom said she would stick around to help.

That day, after a scrumptious lunch of ramen soup and grilled cheese and tomato (even the simplest food tasted like gourmet with the appetite you had as a nursing mother), the buzzer rang. "I must be more nervous than Paty," I told my mom as I started wiping the dining room table. Outside I heard clunky footsteps coming up the five flights to our apartment, and I imagined a stocky mujer. I opened the door and there was this tiny, exotic-looking young woman with huge black platform boots and brown corduroy bell bottoms that looked exactly like the ones I had ordered from a Sears catalog when I was twelve years old. She had thin black painted eyebrows and dark eyeliner à la Marilyn Monroe, with long ebony-colored wavy hair just like mine. She looked like a combination between a modern hip-hopster rocker and a 1960s hippie. She was soft spoken like a fragile bird and she was carrying a Toni Morrison novel.

The first question I asked took both me and her by surprise, but it just rolled off my tongue as soon as she sat down.

"So, what other novels have you read in the past year, Paty?"

We immediately hit it off. It was like Paty was so many parts of me all mish-mashed together. It was even scary. In many ways, I felt more like Paty than I did the person I had recently become—a grown-up woman and mother with a husband, a house, a serious job, and a newborn. Paty was like a younger Mexicana version of me—what I would have been like had I stayed in Mexico and, like Paty, come to this country as a budding teenager. She came from a hard-working family in Veracruz where she had an uncle who was a doctor and a grandfather who was a farmer. Her father had worked in a small business in Mexico. Here he was working long hours making minimum wage washing dishes at a fast-food joint. He had been trying since she was a toddler to get Paty here and her papers had finally come through when she turned eleven.

Paty read J. D. Salinger but listened to rock en español. She ate tacos at home but went in-line skating until midnight through the streets of her Jewish neighborhood in Brooklyn. She had been at the top of her high school class and had been accepted into college, but she didn't get the financial aid she needed. Soon after she started working for us (she was coming two or three half days a week), I spoke to an old professor of mine at Barnard and Paty audited a class on Latin American litera-ture. She received A's on all her work, and she cleaned my house better than I could. She was the real superwoman, I thought. She faced obsta-cles everywhere—her macho father, her traditional mamá, her jealous boyfriend, her family's precarious economic situation—but she had a goal to go to college and do something with her life. Paty's patient and humble dedication motivated me. And now she was part of my familia.

Raul Ariel seemed to get older overnight. Two weeks soon became three and then four. And every little detail of what happened to my son on each day I wrote down in his Mexican baby/date book. Two weeks old: first social outing to las Chicas del Poder meeting (my Latina jour-nalists group). Everyone there wanted to hold my tiny seven-pound baby. Three weeks old: Mami went to get acupuncture for carpal tunnel still left over from pregnancy. I left you with Dad and I dreamed about you while the needles were sticking in my arms. Sandy came to visit and you stared at her dreads through the sunlight. Four weeks old: Your first visit to Boca Chica and your first ride in a snuggly. You stared at your black-and-white cow and your eyes followed it in arc formation (ge-nius!). Five weeks old: Primer baño de tina con mamá. I got in the tub with you and you loved it! You smiled for the first time but not to me. To your visiting tía Bertha Elena. Six weeks old: Your first SoHo art opening for Papi's art show. You wore your latest gift—a Dior baby suit (Mom doesn't even own a Dior—probably never will!) Seven weeks old: Chinese New Year dinner in Chinatown. The firecrackers didn't even phase you. Mom ate with you in snuggly and food fell from chop-sticks in your hair. You didn't care 'cause you slept the entire dinner.

As time passed, I soon realized that I had been given the gift of an almost perfect baby. He hardly ever cried and had settled into his own schedule—sleep for three hours and wake up as if on cue, nurse and burp and diaper changes for two hours and then again sleep for another three. Gérman had volunteered to take over the three A.M. feeding and so at the first sign of Raul Ariel waking in the middle of the night I would flip on the breast pump and in ten minutes hand over to Gérman eight ounces of warm milk that he would give to Raul Ariel in a bottle while he watched reruns on the Sci-Fi channel. Then I would wake up with the baby at eight and Gérman could sleep until nine or even ten o'clock.

I didn't know any other mothers of newborns and just couldn't see myself going to "new mother" lectures so I depended on Gérman and my mom and sister and my *What to Expect in the First Year* book. I did have the most fabulous pediatrician though. My friend Betty, who was born and raised in Chinatown and was a newspaper columnist and a mother of a six-month-old, had recommended Mark to us. Betty knew a lot about natural medicines and acupuncture and Chinese herbs and she told me that Mark was one of the few pediatricians in the country who used a combination of alternative and mainstream treatments for his young patients.

So after my visits with Mark I would stock up on all these new things that I had never even heard of like, flax seed oil and baby primadophilous and homeopathic teething drops and lavender oil to sprinkle on his pillow to help him sleep and fennel tea for his gas and oatmeal for his bath to keep his skin soft and sesame oil for his cradle cap. I trusted Mark like I had never trusted a doctor before, because he acted like a normal human being, not like an authority figure. Anything you need you call me anytime, he would remind me after our monthly visits.

The first nonfrigid day after an unseasonably long and cold winter came in early March when Raul Ariel was just over two months old. I woke up that morning thinking about what the Dominican woman who was the new cashier at the corner bodega had said about Raul Ariel the day before when I took him with me to buy some mango juice.

"Ay, qué bueno! Salió blanquito!" Oh how wonderful! He came out white!

I knew she had the best of intentions but I didn't know what to say.

Thank you?

I didn't think so. So I just smiled. Then she said, "Que Dios lo bendiga," and I thought, What God? The God that likes white babies more?

Why did I have to obsess over every stupid comment made to me by virtual strangers, I was thinking to myself as I pulled the covers off and started to stretch. I looked in the bassinet and saw that Raul Ariel was gone. So was Gérman. They must have gone out to get coffee. I plunked my head on the pillow and thought about the woman from the bodega. When she asked me where I was from I got the same response I have heard a million times: "You're Mexican? Really? You don't look Mexican."

I figured my light-skinned Raul Ariel was going to get the same thing in the future. I'm going to have to teach him the famous response that Mom uses whenever someone says the same thing to her:

"Really? You don't *look* ignorant, but you are!" she says matter-of-factly.

I was lying in bed tumbling all of these ideas around in my head when I heard what had become an unfortunately familiar yet terrifying sound.

Pop! Pop! Pop-pop! Pop! Pop-pop-pop!

Gunfire. It was 9:15 in the morning and Gérman and Raul Ariel were out in the street. I went cold from head to toe, felt like I was sucked into the tiny tube of a vacuum cleaner, like all of the blood had left my system—but in a second I forced my legs to move and I climbed down from our loft bed and ran to the window, keeping my head low. You never know when a bullet can ricochet and yes, reach up to the fifth floor and kill you as you are looking out to see where your husband and son are.

Outside our apartment people were running, some deliberately—the women, the children—some, the teenage guys and older men, more slowly, as if even in this moment of craziness they still wanted to look cool. A gunfight had broken out and my family was nowhere to be seen.

I called 911. They answered. A good sign, at least. (A year before I had called 911 and gotten a recording.) The monotone operator couldn't give a shit about the anguish in my tone. "Just give me the facts, ma'am. If you don't I can't help you."

There has been gunfire . . . several shots . . . coming from a downtown street . . . I can't say who is shot or who is doing the shooting, but
there *is* gunfire. I hung up and called again. I knew that unless the police
got several 911 calls about a shooting they might not even respond. An
officer had told me that one day. "Do you do that for every neighborhood?" I asked the cop sarcastically when he shared this with me. I wondered if I should call a third time but instead I put on my clothes.
Trembling as I put my foot through my overalls, I had horrible images
going on in my mind. Then I wondered if going out was the smartest
thing to do. What if I walked right into the gunfire? What if in trying to
save my family I got myself killed and left my son motherless? I turned
on the TV to the local all-news channel. The sirens of the police and
ambulances were drowning out the anchor's voice. I started to tie my
shoes.

What looked like about ten police cars screeched up the avenue and
the officers jumped out of their cars, scattering like bugs. Gérman must
have gone to get a coffee, I repeated to myself. But had he gone to
Broadway or to the little bodega? Why don't I see him? Why isn't he on
the street? Why? *Where is he? Por qué no aparece?!*

I grabbed my jacket. I couldn't take it anymore. I was going to go
downstairs, y ya! Everything felt like it was in slow motion even though
I felt like I was running everywhere. But I couldn't seem to get things
done quickly enough. I ran to the window one last time and I saw Gérman turning the corner. Raul Ariel was in the snuggly. Gérman looked
away, toward where the gunfire had come from and then he turned his
head and instantly looked up to the window. I opened it frantically and
signaled him with wild arms to come home. *Now!* He waved back as if
nothing had happened. I closed the window and took a deep breath and
felt my heart pulsing quickly against my chest. I shut my eyes and an un-
steady smile started to break. I looked outside the window again and
saw the calm *after* the storm. The gunfire had ended, the police were
there. People started to get on with their lives again. As Gérman
walked down the street I saw him bump into one of our neighbors at the
vegetable stand. They said hello, talked for a few seconds, and then my
neighbor looked up and waved at me. Then they both went back to buying plátanos and avocados and apples. It all felt too surreal. A toddler
was on his plastic bike riding around his grandmother at the bus stop.

Traffic was rumbling by on the street again. Life went on—it picked up right where it left off before the gunshots. I felt like screaming out the window—*Someone was just shot a block away! Stop what you're doing! We have to do something about this!* My head was spinning. I was exhausted but at the same time I felt like my body was on speed.

I heard the announcer on television. "We have this breaking story for you now. A nine-year-old boy has been shot in upper Manhattan. The young boy, whose identity cannot be released until his family is notified, was apparently walking to school when he was caught in a turf dispute between drug dealers in the neighborhood. The boy is apparently in stable condition with a gunshot wound to the shoulder. We have a reporter on the way. Details coming up later in the broadcast . . . "

For a second my brain switched off from "mom" and into "reporter." That could be me, I thought. I could be the reporter on assignment arriving in someone else's neighborhood to report on some incident. Instead, my colleagues would be descending into *my* neighborhood. They would stay for a day or two and then leave and that would be the end of it. The story would be reduced to a two-minute piece on just one more shooting in another "bad" neighborhood. But there was more to the story, of course. This was the story of how this community had slowly been abandoned by police and left in control of the dealers. This wasn't a "bad" neighborhood. This was a barrio that had been left to die on its own and now we were being blamed for it.

"Qué pasó?" I said and rushed toward Gérman and the baby as they walked in the front door. Raul Ariel was asleep, oblivious to what he had just witnessed and to the life-changing sounds he had just heard. Gérman was calm.

"When we heard the shots we were in the corner coffee shop. We stayed inside for a long while and then walked over to come home."

"I thought you had been killed! I was just going to look for you. Qué bueno que nada les pasó."

"You should never go outside when you hear gunshots." I knew he was going to tell me this. "You should never walk into an unpredictable scene like that," he scolded me.

"But I was going crazy up here!"

"Don't ever do that. Ojalá que el otro niño esté bién. I saw his mother being driven to the hospital by the police. It was bad. We should light a candle for him."

I got one of the long votive candles we had on the shelf, the one with the picture of La Virgen de Guadalupe and the Mexican flag on it and we lit it together. We held hands and asked for the dioses to protect the little boy and thanked the gods for protecting us. We kissed on the lips and kissed Raul Ariel's forehead and blew out the match at the same time together. I took Raul Ariel and I squeezed him to my chest. I laid him in his bassinet and watched him for a long while.

In my mind I had these thoughts whirling in my head:

> move out? and leave others to live like this? not fair.
> anger at why it hasn't changed
> angry at the shooters
> promises of FBI
> they did show up quickly (police) but nothing changes—
> what kind of security is that?
> eeriness—kid on plastic tricycle at bus stop
> community gathering, neighbor waves to window as if nothing
> second time raul ariel hears gunshots since his birth—is this
> a new sound my baby must process along with turning to
> the sound of my voice?
> legs are shaky
> angry that it becomes commonplace but what else can you
> do—have to live with it otherwise you go crazy, absolutely crazy

You can't think about it all the time, I rambled in my mind, as if trying to convince myself of something. You would be paralyzed and you would never leave your house. And things do go back to normal. After a few weeks of being shell-shocked you and your community do go back to normal. You adjust your life. You cross the street to avoid bumping into the addicts who look sickly and emaciated. They rush around you with this electric energy that makes them look as if a fire is chasing them and they have got to get some place to put it out, quickly, desperately. The youngbloods, the dealers, they know who you are. They know you are a mom, you have a husband, you are no trouble to them. You are invisible to them. They are looking for customers and for police and for rivals. You become the background scenery.

Most of the time in my barrio, during the day, I don't feel unsafe. I feel angry. Very angry and very sad. If I can point out dealers, drug spots, stash points, customers, cars with suburban teenagers coming to buy on my corner, then why can't the police? It becomes easy to lose hope, to become passive, to distrust everyone. Why should you call the police? What if you end up giving a complaint to one of the cops who is on the take and then he decides you are the problem, not the dealer? Who are you supposed to turn to then for safety and protection? You are isolated. And that's just what everyone wants, after all. From the dealers' perspective, an isolated, scared community is the easiest one to take over.

Moving out of the neighborhood just wasn't an alternative. We couldn't afford to live anywhere else in Manhattan, we had just bought this condo a few years ago, we weren't going to move to the suburbs, and plus, this was my neighborhood. We had made a choice to stay in Manhattan and this was what we could afford. This is what Gérman and I had chosen, but was I putting Raul Ariel's life at risk? Still, leaving New York just wasn't possible. I couldn't even create an image of my family living in a suburb. If I tried to imagine it in my mind, the image would get blurry and fizzle out just at the thought of getting into one of those commuter trains.

No, I was a city girl—born in Mexico City, raised on the South Side of Chicago, and down with Manhattan.

I loved my barrio.

Loved the fact that there were families everywhere, like the Dominican girls who hung out in front of our stoop and who rushed over to kiss el bebé Raul every time they saw us. Loved the old-timers hanging out at the bodegas with the thumping merengue, holding their beers in small paper bags, and who always said buenas tardes and opened the store door for me. Loved the fact that those bodegas felt as if they had been airlifted right out of a barrio in Santo Domingo and placed here in uptown Manhattan. Loved the fact that Mexicanos who spoke Náhuatl drove around on their bikes delivering food, listening to norteñas on their Walkmans. I remember seeing one Mexicano wearing a T-shirt with a faded American flag and the words "You can't touch this, Sadam!" written in big bold letters. Loved the fact that my neighborhood was alive and pumping, full of locura and contradictions, full of energy and life. I didn't need to read Gabriel García Márquez. I lived with wild and magical scenes right here in the middle of New York City.

Where else can you wake up to the sounds of roosters on roofs at four in the morning or see ducks tied to fire escapes? Where else can you find a building named after Diego Rivera and another named after Frida Kahlo on a street named after Duke Ellington? Where else can you see a wild skunk dodging yellow cabs in the middle of a street?

I imagined that one day Raul Ariel was going to ask me this question: Why do we stay here, Ma? Why do we live in this neighborhood?

First of all, mi'jito, I would say to him, because we can't afford to move anyplace else and anyplace else affordable would be the suburbs and the suburbs I know don't have this espíritu and energía that feeds our lives.

We stay here, mi'jito, because this is the place that is full of life and full of the people who make up your world. There are Dominican families, African American families, Mexican workers, Latino artists, Anglo couples, upper-middle-class condo owners living next to families of the working poor. There are men and women of all races in business suits, teen hip-hoppers striding next to young Latino girls in frilly dresses and boys in suits who gather for their Pentecostal services with drums and tambourines. There are old African American men from the South, widowed and lonely, accompanied by their dogs. There are fancy older Cuban and Argentine women who live alone and exchange recipes and Macy's and Bloomingdale's one-day-sales info with one another. There are musicians playing their congas and bass guitars into the evening, and gay couples. There are sirens and yellow cabs and bodegas where Mami y Papi can buy queso para freir, tortillas, yuca, aguacate, cilantro, mangos, chiles, tostadas, arroz y frijoles y con-con from the restaurante on the esquina. You hear Spanish and English and Náhuatl and Creole and Mandarin and Korean and crazy combinations of all of them together. There is hanging out on the stoop and abuelitas who throw you kisses and say "Que Dios lo bendiga" without knowing you. There is music, so much music—from merengue to rap to rock en español to bachatas and baladas to blues and Motown to Sting and Salt-N-Pepa and Boyz II Men and the BarrioBoyz to Dark Latin Groove (DLG) and Marvin Gaye and salsa, so much salsa into the wee hours of the night because here music is not considered a bother, it is considered a sign of life, just like the ridiculous sounds of the out-of-tune and over-modulated ice cream truck that drives Mamá crazy but that she resigns herself to because your father said to her one time "Just think of the joy that sound brings to so many children." There are piragueros and shopping carts filled with flowers and taco stands and hot dog carts and mechanics on the streets and there is color everywhere—hand-painted bodega signs, graffiti murals, spray-painted gibberish that is here one day and gone the next. There are the Jewish men and women, the men with their yarmulkes on Friday nights as they walk past our home on their way to and from temple. There are dominoes and basketball hoops made out of old milk crates and hopscotch and double dutch, which Mami jumps every chance she gets. And there are people everywhere, all the time, all day and all night, people going and coming, from work to school to parties to church to a bembé where maybe right next door the spirit of Yemanya will come down in the celebration and she'll be received in a home with an altar for La Virgen de Guadalupe and there is no contradiction. There is happiness and fear and you learn to live with them both and you learn how to trust your gut and you develop street smarts to avoid trouble but you know that in this life te salvas del rayo pero no de la raya because life comes with death, the two go hand in hand, and you know that and you see it and you hear it and you live it. This is your barrio and your neighborhood and you belong here just like anyone else because this is who you are and will become, and you will be orgulloso—proud.

Or maybe not. Because, yes, this is our barrio, but in so many ways we are outsiders here as well. I know the parishioners from the evangelical church on our corner think I wear pants that are too tight and believe it is a sacrilege that I am a working mom. They dislike Gérman's ponytail and were shocked when they saw one of his paintings. I know that our neighbors who have been living here for many more years than we have, see us as the invaders, young professionals who might yuppify their barrio. I know some people look at us with distrust because we do have more than they have and because we don't always make the time to just shoot the breeze while hanging out in front of the bodega. I am sure they look at us sometimes and hiss that we think we are better than they and that's why we are so private with our lives. I know that even in my own barrio I am sometimes looked at like the real outsider and I don't like the feeling.

So I am not sure where we "fit," but I know this place feels more like home than any other.

Thinking back on my own childhood, I remember I grew up in one of the few truly integrated neighborhoods in Chicago. We ended up there by chance because it was close to the university where my father found work. I spent many afternoons at the JCC, thinking it meant Jay Cee Cee. Only when I got much older did I realize that I was hanging out on the second floor of a synagogue and that J-C-C actually stood for the Jewish Community Center of Sinai Temple. And so I had Jewish friends like Michelle Gittler. And other friends like Elizabeth Takeuchi or Lisa Tyre who had long, straight blond hair, the color of sweet corn, or Teresa who taught me how to do the Grandfather to Sly and the Family Stone.

Back then, I would see people like me only on the weekends when my family would go shopping to a place we called "el barrio Mexicano." All six of us would pack into our dark green station wagon and drive twenty minutes away. I knew I was in el barrio when I would begin to see apartment buildings that were so old they looked bent, with windows that were so dirty and gray you could hardly see the curtains and if you did they always looked ragged and mismatched, if there were any curtains at all.

I remember telling my mom one day, "Mami, I am so glad we don't have to live in el barrio Mexicano. Everything is so dark and dirty." And then I asked, "Mami, why do the Mexicanos have to live here? Por qué tienen que vivir en tanta pobreza? Why do they have to live so poor? And how come *we* don't live here? We're Mexicanos, too." Mom held me close and told me that, yes, we were just like the Mexicans who lived there, but that some people in this world were poor. And that unfortunately, even though Mexicans in this country worked so hard, many of them were still poor and had no choice but to live in these communities.

I was sure I was going to have to give Raul Ariel many explanations about why we lived the way we did. I didn't think it was going to be as easy as just explaining to him the whys of the flowers and rainbows and the sun.

The day of the gunfire I didn't go out, even though it was finally warm in Manhattan. I didn't feel safe. I didn't feel like I could protect my son.

What good was I as a mother if I couldn't do that? I hoped I was making the right decisions about my life. But now it was clear that it wasn't just about me and my life. Staying up late, the feedings, the nursing, the diaper rash and crying spurts—that was all hard. But choosing to make my life on Duke Ellington Boulevard was now more complicated than I could have ever imagined.

Raising Kids Como Los Americanos

Thank the santos for Annie LaMott's book *Operating Instructions*. I kept it near my bed at night and read it so that the author's baby and mine were growing up in the same time frame and I could compare notes. At least this way I felt as if there was someone else out there who wasn't a perfect mother. There were those moments when I did feel like things were smooth and sailing but much of the time I felt simply inadequate. I saw all of these other mothers walking along Broadway, wheeling their babies around in groups of two and three, and wondered why I didn't have any other mom friends. And then I would see a newly arrived Mexicana immigrant around the corner from my house, walking with three young kids, managing a family and a new country and at least looking as if she had it under control. And then there was my son and me—all alone.

My notes in Raul Ariel's baby book continued as the weeks went by: "Constipation woes! First suppository—explosivo! First ah-goo. First time that you laugh and squeal in delight. You touched Mami's face deliberately for the first time. You love to stand on your legs and hold your head up. Your first shower. You loved it! First visit to a dim sum restaurant. First visit to church to say hello to your tocayo Jesús. First shots. Yikes! First day in your life that you feel warm air—it was seventy-four degrees today!"

That happened on April 12, the first fresh blue-sky day in what felt like months. That day I put Raul Ariel in the snuggly and went out to buy him his stroller. I was going to take him for his first-ever visit to the playground. I bought the stroller that the store owner recommended ("It's British," he said. "All Manhattan mothers buy this one!"), strapped my baby in, and walked his little Domini-Mex self to the park.

This was the new me. Mami the full-time mom. The newness of it reminded me of my first day as a working journalist—the day I walked into the NPR offices in Washington. I was excited and scared. And here I was feeling the same thing on my way to the playground.

At the park, it seemed like all the other mothers and nannies knew each other. I stayed to myself and placed Raul Ariel into a swing and we had a sweet fifteen minutes. But then he started pouting and I realized he needed to poo so I lifted him out and held him upright. Moms were beginning to smile at me. I smiled back. This wasn't so bad after all.

Raul Ariel scrunched his face and pushed and I was laughing at him when all of a sudden the poo started slipping out of his diaper and onto his pants. I looked around, embarrassed. This had never happened before. I tried to keep him upright while I grabbed his bag from the stroller and it was only then that I realized that I had forgotten his baby bag!

I had no wipes, no diaper, no change of clothes. Caca was everywhere. New stroller, new outfit, crying baby, and a long ten-block walk home.

Mala madre!

I never left the house again without a lifetime supply of baby needs.

It was just about that time that Gérman and I had one of our biggest fights ever. It was so bad that we stopped talking to each other for twenty-four hours—that had never happened before. And what did we fight about? Raul Ariel's naps!

Gérman wanted to play his music as loud as he usually did when he worked on his paintings. "The baby shouldn't change our lifestyle. He needs to integrate into our lives and not the other way around," he echoed what Dr. Mark had said to us.

"Yes, but Dr. Mark also said that the baby needs to take his naps and if the music is keeping him awake then it's not going to happen!"

Dr. Mark had become the invisible referee for our fights over babydom.

After twenty-four hours of noncommunication, we both broke

down and compromised. The music would stay on but not full volume. And Raul Ariel would take naps in his room with the door closed.

Oh, the joys of co-parenting. Before, women ran the house and that was that. Now everything had to be debated and agreed on in conjunction and a mother's intuition had to be constantly explained to fathers.

It was hard enough just digging deep enough to find out what my mother's intuition was. I knew it had to be there. Somewhere. But now I had to give reasons for everything I did to my baby's father. Ay. More work.

What I did know was that I was in love with my son and every time I nursed him to sleep I would paint the picture of that moment in my mind and say to myself, "Never forget this moment. This is bliss." I would stare at his pursed lips as they sucked, marvel at his dark deer eyes and mile-long eyelashes. I would squeeze him tight and cover his face with besos. Te adoro, te quiero, te adoro, mi pequeño príncipe, I would whisper into his tiny ear.

And when he would wake from his nap I would turn on the music— maybe Juan Luis Guerra, maybe Ana Belem, maybe Tracy Chapman— and dance and sing with him. Mi muchachito is going to have rhythm, I would say to him as he stared at my curls, twirling through the air.

Sometimes I did think I was doing some things right.

On the phone, Bertha Elena gave me tips on stimulating him with colors and sounds. Mom told me not to carry him too much because "se me iba a embrasilar," he was going to get dependent on my arms for everything. Sandy told me to shower him with kisses, Ceci only asked me questions about her advancing pregnancy, Ro squeezed in my phone calls to her in between meetings, and Victor and Graci were busy traveling all over the world going to genetics conferences. But with all the talking on the phone, it wasn't like people were pouring into the house to visit. I got the feeling people didn't want to disturb us because life with a newborn was supposed to be so difficult or because they couldn't deal with us as parents. Nonetheless, I missed many of my friends.

Gérman was my rock. If I couldn't get Raul Ariel to go to sleep, Gérman would do it. If I couldn't get Raul Ariel's burp out, Gérman would do it. If I didn't get around to making dinner, Gérman would do it. Sometimes I thought Gérman was better at mothering than I was. I couldn't imagine doing this alone—as a single mom or doing it alone with a husband who worked all the time. Gérman and I were a team.

But with all my rap about accepting difference and how difference and diversity were good things, I couldn't accept that the way I was mothering was okay, just different. I kept on comparing myself to all the moms I knew and coming up short. I wasn't like my cousins, I wasn't like the moms on TV, I wasn't like the moms in the magazines, I wasn't like my sister, or my mother, of even Ro. And I felt guilty about depending on Gérman so much. *A real mother sacrifices herself for her child*— the never-ending tape that played inside my head said. A real mother would wake up herself at three in the morning to feed the baby. A real mother wouldn't have a babysitter in the house. A real mother would have read all of the books about parenting and be an encyclopedia of information.

I wondered if the comparisons would ever end.

When Raul Ariel was five months old we took him to meet his future girlfriend in Chicago. Ceci had just had a little girl.

"Malu, I don't know what to do," Ceci said when we got together. She looked exhausted with dark rings under her eyes. Her usually flawless face looked gray and wrinkly. She seemed nervous. "My baby won't stop crying. She won't stop nursing. And she won't stay down for more than fifteen minutes at a time. I'm at my wit's end."

And just as my mother had done for me, I told Ceci that what she needed to do was to rest. So I took her daughter in one arm and Raul Ariel in the other and walked into the living room. I told Ceci to go to her bedroom and close the door.

"Sleep, Ceci," I said. "Just take a nap. I'll take care of the both of them."

And while Raul Ariel napped, I held Ceci's baby. And when she started to cry, I thought of my mother when she had held Raul Ariel as a newborn. And I thought of how Mom had just exuded motherly know-how when she held him. And so I tried to do the same thing with Ceci's daughter. I told myself that I knew what I was doing, that I knew how to wrap and hold this newborn and make her go to sleep. All of a sudden I had become my mom. I knew how to do this. It was as if I stepped through some curtain and had made it to the other side. I knew how to mother, not only my own but someone else's. And I gave the gift of sleep to my querida amiga.

It really was a wonderful moment and I told Ceci all about it. She was feeling like I had felt not too long ago (more like days ago), like she was never going to get the hang of it, never going to be able to develop her own mother's intuition. So I decided to tell Ceci that beyond all of the romanticism of the moment and me proving to myself that I could mother two, that there *was* one little practical thing I had done as well that had probably held Ceci's daughter finally sleep.

"Your baby had diaper rash, Ceci. So yeah, I have great motherly arms that can rock a crying newborn to sleep and all that, but the real secret is that I put Balmex on her colita!"

It was great to be back at my old apartment in Chicago with my family. Mom immediately started doing things with Raul Ariel that I would have never done. She got him into a little high chair (But he can't even sit up yet! I said anxiously) and stuffed pillows all around him so that he was upright and then she gave him a hard roll to play with. "Ma, he doesn't even eat yet. How can you give him food? He's going to choke. Something is going to happen to him! He's too young to eat." And before I could finish listing my worries, Raul Ariel had grabbed the bread and was gnawing at it with gusto!

Then she pulled out a banana. "Un poquito, nada más, Malulis! Nothing is going to happen to him. This is what we used to do in México. We always started con un poquito de platanito."

"Mom, are you sure? Our doctor said he didn't have to eat solids for another month and he said to start him off with orange veggies, not fruit!"

Raul Ariel loved the banana.

And that night when I gave him his bath, Mom said, "Tu abuelita always said to let the baby taste a little of his bath water. It makes them talk sooner."

"Mami! No!"

But before I knew it Raul Ariel was smacking his lips and smiling in the tub. And a minute later he made a garbled attempt at a word.

Later, Mom and I talked as we cleaned up the kitchen. She had made her exquisite picadillo, Mexican-style ground beef with spices and raisins. I had eaten six tacos and was about to burst.

"I don't know how you did it, Mom. Four kids, in a new country, all alone, with Dad working all the time. Didn't you go through massive culture shock? Weren't you sad? Did you ever feel like you could never get things right? Like the mothers all around you knew more than you did?"

"You know what, mi'jita? I just did what I had to do. My feelings came last. And by the end of the day I was too tired to think about them. You women today suffer more. Pobrecitas! It was easier to be ig-norant like I was."

"But Mom, you weren't ignorant. You were just young."

"Bueno, mi'jita. I'll never forget the time when my first American neighbor told me that I should go read some psychology books. She said she had never seen a mother as compulsive as me.

"I couldn't answer because I didn't even know what the word *psy-chology* meant," Mom said to me, laughing. She proceeded to tell me the story.

The year was 1958 and it was Dad's first sabbatical at the University of Chicago and their first time living in the United States. Every morn-ing, Mami told me, she used to wake up and clean the entire apartment. She made the beds every day the way she was taught in Mexico. The sheets would all come off and be sacudidos out the window and then put on again. Changed and washed every week, Mami would iron them before putting them on the beds. My sister and brother would be dressed up in starched clean clothes every day—my four-year-old sister in petticoats and white patent-leather shoes; my brother, who was two, in crisp shirts and suspenders, his white shoelaces washed every night and hung on the bannister to dry. This is how Mom would take them out to play in the backyard. But my sister, Bertha Elena, never played in the dirt. And my brother Raul had never been in a sandbox because sandboxes didn't exist in Mexico. And when it was time for meals, Mom spoon-fed them every meal, every day, every week—just as my tías did in Mexico.

The upstairs neighbor would see my mom doing all of this and, of course, thought she was manic and obsessive. Ruth, the mother of a three-year-old, was a graduate student in psychology. She was also a

Jewish bohemian and decided she was going to be my mother's first teacher in America. They couldn't have possibly been more different.

Mami said she was open to this new experience sin prejuicios, without prejudice. She had to *learn* how to become a part of this strange place. And why not? This country was her new home. She was open and willing to learn. Maybe it was because she was a youngster herself, a mother of two and just twenty years old. Or maybe it was because it has always been my mother's character to be willing to try anything new. Or maybe it was because my mother was profoundly insecure about who she was and the new life she was leading in el Norte and she wanted to blend in as quickly as possible.

Ruth loaned my mom her child-psychology books. She talked to Mom about the importance of giving children their independence, of letting them experiment, how this helped build character. She explained that an apartment didn't need to be cleaned constantly. That the time she spent doing that might be better spent playing with my brother and sister, playing games that would stimulate their creative and intellectual development. She told Mom about how her kids should be put on a schedule because that's what Dr. Spock recommended. Mom went home and looked up the word schedule in the book Ruth had given her. All night she tried to understand how to pronounce it. *SSS-cheh-dool . . . sss-cheh-dool,* she repeated to herself. What did this word mean? *Sss-cheh-dool?* My father, whose English was just a bit better than Mom's, had no idea what word my mom was trying to say.

One night, Mom remembers, she put on a Cri Crí record, the Mexican singing grasshopper that sang children's songs, the same ones Mami listened to on the radio when she was a child growing up. In her small Chicago apartment, while everyone else was asleep, she sat next to the portable phonograph, listening to the scratchy Cri Crí rhymes and cried. She missed Mexico, she missed her mother, she missed the place where no one questioned her or called her words she didn't understand, like *obsessive.*

Ruth knew more about raising children than Mami, she thought. She would try doing things her way, the American way. She was alone, away from her family who only knew how to raise kids à la Mexicana. No one questioned how kids were raised back home—así se hace y punto. It was done that way and that was that, period. She decided there might be no better time to try something new. Maybe Ruth and this Dr. Spock were right.

So in no time, my brother was wearing sweatpants and playing in the mud. My sister discovered the sandbox, but she asked my mom to please let her wear her petticoats and white shoes while she played there. They also started to eat by themselves and they liked it.

How gringo this all was. But Mom said she liked it, too. She felt like she was suddenly more sophisticated than her sisters back in Mexico. Así lo hacen los Americanos, she would say to them when she went back home and told them all she had learned. She would even take them a few jars of precooked Gerber food. My aunts would never think of feeding their babies this.

My father barely noticed this seismic shift in his newly Americanized household. He was busy at work with the microscope, developing his specialty of studying the inner ear. But when they went back to Mexico after spending the year in Chicago, there were many people who noticed and the criticisms were heaped on my mom fast and furious. How could she do this to her children? Let them eat on their own? Give them food out of a jar? Let them get dirty and not change their clothes? Estás muy rara, Berta, they would say. You are acting strange. Los Americanos are getting to you. But don't let them. Remember your traditions, remember that we have been raising our children like this for decades and we haven't changed and our children are fine.

Just as quickly as she had embraced the American ways of childrearing, Mom let them go soon after she had returned to Mexico. She had two more children and raised them à la Mexicana. Good-bye sss-cheh-dools, Dr. Spock, Gerber foods, and psychology. Back to "así se hace y punto." No more discussions with her sisters, no more accusations of becoming agringada, a gringa.

But then, four years later, la crisis occurred in Mexico and life changed forever.

When it happened Mom was the mother of four and happy with her life. The family had been struggling financially—there is no fortune to be made as a research medical doctor—but my father had been promised a job in the new hospital that was being built by the Mexican government. Finally, they would be able to make ends meet. Just as they were putting the finishing touches on the hospital construction, a new

Mexican president was ushered in and the hospital was no longer on the new president's "to do" list and so it lay idle and my father was out of a job. Chicago was the one place where he knew he could continue his work.

He made arrangements with the hospital there and left before my mom to find a place to live. Three weeks later, we left Mexico to join him in our new home.

I was just about a year old when all of this happened. My sister was eight, my brothers, six and three. Alone with the four of us, Mom got on a plane. Apparently my brother screamed the entire flight, *un-cae, un-cae!*—toddler speak in Spanish for, We're falling! My sister took care of him while my other brother insisted on banging on the pilot's door. He wanted to help them fly the plane. I had just gotten over a bad skin rash, a reaction to the old wool blankets I had used the last few days in Mexico. Our blankets had been packed up in the suitcases for days, waiting for the airport.

We flew into Dallas where we needed to change planes for Chicago. We had just enough time to make the connecting flight. But first we had to pass through immigration. All of our green cards were in order and everything was moving ahead smoothly until the immigration officer got to me. My face still had visible patches of red from the rash. The man said it looked like I had the German measles. No, my mother tried to explain in her unpracticed English. It was just a rash. Una irritación! I had had my measles vaccine already. The proof was the spot on my ankle where the vaccine left its scar. Mami tried to explain that that was the fad now in Mexico—the vaccine in the shoulder left those dimple scars that didn't look nice on a young girl's arm.

"Well, I'm sorry, ma'am, but we are going to have to put her in quarantine. You'll have to leave your daughter here for a week."

With three other kids grabbing at her skirt, telling her it was time to go, that the plane was going to leave, and with a long line of angry people behind us, my mother clung to me and told the man that there was no way she was going to leave her daughter with him or anyone else. She had to be on that flight to Chicago with all four of her kids. Y ya!

The officer nearly grabbed me out of my mother's arms, but I think he was too afraid to touch me, fearful that he would get whatever god-awful sickness he thought I had. He called in his supervisor because

Mami would not budge. She was holding her ground, defending her territory—in tears.

They let her go only because she told them that her husband was a doctor. But she was given a form and told sternly that she had to report to the board of health as soon as she got to Chicago to prove that I was okay. Otherwise they would come looking for her—or rather, for me. We made it to the plane and we were off to Chicago.

One night during our visit to Chicago, after Raul Ariel had fallen to sleep, I stayed up looking through old boxes in what had been my room when I was growing up. As I picked through old pictures from grammar school and secret love notes from high school boyfriends, I thought about how my own experience growing up had been shaped by the very particular choices Mom had made for herself and for all of us. Just as Raul Ariel's experience would be shaped by my choices.

I opened up the boxes, laid out old dolls and photographs, and let my mind wander. I thought of friends, both old and new, and how important they were in my life. It was Mami who had been the one who taught me *how* to make friends, I realized.

It was the sixties when I was growing up and Chicago was a divided city but my mother was a woman of little prejudice and this she taught to us, not through lessons in a book or with words, but in the way she lived her life. Our parents seemed to be friends with everyone, and every weekend I looked forward to visiting someone else's house.

Like Peter and Pamela's, for instance.

"People we knew used to call Peter and Pamela white trash," Mami had once told me. "I didn't know what that meant back then but I knew it wasn't anything good. I just kept those words to myself. But, when we would go visit Peter and Pamela, *they* in turn would say horrible things about Black people. And you know we had friends who were Black. I'll never forget the day that Pamela said she wished all the Black people in the country would fall into a bucket of bleach. I told her that was a horrible thing to say but she just shushed me. I always felt as if we were in the middle, hearing people saying such nasty things. But all of these different people were our friends and yours, too."

I remembered that Pamela was twice as tall as Mami, with a head twice as long as mine and a smile that reminded me of the Joker from *Batman*. She wore black glasses that curled up in the corners and that had little pieces of crystal that made it look like there were stars on her face. Pamela taught Mom how to make fried chicken. They would spend most of their time in the kitchen. Sometimes I would see Pamela sitting hunched over the kitchen table, her shoulders shaking. Mami would stand next to her and rub her back. I didn't realize then that she was crying. I thought adults didn't cry since I had never seen Mom or Dad do it.

Peter was the manager at the gas station where Papi went every week to fill up the family car. He had a big belly and his hair always looked wet because of the gel he wore in it every day. At his house he would sit in front of the TV, smoking, talking to Dad about sports, and Dad would listen even though he didn't really care for baseball or football. But he would listen, mostly, because Peter didn't understand Dad too well because of his accent, and he would always ask one of us kids to tell him what Dad was trying to say. So Dad just sat and listened while we played hide and seek with their six kids in the two-floor, two-bedroom, crooked white house.

I remember Peter and Pamela were the only friends of my parents who let us call them by their first names. I liked them a lot. But then one day they moved and didn't tell us where they were going. I cried because I missed Suzie, the girl my age who laughed like a seal. Only then did Mom explain to me that Suzie and her brother who died (he got run over by a car) were mentally retarded. Peter and Pamela moved away because the kids from their neighborhood used to tease Suzie too much and recently Suzie tried to run onto the same highway where her brother got killed, and it wasn't because she was running after a ball. It was because she was running away from kids who were calling her names. Peter and Pamela left to get away from that highway.

We didn't live near a highway, but there was a busy street on our route to school and there worked a crossing guard named Lorraine. She was short and round and dark, and we used to give her hugs and kisses on her soft face underneath her white crossing guard hat. One day Mami had to take my sister to the doctor for an emergency, and she had no one to leave my brothers and me with, so she asked Lorraine if we could stay with her at the corner until she came back. Lorraine offered to take us home and that was how our friendship began. After that day, Lorraine would always come to the house to take care of us, and she became like our second mother and all the kids at school thought it was strange that we would become friends with the school crossing guard.

Lorraine became my mother's best friend and a part of our family.

One Thanksgiving we spent with Lorraine in her apartment on the tenth floor of the Cabrini Green housing project. I remember the elevator was dirty and smelled and the windows had black grating over them so everything looked dark. We listened to Motown and Lorraine put on boxing gloves and started to teach my brother how to box. He had been beaten up in school a couple of times because he was a smart aleck and Lorraine told him he had to learn how to defend himself. My sister, who was by then a teenager, said that when she told her friends she was going to Lorraine's house in the projects, they all said she was going to come back with cooties.

All I knew was that I loved Lorraine and I knew Mami did as well and this was Lorraine's house and she had invited us here.

I always thought that what saved my mother from suffering in her new country was her ignorance and her naïveté. That what allowed her to be so open and accepting of so many people was the fact that she wasn't worldly enough to know prejudice. It wasn't her ignorance that kept her from being judgmental I realized. Her openness was part of her, part of her experience handed down to her by my own grandmother who was nicknamed la pata del perro, a dog's foot, because she was always taking her kids on one adventure or another, like a stray dog traveling the streets. Mami grew up traveling throughout Mexico, spending nights in pueblos, sharing buses and bedrooms with the peasants who lived in the countryside. I doubt that Mom grew up feeling superior to people. This was instilled in her as a child, by my abuelita.

The next morning in Chicago we all took a walk to the beach so that Raul Ariel could see Lake Michigan. Dad carried Raul Ariel in his arms the same way I had seen him carry me in the picture in our family photo album.

This trip home was all about memories.

We passed by the first apartment we lived in when we arrived here. I had an image in my head of when I was four years old. I am wearing pink-plastic high-heeled glittering slippers that Mami bought me at Woolworth's. I have a pair of pink nylon pajama pants on my head, my make-believe long locks of straight blond hair. I am wearing an old petticoat and skirt and twirling in circles in the kitchen, around the portable dishwasher, on the old rust-colored linoleum floor. I am singing, with a proper English accent, all of the lyrics of the Hollywood musicals that I love. My favorite was "I could have danced all night, I could have danced all night, and still have asked for more . . . !" I believe I am Eliza Doolittle, I am the Fair Lady, I am Audrey Hepburn. I *am* her. The next day I am Julie Andrews and my husband is the gorgeous Dick Van Dyke. I ride a pink horse that takes me down a cobblestone lane into a beautiful park where everything looks like it is made of candy. I can sing *supercalifragilisticexpialidocious,* repeating it faster and faster and faster because I can speak English. Yes, I can! I am Mary Poppins. I am that tall, graceful, sophisticated lady with the frilly umbrella. And as I get older I fall in love with Michael Jackson, Elton John, David Bowie. I dress up in high school on Saturday nights to go see *The Rocky Horror Picture Show.* I wear one of my mother's old black slips over a white T-shirt and paint my lips ruby red. Mami watches me as I become all of these things and she lets me be. She let me *be.*

I look at Raul Ariel and I think, if he ever wants to become a Power Ranger I will have a fit.

I'm already worrying about letting Raul Ariel watch Barney when he gets a little older. I want to keep him far away from the claws of popular, commercialized culture. I hide the Mickey Mouse doll a friend gave him and replace it with a Mayan one. Am I wrong? Am I crazy? How long am I going to do this for, I wonder?

I wish I could mother my son the way my mother mothered me. Just let things be.

But when I think about it, I find it hard to remember that Mom ever played with me. The message from all of the books and magazines is all about quality time with your children. About how important it is for you to just play with your kids.

And I realize that I don't often make time just to play with Raul

Ariel. Our time together is often spent doing things—going shopping, cooking, cleaning up, bathing, nursing. I don't feel like it comes naturally to just sit and play with him for hours on end. Paty the babysitter does that. Maybe that's another reason why I feel like I'm an inadequate mother.

Back at home, I ask Mom if she ever made the time just to play with me.

"Pues, I didn't have that much time, mi reina. I was raising three other kids and running the entire household by myself," she says. "But I gave you other things, mi'jita," she says and gives me a hug. She takes my face in her hand and kisses me tenderly on the cheek.

"Yeah, Mom, you did," I said, and kissed her back.

It's true that I couldn't remember the times Mami played jacks with me, but I could remember specific moments of finding solace in her arms, her voice, her scent.

I remember that I loved to knead my small hands into the softness of her upper arms. I would squeeze her tight and she would squeeze back and cover my face with soft delicate kisses. Sometimes her kisses would be snuggly ones, hard and fast all over my neck and arms, ending up with my fingertips. Some nights when I was feeling especially needy for comfort I would call to Mami from my bed and tell her that my legs were hurting because I could feel them growing. She would bring in the alcohol that she bought in Mexico (made specifically for growing pains she would tell me), and then she would wet her hands in it and rub my legs from top to bottom. Up and down my legs, the cool alcohol lifting away my imaginary growing pains. Manos sobadoras, my mother has—like the hands of the medicine women in Mexico—las sobadoras.

"Sóbame aquí, Mami. Sóbame más, no pares," I would say to Mom. "Massage me here, Mom. Massage me more. Don't stop." And she wouldn't until I was fast asleep.

I remember that every night, Mom was there to tuck me in and bless me the way she had been taught by her mother. She would start by making a cross on my forehead, thumb and forefinger together. Then she would touch my lips with the same tender movement, and finally make another imaginary cross in front of my chest. She would whisper "Por la señal de la santa cruz, de nuestros enemigos, líbranos señor, Dios nuestro" so softly that it was only through sensing her breath that I knew she was talking. And then she would finish by blessing me in the name of the Father, the Son, and the Holy Ghost. "En el nombre del Padre, del Hijo, del Espíritu Santo." A kiss on her warm fingers and then Amén. We would always stare into each other's eyes for a long while after that and then she would come close to me and hug me again, another kiss on both cheeks, a long stroke with her hands through my hair. I would snuggle into bed and she would tuck the sheet tight across my body so I could barely move, immobilized under the covers, as if I was a newborn again and she was wrapping me papoose-style in a blanket. "Más apretado, Mami. Tighter, Mami. Make it tighter." And she would.

It is what I, without realizing until that very moment, give to my son already. Limitless closeness with hugs and kisses and my own manos sobadoras. My own long, luxurious stroking of his hair, my fingers sweeping down his eyes and nose until he is mesmerized into profound sleep. The interlocked eyes as he nurses. Giving him love the way I know how, the way I was taught. This I do know how to do. This I can give because it was given to me. This is my way of mothering and it is good and it is right, I say to myself.

Our last night in Chicago, after bathing Raul Ariel and singing to him and nursing him in my arms until he falls off into a deep, deep sleep, I understand what a mother's real entrega is to her child. I think for the first time in my life and in my son's, I understand how important a mother's touch, *my* touch, can be. That I-am-here-for-you-right-now-and-nothing-can-pull-me-away-from-you-not-even-wild-horses-I-promise feeling. I understand that ten minutes of entrega can make up for hours of being away and at that moment, as I lay intertwined with my son, I stopped feeling inadequate and guilty. I felt like the sensation left my body, made its way out of my shoulders and fizzled straight up into the sky. I was liberated. Free from that damning, depleting mother's guilt. I made a promise to myself to remember this moment, to remember what this felt like, to remember that just in holding Raul Ariel close I was already creating memory for him—a sense of memory of touch and smell and love. I was giving him *my* mother's smell, the aroma of sweet milk and mother that he would always look for when he came to me and nuzzled close, the particular scent I would exude from now on until the day I

died. And only I could give that to him. I laid my son down in bed and
tucked him in tight as only I knew how and gave him lingering kisses on
his forehead, his eyes, his cheeks, and his lips. Then I went out to the living room, sat next to my mom, and hugged her.

Without thinking, she pulled up one of my legs and put it across her
lap and started giving it long, determined strokes, just as she had done
when I was a child. My memory of her mothering kicked in in an instant. I was a child again.

I dozed off in my mother's arms. I slept like a baby and so did Raul
Ariel, smothered in kisses and soft sobadora hands, tucked in bed so
tight so that not even his dreams could disturb him. My freedom from
mother's guilt let me rest, peacefully.

The First Ceremony

Raul Ariel was six months old now and I still hadn't sent out his birth announcement. We finally chose an adorable picture of him and I wrote a short paragraph about how he was a spirit of calmness and curiosity. I translated it into Spanish, Gérman helped me design it, and we picked out bright yellow paper and purple envelopes. It was all set. I spent four nights addressing envelopes, folding the announcement, licking stamps, and all. Misión cumplida.

Several days later Papi called me.

"Cómo se te ocurre? Qué puntadas las tuyas, Maria de Lourdes!" Oh, oh. Dad is using my full name. I know this is something serious. "What were you thinking when you chose that photo of Raul Ariel naked to send for his birth announcement?" It was an early morning scolding from Papi, complete with his ultraserious tone—a surefire way to set the rest of my day off kilter. I rolled my eyes and took a deep breath.

"Ay, Papi. Come on. It's a great photo. So what if he is naked! He's only six months old. How could anyone be offended by that? Por favor!"

The thought hadn't crossed my mind until this very moment, but then of course it made sense that Papi would throw chispas about it. No nudity was an accepted part of our extended Mexico-based family rules. Just part of the rituals and traditions that have been passed on for decades. Engraved in my familia like letters in gold.

"Mi'jita, I like the photo but think about your relatives. Your abuelita called me from Tampico and was speechless. She told me she won't be able to show the photo to anyone. She opened up your letter while her amigas were over for a game of canasta and she heard them all gasping. Then she saw the photo and started gasping herself."

"Papi, I know you are kidding me, right? No puede ser!"

"I am not kidding you! You are going to have to send me some different photos so I can take them down to Tampico next week when I go. Your abuelita says she can think of no other way to deal with semejante desgracia. I don't know what you were thinking Maria de Lourdes. Really. Siempre te salen estas locuras y no aprendes."

So I got another photo of Raul Ariel, fully dressed and smiling, and slipped it into an envelope. This is absolutely crazy, I thought to myself as I licked the envelope. Abuelita is, sadly, bordering on senility. The last time I visited her she couldn't remember who I was. "You're my granddaughter who lives in Chicago, right? Your father is Raulito, right? Dime, mi'jita, just once again, cómo te llamas? What's your name? And where do you live? And who is that man you are with? He looks like such a nice man but why does he wear his hair in a ponytail?"

"Abuelita, that's my husband."

"No me digas! When did you get married? Ay, Dios! No me invitaron a la boda! Why wasn't I invited to the wedding?" she whispers in my ear indignantly.

"We've been married six years. And you were there when it happened," I whispered back.

Mi abuelita is senile, yes. She can't even remember her own name, much less the name of a great-grandson named after her husband. But she can't forget that public nudity, under any circumstances, is not acceptable. Sólo los pobres tienen que andar desnudos. Only the poor have to go naked, she would always say.

It's just as well that no one from Mexico was planning on coming up for Raul Ariel's naming ceremony, I thought. First of all, they would all want to know, what *is* a naming ceremony? And second of all, wasn't Raul Ariel going to get baptized in a church? A Catholic church, como manda Dios?

I could just imagine the looks I would get if I told them I was borrowing an African tradition by doing a naming ceremony. "You and your locuras, Maria," they would be thinking. "Why does she have to be so weird? That's what happens when you grow up en los Estados Unidos.

All that freedom and libertinaje—you lose your traditions and what you believe in."

The freedom to choose and make and create new traditions and rituals and call them your own. Yes, that certainly *is* strange.

When Gérman and I got married in 1991, we created our own marriage ritual. We sat down one night and thought about the different spiritual traditions that made up who we were. There was Catholicism. But there was also Yoruba, Santería, and indigenous beliefs from the Caribbean and Mexico. We knew that what unified these beliefs was that they were based on nature. But we also felt close to the Catholic tradition of padrinos, godparents who are supposed to watch over your marriage in the name of the faith. We combined these two traditions and ended up choosing four pairs of marriage godparents, one for each of the elements—fire, water, air, earth. At the ceremony, we formed a circle, with each set of godparents standing on the four cardinal points. The godparents had to give us something symbolic for each element. For fire we lit candles. For earth, we brought dirt from our birth places and potted a plant. For water, we were blessed with holy water. For air, we let two white doves go free. (Poor little doves. We bought them at a hen house in Spanish Harlem. They would have been made into stew if not for our wedding.) We had Caribbean drumming and we were intertwined with a white lace lasso from Mexico, just like the kind my parents used at their marriage ceremony and which is used all over Mexico. Gérman was dressed in white in a traditional Venezuelan liki-liki (like a Nehru suit), and I wore a purple Tehuana dress, the kind Frida Kahlo used to wear, my hair tied back with colored ribbons. We did it all on a hill in Central Park in the middle of a scorching 105 degree day. The tears flowed, but my uncle and aunt from Mexico stood and watched our ceremony with their arms folded across their chests and sour looks on their faces.

"Where was Jesús Cristo? Where was God?" they asked after the ceremony.

"Everywhere," I said to them. "Didn't you see them? Didn't you feel their presence?"

Scorns. You and your locuras, Maria de Lourdes . . .

For Raul Ariel's naming ceremony we decided to stick with our, now traditional, ceremony. We chose four sets of godparents also, there was holy water, dirt from Mexico City, Santo Domingo, New York City, and Bethlehem, Connecticut, and there were candles and drums and a lone white dove.

There was also Hurricane Bertha, so appropriately named after my mother, so we couldn't use Central Park. Instead we all crammed into our apartment, our guests and padrinos and madrinas drenched, while the violent gusts of wind and torrential showers darkened the noonday streets outside. There hadn't been a storm like this in New York for years. No one, absolutely no one, was out in the streets. Except for the people coming to our naming ceremony.

Two sets of godparents, Ceci and her husband, and Sandy and her husband, were stuck at the airport, so we asked other friends to join us as padrinos. And one by one our guests poured in, literally. They had to wring out their clothes and socks. There was Patricia, a Brazilian choreographer, and her Ecuadorian-Californian performance artist–companion George, who arrived first. Then came Susan and Bert, a middle-aged Jewish couple who were close friends of ours. And Joe and Judy (we met at our Lamaze classes) and their baby, Sammy, who showed up in bright yellow rain suits. Ismael, a childhood friend of Gérman's from the Dominican Republic, brought his conga and so did Alfredo, a young Panamanian drummer, also a friend of Gérman's. Our downstairs neighbors, a couple from Puerto Rico who were artists, showed up with their two boys, and they were the only dry people there. Paty, our hip-hop-hippie nanny (wearing hip huggers and showing off her newly pierced belly button) showed up with her mom, her sister, and her two nephews. David, my musician friend from college, one of my oldest and dearest friends, an existential lawyer–housing rights activist came ready to sing a song. And then there were the padrinos and madrinas and my mom and dad and my sister with her two kids.

Guadalupe, a fifty-year-old Mexican artist and writer named after the Virgin of Guadalupe, who was now in her first year of initiation into the Yoruba religion, started off the ceremony. Dressed all in white, she took the dirt from Raul Ariel's birthplace (and some we had left over from Santo Domingo and Mexico) and made a small altar on the floor. She brought a small wooden African pot and inside put cola nuts and all sorts of other traditional good luck gifts. She spoke to Raul Ariel of the importance of earth, of grounding, of home, of roots, and while she did that she made a mark on Raul Ariel's forehead with white chalk made from eggshells. He looked exotic with the face paint, but he was wearing a Russian lace outfit that Susan and Bert had brought back from Saint Petersburg. What a combination.

My sister and one of Gérman's closest friends from the Dominican Republic, Pedro, were the padrinos of fire. Bertha Elena lit the candle and placed it over Raul Ariel's head and declared her love and commitment to my son while her own two children watched in wonder. Pedro, a health insurance salesman who belonged to a Japanese religious sect that believes in the healing power of energy and light, spoke to Raul Ariel in a combination of Japanese prayer, Dominican proverbs, and New York slang as he kneeled in front of Raul Ariel as a gesture of respect.

Our friends Graci and Victor were the Jewish padrinos of water. They brought a little blue-and-white vase and filled it with holy water, which they had blessed themselves. Like a baptism, they poured some over Raul Ariel's head and kissed him.

Adaluz, my therapist turned family friend, held on to the white dove. Adaluz was raised believing in Santería and Catholicism, and so she spoke to Raul Ariel about Obatalá and Jesus Christ, moving between these two religious icons with ease and fluidity. Freedom in flight, freedom to be, freedom to move and grow and learn and change is what the wind and dove symbolize, she said to Raul Ariel in sentences that combined English and Spanish. When she was done talking, we opened the window and the fierce gushes of wind blew across everyone's faces, but it was time to let the dove go. Adaluz stretched her arms to the open window and spread her palms to the thunderous skies and let the dove go. But it flew out of her hands for only a second and then flew right back and perched on the open window. "He's not ready to leave us yet," said Adaluz, and the white dove just stayed and watched us all until the ceremony was finished.

Once the padrinos had all presented their gifts to Raul Ariel, my mom and dad presented him with his name. Mami gave Raul Ariel a jar of ocean water that she had saved and told him she was his madrina del mar, his godmother of the ocean. My father took out a crumpled piece of white paper from his guayabera shirt pocket and said that he was passing on his name to the new generation of Rauls. The generation born in a new land, a new generation for the next millennium that began with Raul Ariel.

And then everyone who wanted to say or give something to Raul Ariel was invited into the circle. People stepped forward and kissed him and lay candles and flowers and food at our feet to give to our son. Nothing was written or rehearsed but every word was heavy with love for this child we were welcoming to our world. We were creating a new kind of family for him. These people would be his familia now, his mentors and teachers and caretakers, the people who made up his days and nights, the people who may not have been tied by blood but instead by love, and to be frank, by the convenience of proximity.

When I called Ro to invite her to the naming ceremony days before, she told me about what she did with her own kids. "I may not go to church every Sunday but let me tell you, it was never a consideration *not* to baptize them," she said. "They had to be Cristianos, not Moros!"

Christians, not Moors! What? In 1996 modern America?

"Ro, are you serious?"

"Oh yeah, honey. Mom said she would have it no other way, and to be honest with you, the stuff is so much in my blood that if I didn't have them baptized in church I would have forever worried about their almas and the mal de ojo." The evil eye.

It made me think about the story of tía Maria Covadonga who, on a visit to Chicago from Mexico when I was a child, took two young Jewish friends of mine to church one day to have them baptized. "No podían vivir así, en las tinieblas—they can't live like this, in the fog of religious obscurity!" And so she had them baptized that afternoon behind their parents' backs. And she didn't tell anyone about it. She thought she was doing it for their own good.

Ro told me she wasn't going to be able to make it to the naming ceremony and seemed to be having a hard time telling why.

Finally, she did.

"Maria, I have been invited to go on a media tour of Disneyland and I have never been before. I know you can understand," she said.

"Well, you know I love you, Ro, but no I can't understand. See, I have never been to Disneyland. And I don't have any plans to take Raul Ariel there, either. That's another tradition I am creating. Naming ceremonies and Disneyland boycotts."

I never went to Disneyland as a child not because my parents were boycotting but because we simply couldn't afford it. I remember asking my mom to please take me there. She said, "Why do you want to go to Disneyland to see all those people dressed up in make-believe costumes when we take you to Mexico every year and you see real and exciting things happening right before your very eyes? If you had to choose between Mexico and Disneyland, what would you choose?" My head said Disneyland but my heart said Mexico, but I never asked again and I erased Disneyland from my mind. As I got older I started to wear my "Disneylandlessness" as a badge.

When Ro came back from Disneyland we had a conversation about baptisms, rituals, holy water, Mickey, and Minnie.

"Keeping your children away from Disneyland is not a tradition!" Ro laughed.

"It has been in my household! And why not keep it alive? I want Raul Ariel to find magic in something other than a hugely expensive theme park. I'll spend my money and take him on a trip to Bali or to see the pyramids in Mexico."

"You know, I used to be like you, Maria. I never went to Disneyland when I was growing up because we couldn't afford it. But I went last week because I wanted to see what it was all about. And it is beautiful, I have to tell you. It is a fantasy land. It is like nothing you've ever seen before.

"But here is what I realized as I was walking alone through the streets of Disneyland," she continued. "Here were all of these adults who as kids had come here and had great memories of Disneyland. And I realized that there was this palatial gap between them and me because this was part of *the* American experience of growing up, and even though I grew up here I didn't have it. And now that I can afford to take my kids to Disneyland, I don't want them to feel like the outsider that I did because I never could go. If they are growing up here then I want them to grow up with the same American experiences that their friends are going to have. I don't want to deprive them of that and make them feel like the oddballs. Besides, if I was excited about being there and almost peeing in my pants for joy when I walked through the Disneyland gates, then think about how a six-year-old will feel. Why not give them that joy?"

I wondered if Ro had a point. Maybe it was time to jump off my Disneyland-boycott-mania.

"Give it up already, Maria," said Ro, always poignant and to the point. "Next time we'll go together and it will be the Bronx-Nuyorican-Domini-Mex-Manhattanite invasion of Disneylandia!"

But the naming ceremony went on without Ro, though I missed her. The afternoon of the ceremony ended with a song written by my friend David, who always joked that he was my only "white male friend." That wasn't true but nevertheless, out of everyone at the naming ceremony, it was David who summed it all up the best with his song.

WELCOME TO THE WORLD

Welcome to the world, Raul Ariel
glad to have you here.
Welcome to the earth, water, fire, and air.
Welcome to our lives,
glad you came along,
may your mind be wise and your heart be strong.
Through your eyes you will see
everything that is true.
Through your eyes we will see,
everything as if new.
So much to touch
taste, smell, and hear
to see and to feel
to make your own and to share.
Sunrise, blue skies
burger and French fries.
Salsa, merengue
café con leche.
Mingus, Coltrane
riding on an airplane.
Beso de tu novia

Abrazo de un amigo.
Libros, pájaros, perros, y gatos.
Los mares, los ríos
el sol y el dios.
La lucha for freedom
and justice and peace
a spacious apartment
with a rent-control lease.
Conversation, education
summer vacation.
Neruda y Borges
árboles y flores.
Béisbol y fútbol
hanging out at the mall (not!)
Mercedes Sosa
Celia Cruz
rock 'n' roll
rhythm and blues.
The canyons, the mountains
waterfalls and fountains.
The Beatles and Dylan
just sittin' and chillin'.
Santo Domingo y México
NeuvaYork y San Francisco.
Artistas, periodistas
y más y más y más y más . . .
Bienvenido al mundo, Raul Ariel
Welcome to the world, Raul Ariel!

La Política

Oh yes, I definitely had those mother-and-son Madonna moments of swaying my baby into perfect slumber. But then those idyllic moments of ten minutes and he's out, became interminably long. I would rock him for a half hour and the second I would put him into his loft-crib he would start screaming at me. (How *dare* you leave me like this, Ma?) And so I would pick him up and start all over for another half hour. And he was often still waking up in the middle of the night and wouldn't go back to sleep unless I nursed him for another seemingly endless hour. During the day I began to feel like an angry zombie. I would look into my son's big eyes and be overwhelmed by a desire to force them shut with superglue. Sleep deprivation was having its effect.

Before becoming a mom, I had heard the horror stories from friends who had kids—"Ay, I was up at five A.M. this morning!" or "I couldn't get the baby to sleep until midnight!" or "My son is four years old and he still wakes up four times a night!"—and I thought, I will never let that happen to me. I had listened carefully to all of their sleep-problem-solution strategies. The family bed, the merry-go-round bed (one friend told me she never knew what bed she and her husband and her kids were going to end up sleeping in and who was going to wake up with whom), the rock-them-to-sleep plan, the Ferber-method, the old-style method, the newest method, the this-method and the that-method. I just wanted a friggin' method, already!

One night I told Gérman I thought we should do the family bed. Maybe he would sleep through the night like this? And besides (according to the latest fad book), wasn't it part of the Latin American tradition of the poor to all sleep in the same bed? Wouldn't this be another way of going back to our roots?

"Whose roots?" he laughed. "I didn't sleep with my parents. Did you?"

"No," I said, and remembered that actually my parents' bed was off-limits to us kids, except for Saturday and Sunday mornings when we would all pile in for our cosquilla fights, to see who could make the other laugh the most.

"Well, I feel the same way as your parents," Gérman stated. "Nuestra cama es santa. Our bed is ours and ours only."

Mom told me she did it the same way abuelita had.

"Hay que dejarlos llorar para que encuentren su sueño," was what abuelita had told my mom and my mom had told me. You have to let them cry until they find the sandman.

Dr. Mark was from the same school of thought. "If you can tolerate some tears, it's the fastest and most effective way to teach children how to sleep through the night and on their own."

After talking about it for several days, Gérman and I finally agreed to try it. One night a few weeks after the naming ceremony, in the middle of summer, when all of our house guests had left and we were getting back into our routine, we kissed Raul Ariel good night, I nursed him, and then, while he was still awake, left him in his ocean blue–loft-crib.

I closed the door and he started crying. In the next room, Gérman had two beers waiting (my sister had said it would help us cope), and a movie all set to go in the VCR. He cried for forty-five minutes and then was out. It was agony. At one point I put some earplugs in because I couldn't take it anymore, but I was adamant about not breaking down. Everyone had told me it only takes longer if you keep going back. They said I needed to have "stealth determination." (Aha! The military sleep plan!)

The phrase from one of the books that I repeated to myself over and over again that night went something like, "You tolerate your child crying after he gets his shots because you know that the shots are ultimately good for him. Letting a child learn how to sleep is a good thing. Tolerating tears is fine when teaching a baby to sleep on their own. You are not a bad parent because of this."

I certainly felt like one though, and I thought, if anyone from the child welfare office knew we were doing this they would surely take our son away.

But in less than a week Raul Ariel was sleeping on his own and all through the night, down at 7:30 P.M. and up at 6:30 A.M. The only people I confessed to trying this method were the people who I knew for a fact believed in the same "crying it out" philosophy. Victor and Graci congratulated us. So did Mom and Dad. As did our neighbors in Boca Chica who had two toddlers themselves.

But I never uttered a word about our sleeping style to any other parent who did it differently. The one time I did, a mother called me cruel.

I hadn't realized that sleep was such a political issue.

How you put your kids to sleep, where you put your kids to sleep, when you put them to sleep—seemed to be the modern dividing lines among parents and parenting styles.

Because we were all sleeping better I now had some additional energy and decided I needed to devote it to myself. (What an un-Mexican-madre thing to do!) I had had enough of my full-figured womanly body, even though in my neighborhood I seemed to be attracting more street comentarios because of my full rump and thighs. ("Ay, mamita, si cocinas como caminas quiero comerme tu cena! If you cook the way you walk then I want your dinner!") And for a while there I had enjoyed filling out dresses that before used to hang on my chest and dangle on my hips. It had been an interesting experiment to look like my mom, with full, meaty upper arms and shoulders, and to walk around with my Marilyn Monroe-esque rounded tummy. Pero, enough already. So, I became a member of my local exercise studio and started doing step aerobics four times a week. The first thing I noticed was that I was getting strong again. And that felt great. I could carry Raul Ariel and not feel as if my back was breaking and getting up the five flights to our apartment soon became a breeze. For me the excercising was about feeling fuerte. The fact that I was looking better was like an added bonus. After a month, I was a full-fledged step addict, hooked on that endorphin rush.

At the same time, I started going to the library to write, three to four days a week. I had told myself, before Raul Ariel was born, that I would start my writing projects when he was four months old. I had procrastinated for another two. It was time now and there were no more excuses. If there was ever going to be a space in my life when I could write not as a reporter but as a storyteller then this would be it. I had all of these ideas and I had a dream that one day I could actually put them on paper. It was something I had wanted to try for myself.

But, of course, I began to feel guilty. How selfish of me to be more concerned about my career and my body than about my baby. I pushed myself, though, everyday. "If you don't do this now," I would say to myself as I walked out the door leaving Raul Ariel behind, "then you can kiss your writer's sueño away." Somedays I would miss him so much that I would leave the library after just an hour of writing. Ni modo.

It took me a few weeks to get into it, but soon I started to look forward to my time in the library. I was doing a lot of stream-of-conciousness work and I was consumed with my memories. I would write and write and write and then run off to the playground to see if I could catch up with the baby and Paty, but inevitably I would show up just as they were leaving, or just as Raul Ariel was beginning to take his nap, and often I would miss them entirely.

If I was in the gym, I'd be thinking about my writing. If I was writing, I'd be thinking about being with Raul Ariel. If I was with Raul Ariel, I'd be thinking about what projects I might be able to take on to start bringing some money into the house. I began to feel as if I was never in one place or the other.

And along with everything else, I was going through a prolonged phase of constantly comparing myself to my cousins in Mexico. They were simply mothers y ya. Why couldn't I focus on Raul Ariel and have that be it? Why did I have to set these goals of writing when I should instead be using my leave to take care of my baby?

But the older Raul Ariel got and the more work it was to care for him, I realized that I needed time away from him to maintain my sanity.

A woman I had worked out with told me she had gone back to work when her baby was just two months old. My heart broke. "Wasn't that incredibly difficult?" I had asked.

"No! She cried all the time. I wanted to get away from her!"

It sounded so cold.

And yet, in essence, now I was feeling the same way.

The Mexican way. The American way. The Mexican way. The American way.

Why, I thought to myself, wasn't I happy just being a mom? Was I really so ambitious about my career? Why wasn't it a natural part of me to be ambitious about being a full-time mother?

It was around this time that we packed up the car and drove down to Washington, D.C.. to visit madrina Sandy (she wasn't able to make the naming ceremony, but she was Raul Ariel's madrina of the earth) and to take Raul Ariel to his first-ever demonstration. Even though he wasn't an immigrant, this American-born son of two immigrants would be protesting for immigrant rights in front of the White House.

In Washington we spent the night at Sandy's house, and Raul Ariel was fascinated by all of her African masks. And he loved to play peek-a-boo with Sandy's dreads. That night Raul Ariel slept with Gérman and me on a mattress on the floor. It was our first experience with a family bed. I loved it!

Maybe the family bed wasn't so bad after all, I told Gérman that morning in D.C.

"Ni se te ocura," he said and kissed me lightly on the lips. "I want you in my bed all for myself." He squeezed me tight.

"Ooohhhh, that's nice," I said, and kissed his neck. It had been months since we had made love. The urge was returning. I was a woman again. Why make it more difficult by adding a third person to our bed?

We made our way to the demonstration and met Graci and Victor and their two kids there. This was the first demonstration I had been to as a nonreporter in ten years. Today I was just a mom and an immigrant. It was Gérman's first demo in the United States as well. And he was going to make this a Caribbean-style marcha.

"Put the snare drum over my head," he told me before we joined the march. "And then strap Raul Ariel in the back carrier. And you carry the cow bell and give Graci and Victor the claves and whistles."

We started marching behind Gérman, with him leading us like the Pied Piper, and within a few blocks we caught up with the crowds. Gérman was banging out rhythms better than the leader of a high school marching band, and Raul Ariel was screaming with glee, bouncing in his carrier, wearing the Curious George overalls and kente cloth baseball hat that Sandy had given him. He carried a flag in each hand—one Dominican, one Mexican. And on the back of his back carrier, Gérman had taped an American one.

There we were, our own little clan, marching to the rhythm of samba, making our way through all of the different other groups trekking to the White House. We passed Janitors for Justice, a group of former gang members, a group of Irish immigrants, a group of Catholic priests dressed in white and black, some Pentecostal marchers, university students, immigrant gays and lesbians, Aztec dancers, babies and their grandparents.

I wondered what Raul Ariel would remember about this day. Probably nothing. But I wanted him to have this experience and this memory, even if just in photographs. Just as I had.

When I was eight years old, Mami wrote a letter to my third-grade teacher excusing me from school to go to a demonstration to see César Chávez. I remember the look on Mrs. Carroll's face when I handed her that note. Mrs. Carroll, my teacher, was filled with disdain. I felt an inch tall. But luckily, several other kids in my class had brought letters from home excusing them from class for the demonstration as well. Mrs. Carroll wore a look that said "Your mother is a bad parent."

I did miss a day of school but what I learned that day of the demonstration changed my life. I learned that in the United States if something is wrong you are allowed to speak up about it, which was a total contradiction to what my cousins had told me about was happening in Mexico. They showed me the newspaper clippings about a demonstration that looked just like the one I had been at in Chicago—people carrying posters, chanting, singing—but in Mexico it ended with hundreds of people being shot by the military. I learned that in the country where I was born, silence was rewarded with life.

I wanted to teach Raul Ariel what Mami had taught me. I wanted to follow in her footsteps and in her tradition.

During the drive back from D.C., Raul Ariel slept for three hours, and Gérman and I gabbed like friends who hadn't seen each other in years. Raul Ariel was nine months old and my husband and I were reconnecting, beginning to feel almost normal again.

"I don't want to go back to work yet," I told him in the car. "I don't feel ready. I feel like I haven't spent enough time with my writing and now, I have to go back to work in six weeks and I haven't produced anything substantial. And just the thought of being away from Raul Ariel five full days a week rips me apart. And having to go back to the office and the daily battles—I don't have the energy for that."

I looked out the window.

"On the other hand, honey, I have to tell you that I miss reporting. I miss interviewing people, I miss hearing people's stories. I miss being on the air. I miss the rush. I just wish I could tell the stories that I want to tell, how I want to tell them, without all the office politics."

"Why don't you just quit?" Gérman asked me.

"Because I do love what I do. I'm just tired of the bullshit."

I had heard other first-time mothers talk about how they had lost their tolerance for bullshit on the job once they had become mothers. I never thought I would feel the same way, but here I was. And it felt good.

But it was frustrating. Such conflicted feelings. I felt like my heart was getting squeezed tighter and tighter with each day that passed, as the Big Day got closer and closer.

Then, two weeks later, I received a message on my machine. An executive with CNN wanted to meet me.

A shiver of joy and excitement rippled through my body.

CNN wanted to see an audition piece and so they assigned me a producer and a crew and within days I was a reporter again. I worked for seven days straight, from nine to six—the longest time I had been away from Raul Ariel (and thanks to my breast pump I could do it—at least physically). But my heart was getting squeezed even more. Every day when I would walk out the door I would brush his face and neck and hands and feet with kisses before leaving. I missed him terribly, but I was wildly excited to be reporting again and intrigued by this new opportunity.

Yes, this might mean a job offer. Yes, this might mean a huge career change. Yes, this was the opportunity of a lifetime.

But I was also thinking this might be my chance to buy myself more time. It would buy me more time to be with Raul Ariel. And it would buy me more time to write.

"Los bebés traen regalos cuando nacen," Gérman told me. "Babies always come with gifts. Look at how many wonderful gifts your son is bringing you."

He was right. I felt very blessed. I was the luckiest woman around. The santos were shining on me.

But the last day of the audition story, when the piece was all finished and edited, I came home late, ready to reconnect with my son after seven days of being away, and when I extended my arms out to him as Paty answered the front door carrying Raul Ariel, he turned away from me. And when I tried to take him from Paty, he started crying even harder.

I was devastated.

I didn't want Paty to see me crying so I took off to the bathroom. Five minutes later, I came out and tried again. The same thing happened.

A wildness overcame me, a fierce territoriality and I grabbed Raul Ariel out of Paty's arms even though he was screaming. I took him to his room and started kissing him. I tried to nurse him. Impossible. He was too upset. I tried to entertain him. Nada.

I couldn't let him go. He was going to be with me and love me right then and there and that was it! Y se acabó!

Finally he calmed down and crawled into my arms and I nursed him to sleep. I hadn't done that since we had "taught" him how to go to sleep on his own.

I was a mala madre for being away from him, mala madre for forcing him into my arms, and a mala madre for now breaking with our own sleep rules and letting him fall asleep in my arms.

That night I called Ro, who was staying late at the office. She was working with her reporters on a breaking story but she made time to take my call.

"Ro, today for the first time Raul Ariel turned away from me when I tried to hug him. I'm a wreck." I felt a lump in my throat.

"Ay, chica, no te preocupes! All kids do that! It's not the end of the world," she said, sounding good-natured. Deadlines never seemed to phase her.

"But Ro! I feel like he is separating from me. I feel like he is letting me know that he is angry that I've been working all these days. How could he prefer los brazos de la nana over mine? His babysitter's arms over mine?" I could feel the tears slowly flooding my eyes.

"Maria, what you need to realize is that it's a good sign that Raul Ariel is doing that. You need to realize that your son is showing you that he is capable of loving many people. Can't you see that this shows that you have done a good job of giving your son an emotional base so that he feels secure enough to love other people?"

"No, Ro. I can't see that right now."

"Chica, your son is going to love many people in his life. Lots of different people. His babysitter, his father, his abuelos, his tías, his godparents. But he will never love anyone like he loves you. You are his mother! No one can replace his love for his mother."

"Well, if that's the case then why doesn't he want to be with me?"

"It's a good time for you to understand that Raul Ariel is growing up. And you should be happy that he can express his emotions. It's absolutely normal, nena."

Ro sounded so calm, her voice like a warm blanket wrapping itself around my sadness. How she could do that in the middle of her office with reporters swarming around her and a deadline to meet was beyond me.

I asked her again and again and she repeated the same things over and over, until finally, I had settled down enough to say good-bye, nevertheless feeling saddened by Raul Ariel's "maturity."

"Gracias, nena. For everything," I said.

"Take it easy, girl. Don't beat yourself up so much. Love you. Bye."

I spent the entire next day with Raul Ariel in the park. He didn't even seem to remember what had happened the day before. All was forgiven.

That night, when I took him to bed, I broke all of the rules. The rules that I had set up for myself, the rules that my mother had told me about, the rules my abuelita had followed, the rules the sleep doctors had written books about.

I climbed into his little loft bed with him, hugged him, sang to him, and nursed him until he fell asleep.

Sacrilege!

I kept it a secret. No one will find out that this mom who follows the let-them-fall-asleep-on-their-own guidelines was now putting her son to sleep in her *arms!* And on her *breast!* I would never be able to tell Dr. Mark or my mom. I had caved in.

But here is what I didn't understand. Why should I feel guilty about putting my son to sleep like this? Why couldn't I put Raul Ariel to sleep any damn way I chose? It felt so good to be so close to my son and hold him after days of not seeing him.

The voices in the back of my head said "You're going to make him into a spoiled baby who will always need his mamá to go to sleep, You're going to get him accustomed to your arms and then he will never want to separate from you—lo vas a embrasilar—You're going to make him into an arm-child.

Shut the hell up! I said to the voices. So night after night I would hold him close, nurse him, look lovingly into his eyes, and sing "Gracias a la vida" into his tiny ear. And he loved it. And so did I.

Sleep was political. But a mother's arms, a mother's breast—that was the best way to get around the guilt factor. And for me, it worked, at least for a while.

MÉXICO

It was the beginning of November and I had less than a month to go before I was supposed to go back to work. I was nerve-wracked. I hadn't heard back from CNN and the clock was ticking down to my return to work deadline. Mom and Dad were going to Mexico to celebrate my great-aunt's one hundredth birthday and they invited me and the baby to join them for my last vacation before returning to work.

Gérman drove Raul Ariel and me to the airport early in the morning. He had mixed feelings about our leaving. On the one hand, he would get a chance to stay home alone and paint with no interruptions and he could listen to music all day long at whatever volume he chose. On the other, this would be the first time he would be alone without his familia.

He had been picking up the slack with the baby for the past two weeks when I had been working so hard on the TV story. I knew he needed some time for himself. And I was looking to reconnect with Raul Ariel again. So we kissed and hugged Papá good-bye and made our way to the plane.

Raul Ariel was a trouper during the entire trip. No screaming at all. He just played and slept. Everyone sitting around me on the plane looked relieved. I was, too.

We met up with Mom and Dad at the Mexico City airport and boarded a plane together for Tampico, Papi's hometown. Raul Ariel dozed in Dad's arms in the airplane and I moved one seat closer to him. I was glad to be near my father, happy to be with him in Mexico. It brought back the best memories I had of growing up. All six of us piled into an overloaded station wagon, driving through Mexico for weeks and weeks. Dad was always the happiest during our time in Mexico.

I wondered whether or not Raul Ariel would have the same kind of longing for Mexico that I did. I wondered if milestones in his life would happen to him in Mexico, as they did for me. I wondered if his Mexican cousins would become his best friends (and his biggest critics) just as mine had been. I made a silent vow to take Raul Ariel to Mexico every year.

This was my first time back to Mexico as a mom and that, too, was a huge milestone. Now that I was a mother, I imagined I would finally be taken seriously and respected as a grown woman. I wanted my cousins and aunts and uncles to see that Malulis, the youngest of the gringo cousins, had assumed the womanly responsibilities that were expected of her.

I still felt I had a lot to prove.

This was also the first trip back to Tampico for all of us since my grandfather Raul had died. It was hard, but especially so for my father, to be there without my abuelito. But his spirit, I would realize later, was everywhere, and much more powerful than I could have ever imagined.

In Tampico, the whole family—grandma, tías, primas, primos, sobrinos, fifteen in all—had come to meet us at the airport. Raul Ariel was feliz! He floated from one pair of arms to another—from cousins to aunts to uncles—and once we got home, was happy to be carried in the arms of the women who worked in my grandmother's home, the women who cooked, who cleaned, who did the laundry. They were the women my cousins barely spoke to unless they were telling them what to do. I always wanted to be near them, watching what they were doing, listening in on their conversations. Our first two days there, Raul Ariel spent hours in the kitchen with me as we talked about recipes or old wives' tales or their stories of how they were raised. When Raul Ariel's cousins would show up he would be whisked out to the yard to sit and eat mangoes under the shade of the huge mango tree in my grandmother's garden, just as I had done as a child.

I thought about how some circles were coming to a close and others were just opening up.

Raul Ariel was sleeping in my grandfather's house, tumbling over his old furniture, crawling on the floors my grandfather had shuffled by on, and sitting on the plastic-covered sofa that abuelito himself had picked out. He was standing on the counter in my grandfather's bathroom, playing with Abuelito's shaving brush, the smell of humidity and after-shave lotion impregnated in the walls. Abuelito was still everywhere.

A few days into our visit, we drove to the cemetery with my tía Licha, my father's sister. The Tampico cemetery was on a hill right in the middle of town. I had never been to this cemetery before and like much of Tampico these days, the cemetery was under construction. There were parts of the cemetery that were clean and orderly with ce-ment mausoleums (some of them with two floors even) where entire families were buried. The little walkways on this side of the cemetery were made out of clean white marble. Fresh flowers lined the plots. Some of the plots looked like small buildings, with electricity and bright lights shining on the faces of marble Marys and Jesuses. And also just like the rest of Tampico, the cemetery was divided between the rich and the poor. My father's family had always been someplace in be-tween. There was money to pay for people to cook and clean for my el-derly grandmother. But that didn't mean that the money was there to bury our dead in the posh part of the tombs.

On our side of the cemetery, it looked as if there had been an earth-quake that very morning. Tombstones were twisted and leaning off to the side, dried flowers sat in waterless plastic vases, and weeds made it difficult to see where one plot ended and another began. The traffic just down the hill was thick and noisy; tubes of black exhaust from the crowded buses rose over our heads. I carried Raul Ariel on my backcar-rier and he tipped and rocked as we picked our way to my grandfather's resting place. I held on to my father who was silent.

Papi stood at the bottom of the gray slab with my grandfather's name on it. My aunt was jabbering away about the plots as if they were pieces of real estate, mumbling away in a low monotone about how much she had paid for it, about how she was going to clean up the walkway, about how the one next to abuelito's was for Grandma. I stood next to my fa-ther and for the first time didn't hold on to him but instead held him up, ever so slightly, as I held my Raul on my back.

Where will *we* go? I thought to myself. Where will Dad go? Here, in downtown Tampico? Or in Chicago, a home that is home but that my dad still doesn't exactly think of as home? If we come from the salt of the earth, then which earth do we go back to? And does it matter? Those were my thoughts as I watched my dad choke back his tears as he said goody-bye to his other tocayo.

Back at home that night, as I had done the night before, I took a bottle of mineral water with me to my bed. I had forgotten to ask who had come into my room and finished off half of the bottle the night before. Whoever it was should have at least put the plastic cap back on so as not to let all the gas out. Strange, I thought. I couldn't imagine that my father, mother, grandmother or aunt would drink from a bottle by my bed. And I doubted the woman who cleaned would have done it, either. Whatever. It was not important. I hugged Raul Ariel, who was snoring gently in the big bed we were sharing, said a quiet prayer for my abuelito Raul, and went to sleep in the tropical heat.

The next morning I woke up to the smell of fried tortillas. Why is it, I wondered, that things in Mexico just smell and taste better? If Raul Ariel ever asked me this I would just tell him that the food down here is made con mucho amor. I sat up, rubbed my eyes, and looked at the night table. The bottle of mineral water was there but the plastic cap was sitting right next to it. I hadn't had a drink since I had put the bottle there the night before. It must have been Mom, I thought to myself. We had bought a set of these plastic caps at Woolworth's when I was a kid as a gift to my grandfather. I hadn't seen, much less used, one of these old-fashioned bottle caps for years. I put the cap back on and took Raul Ariel down for chilaquiles and fresh homemade salsa.

That afternoon we took Raul Ariel to the plaza so he could see the globero, the balloon man. I had always loved to see the globeros in the plaza, walking with deliberate pause, carrying a hundred balloons of all different colors and shapes. I would always wonder how it was that the man didn't fly away and how it was that you could choose your balloon from all of the ones floating in the sky and that the globero knew exactly which string to pull to bring down just the one that you had chosen. Raul Ariel was a little frightened by him, though, and I thought that's why he needs to come to Mexico often. Pa' que no le tenga miedo a los globeros. So he won't be frightened by globeros.

That evening, when I went upstairs to bed, the bottle was still on my nightstand but the cap was off again. I sat down and the first image that popped into my mind was my grandfather. I smiled, looked up at the ceiling, and whispered, "Qué onda, abue? Hey, grandpa, we're here in your house with your baby namesake and we miss you." I figured it was Grandpa's spirit who was playing this game.

The next morning I double-checked and asked everyone in the house if they had been drinking my water. Everyone said no.

I was glowing inside. My grandfather had been such a pragmatist that I never thought he would become a jokester ghost. On the other hand, I was not entirely convinced that this is what was happening and I didn't dare mention the incident—or my theory—to my equally pragmatic relatives.

But the night we were leaving I decided to ask my cousin. Bertha Alicia was my same age and she had been the closest of all of us to abuelito Raul. She listened closely to my story and then said, "It was mi abuelito! It had to be because he loved those Woolworth bottle caps so much that he would often open Coke bottles just so he could put the plastic caps on himself."

I was quietly elated—happy that abuelito had obviously taken notice that his great-grandson namesake was in his house. I thought about the celebration of the Day of the Dead that had just passed. I decided I would buy Raul Ariel a sugar-candied skull in Mexico City when we got there and put the name ABUELITO RAUL in blue letters across its forehead.

When we arrived in Mexico City, after our stay in Tampico, Raul Ariel met more cousins. He had never been as social as I was seeing him here. I wondered if it had to do with the language issue. We only spoke to Raul Ariel in Spanish. And he didn't have many Spanish-speaking friends back in New York where he often seemed shy with other babies. Maybe he was flourishing here because all of the children spoke his same language. We knew we wanted him to have Spanish as his first language, but I wondered if we were hindering his social skills as a result.

Of course, there were rough moments during my trip back to Mexico as a mom. Yes, everyone congratulated me and told me how beautiful my son was, but everyone also kept asking me why I was still breast-feeding. Mexico was where I had learned to accept nursing and yet here I was being criticized for doing it for so many months. I didn't get it. Everywhere I went I seemed to get mixed messages and felt I'd never get it straight.

Mom told me, "Oh, mi'jita, in Mexico it's right to nurse but they are so class-conscious that the rich only nurse for four months or so. Then they stop and give them American-made formula. If you breast-feed for longer than six months they tend to look at you as someone who can't afford to buy food."

All of these middle-class Mexican mothering secrets I didn't know about until now.

And then everyone also wanted to know when I was going to cut Raul Ariel's hair. I had thought it was Mexican tradition not to cut a baby's hair until it was one year old, so here I was following this tradition but then I was criticized for it. "That's the old people's tradition, Malulis," one cousin said to me. "You don't have to do that. Go get your son a corte so he stops looking like a hippy."

And then on one particularly difficult day when Raul Ariel was cranky out of his wits and I was too, my tía Gloria called me "neurotica." "Te pareces a esas mamás gringas que se preocupan de todo y no se saben tranquilizar." You look just like those gringa moms who worry about everything and don't know how to relax.

And when I carried Raul Ariel in a reboso, the way all Mexican women (except for my cousins, obviously) carry their babies, they all laughed at me. "Ay, qué chistosa está Maria de Lourdes," my cousin said, rolling her eyes.

Ay. Ay ay ay. I should have expected all of this.

Mexico was family and magic and love and affection and color and smells and the home of my ancestors. But Mexico still remained the place where I was often judged most severely, where I was again, an outsider. It was the place where I was most criticized for not conforming, where the rigid lines of cultural and class traditions were the most constricting. But how could I conform? I was a mishmash of the Mexican middle class, Latino gringo, yuppy American, and a New Yorker. As in every trip I made to Mexico, I went there expecting to feel like this place was my home and came away convinced that it wasn't, but as soon as I arrived in New York, I was longing for the sense of Mexico as homeland all over again.

I wondered if I was going to force all of this on innocent Raul Ariel.

Maybe I shouldn't make Mexico such a huge part of his existence, I thought on our flight back while he slept in my arms, his long lashes laying against his cheeks. He doesn't need to go there to see his family. He wasn't like me who grew up with all of my family living in Mexico and so I *had* to go back to see my grandparents and aunts and uncles. Raul Ariel could see his grandparents, aunts, and uncles by crossing the borders between states and not countries.

But I can't let go of Mexico, I thought as I shifted him from one side to the other, trying to get comfortable in the cramped airplane seat. It's part of who I am. Maybe it will help him to know that Mexico is not his home, that it's not where he was born, it's not his motherland. His homeland is New York City. And Mexico is just a place for visitas.

 A Mother's Power

Gérman was waiting for us at the baggage claim in the airport, looking radiant and vibrant and sexy, too. Am I ready to be feeling *this,* I thought, as I hugged him back and then passed Raul Ariel into his strong arms. It was good to be home, good to be back in New York, good to be with my familia again.

As soon as we had packed up the car, Gérman turned to me and said: "You'll never guess who called you today?"

"Who, honey?" I said, a smile taking over my face. Maybe this was the good news I was hoping for.

"The TV people! They want you to fly down in two days for an interview."

"Yeaaaahhhhhhhh!" I screamed. "Honey, can you imagine! This is incredible! Oh, my god! This is fabulous!"

Raul Ariel applauded from his car seat. Gérman started chanting. "Mamá's gonna get a new job! Mamá's gonna get a new job! La-la-la-la-lala!"

We sang the whole drive home from the airport, put the salsa station on full volume, and Gérman took out the cowbell he kept under the driver's seat and pounded away on it at the stoplights. Raul Ariel was laughing a carcajadas. He had learned this full guttural laugh from his cousins and it sounded hilarious. Once at home, I gave Gérman his present (I bought him a wooden mask for our mask collection), bathed Raul Ariel, and put on his pajamas. Then we put on the Cri-Crí CD we had brought back and started marching around the living room, acting out the song about the animal orchestra.

Being away had done us all some good. Gérman was happy to have had some downtime, I had had a chance to bond with my son, and Raul Ariel was glad to have his mamá and papá together again. Later on, I put Raul Ariel to sleep.

We ordered dinner from our local Italian place and I savored my arugula-and-goat cheese salad and pasta e fagiole soup. I had to start eating light again. The way I was eating in Mexico, I was sure I had put on at least five pounds.

But then as things wound down and I started to unpack, I felt a knot start to form in my stomach.

"Amor, qué te pasa? Why do you look so worried all of a sudden?" Gérman said to me, as the pile of dirty laundry from our trip mushroomed out of our suitcase. "You should be happy about this job offer but instead you look panicked. No te entiendo, honey."

"It's just that it's a big change. And what if they don't end up offering me the job? What if I blow it? And what if I don't like it? What if I miss my radio work?" I took a deep breath and rolled my head to release the tension.

"Sometimes I think you'll never be happy. You always find something to worry or complain about. Por qué será que eres así?"

"I don't know why I'm like that, honey," I snapped, and threw some more clothes into the pile. Gérman was right. If I was given a dozen roses I would always focus on the one that was wilting.

"You're just like your father, Malu. Such a worrier. Life is too short," he said, walking away from me.

I *was* so much like my father, I thought as I stuffed the dirty clothes into the laundry bag. He was a brilliant man and yet he was such a worrier. When we were growing up, Dad would worry every year if he was going to get the next grant to continue doing his research. Each spring, he would get into these terrible moods. After dinner he would rub his temples trying to make his headaches go away. Night after night after night. We all knew what it meant. His grant was up for review. I had no idea what a grant was back then. All I knew was that Dad was worried and he would worry for several months straight.

It was the same thing before our yearly trips to Mexico. Instead of being excited, two months before we would leave Dad would start with his preocupaciones.

"Berta, I'm not going to let you overload the car this year. Last year the car was so heavy that the muffler was almost touching the ground."

For two long months we would hear complaints from Dad. Meanwhile, Mom was buying presents for the whole family and getting lists of what they wanted from the States—Hershey kisses for my grandfather, underwear and nightgowns for my aunts, Tonka trucks for my primos, pantuflas for grandma's feet, dolls from Sears for my primas. Mom would buy stuff every week and then stash it in the back of the hallway closet, out of sight. And then a month before our departure she would start packing the maletas and spreading out the gifts among our clothes so Dad wouldn't notice. And she always took at least one huge maleta with old clothes to give away to people we met along the drive. At the gas stations in small towns when the kids would beg for money, Mom would pull out some clothes and give them away. While Dad filled the car with gas, Mom would talk to the children, telling them that they had to continue going to school. Begging wasn't a way to make a living, she would say.

I was a lot like my mother, I thought. But there was no doubt that I had also made Papi's worst traits my own.

I was quiet. If I had taken this from my father and had made it my own, then there was a good chance that I could pass this on to my son. I didn't want him to become a worrier. I wanted Raul Ariel to have Gérman's strength.

I stopped unpacking and started to fill the tub with warm water. I rounded up some candles and lit some incense in the bathroom. I put some drops of lavender in the water. I turned off the lights and slid slowly into the bath.

Se acabó, I said to myself, as the lavender scent washed over me. Se acabó. I may not be able to get rid of my own anxieties, pero I'm going to try as hard as I can not to let Raul Ariel see them. And I'm going to stop being such a worrier. I let myself sink deeper into the tub, the warm water reaching up to my neck. After a long while in silence and candlelight darkness, I stood up, flipped on the light, and turned my shower radio on to my favorite soul station. Marvin Gaye was singing "Mercy Mercy Me." I took a long, slow breath.

The next morning, I went out and bought my first business suit. If I was going to work in television I decided I needed to look the part on the day of my interview.

I got on the plane for the day trip the next morning and pulled out my notebook. How was I going to sell myself to these people, I thought? What am I going to talk about that makes me unique so that they'll want to hire me? I made a list. I've won all kinds of awards. I'm a good story-teller. I have sources everywhere. But then I felt a little stupid. They had approached me, I thought. So why did I feel like I had to prove myself?

I looked out the window as the plane took off and the Manhattan sky-line disappeared behind me.

I wasn't going to do it, I decided. I wasn't going to be the little girl trying to say and do the right thing. I was an award-winning journalist who had a wonderful job already. Plus I was a mother who had birthed and was raising a son—the most difficult job in the world. Why should I feel anything but powerful? I was going to turn the tables. I was going to be the one in the position of strength for once in my life.

And so I made a list of questions that *I* was going to ask my future bosses. I heeded Gérman's words. He always told me, the more cocky and less interested you seem the more people want you, the more they think that you really are the greatest thing around. I had seen him do it time and again when galleries would call and talk down to him, as if he was just some measly 'Latino' artist. And then he would do the power switch on them and he would raise his voice a notch and tell them that he was very busy and didn't have time to send them anything and the tougher he got, the more they wanted him.

I was going to pull a Gérman Perez. I was going to prove it to my hus-band and to my son and to myself that I could do this. How would I ever be able to teach Raul Ariel to do it for himself if I didn't know how to do it for myself?

En nombre de mi familia, I'm going to do this. I smiled to myself.

And so during the rest of the plane ride I talked myself into believ-ing I was the most qualified person for this job so that by the time I had to go and meet all of the bigwigs I actually did think I was the greatest reporter that ever lived.

During the interviews, I was strong and poised and I don't think I came across as someone who was desperate for work. (I felt as though

I was having an out-of-body experience the whole time I was there, but I never flinched.) I never tried to sell myself but instead posed questions to the men sitting behind their desks. We had one-on-one conversations, not top-down ones. I let them know I felt like their equal. And it worked. At the end of the day (when my body finally came down from orbit) they asked me to come on board. I told them I would get back to them with the specifics, but I did say I wouldn't be able to start for another six months. They said fine. I was happy beyond belief.

After thirty-six, I was finally taking myself seriously. And so it seemed, was everyone else. Maybe people had been taking me seriously all along. Maybe it was just that I was really the last one to finally "get it."

Step One-Two-Three, Virgencita

The day before Thanksgiving, while everyone had holiday cheer and commuter rush on their minds, our cats, Gachica and Pachuco, became ill with some sort of stomach virus. There was cat poo and puke everywhere and Raul Ariel found the whole crazy scene hilarious. I was swearing at the cats (Pinche Pachuco! Coño Gachica!) at seven in the morning, rushing behind them with paper towels in hand and Raul Ariel crawling behind me squeaking like a mouse. I grabbed both of the cats and stuffed them into a carrier, put Raul Ariel on my back, maneuvered down the five flights of stairs, and got everyone in the car for the drive to the ASPCA. As part of my new sense of self-esteem, I wanted to give Gérman a break and let him sleep late and prove to him that even though I depended on him for so much, there were some things *I could do on my own.*

I figured this would also give me another chance to spend some quality time with Raul Ariel, who was amazing me with his budding intellect. I would watch him as he pushed himself fearlessly to try and walk, or as he took his books and turned the pages and made baby talk as if he was reading. I could hardly believe that he was almost one year old.

I had decided that since I couldn't be with him day in and day out, I would do special things and take interesting adventures with him. He would remember me by my grandmother's nickname—I would be "Maria la de la pata del perro"—always on an adventure just for Mom and Raul Ariel. A trip to the ASPCA would be a fun thing to do. I imagined he could play with the animals while we waited to be seen. I had a romantic image of the morning we would spend together—just Mommy and Raul Ariel.

Of course he fell asleep in the car and it started raining, and the cats were hissing and screeching nonstop. By the time I got us all into the ASPCA, I was in a terrible mood.

After an hour of waiting, my number was finally called and at the same time Raul Ariel woke up crying, my cats started screeching again and I had to haul all of us into the vet's office. I walked in pushing a crying Raul Ariel in the stroller and carrying a big bag with both meowing cats on my shoulder.

The vet looked at me in wonder. "Wow! How did you manage to get here—with the kid, the cats, the stroller, the bags? How do you even get out of the house? And you look so composed."

I smiled and realized that sometimes I actually could do it all. Or at least look like I did.

Two weeks after a low-key Thanksgiving celebration in Boca Chica was the celebration of La Virgen de Guadalupe. Usually I would go down to Fourteenth Street to the Guadalupe church where the Mexicanos took over the entire street for the celebration. But a Puerto Rican neighbor of mine told me that his Catholic church on Ninety-sixth Street was going to have mariachis for la virgen during Sunday-morning Mass. Another adventure for Raul Ariel.

That day Raul Ariel woke up and was incredibly cranky. It was the first time in his less-than-year-old life that he seemed to be asserting his independence and his newfound knowledge that if he wanted to, he could be angry or pissed off or just plain nasty.

I was aghast. Where had my sweet, happy baby disappeared to?

"I don't think you should take him to church this morning," said Gérman. "Va a ser un problema. Te va a dar mucha guerra." In Spanish you say that a cranky baby is going to put you through a war. Gérman was giving me fair warning that my morning could easily turn into a disaster.

I didn't care. I had settled in my mind that I wanted Raul Ariel to celebrate la virgen no matter what.

"Eres una cabeza dura," Gérman repeated over and over. What a hard head.

"Yes, I know, honey, but this is important. I want him to see la virgen and los mariachis."

The morning was one huge pleito. Raul Ariel was screaming from the time I put on his clothes to walking down the five flights of stairs. He was screaming so loud in the hallway that one of my neighbors opened her door and asked if there was a problem.

"Oh no," I said as if this was the most natural thing to be happening on an otherwise quiet Sunday morning. "We're just going to church to see la virgen."

"Good luck," she said.

I smiled. I probably should turn back, I thought for a split second. But cabeza dura that I am, there was no stopping me. I was in Guadalupe-frenzy.

Raul Ariel cried during the five-minute cab ride. I tried making up a song to calm both me and the baby. "Vámos a la virgen—ta-ta-da-da. Vámos a la virgen—ta-ta-da-da!" Nada. I felt self-conscious. The cab driver probably thinks he should call child welfare to report me, I thought. But I'm just trying to have an aventura with my son, I can see myself pleading with the social worker.

We got out of the cab and Raul Ariel finally stopped his wailing as soon as he saw the dozens of balloons floating in the sky. It was a globero, right there on Amsterdam Avenue and Ninety-Sixth Street! And he wasn't afraid as he had been in Tampico. He was laughing like all of the rest of the niñas and niños. The steps in front of the church had been transformed. There were women selling tamales out of shopping carts, men selling roses out of another, another man selling cassettes out of a little box he carried around his waist, a van selling tacos with a big painted sign that said TACOS SOBRE RUEDAS, tacos on wheels. It was like I was back in Mexico. The boys and girls were all dressed up with painted mustaches or colorful braids. Raul Ariel was content final-mente. Thank God. So was I.

Inside the huge church, I got in the long line of people and slowly walked all the way to the front altar and I knelt down in front of la vir-gen statue with Raul Ariel in my arms. She was covered in flowers and dozens of candles lay at her feet. I gave Raul Ariel the flowers I had bought outside and he threw them at la virgen, almost knocking her over. He laughed and I scooped him up and scooted off.

We took our place in the pew and the mariachis started. But of course, when the trumpets started blaring, Raul Ariel did, too. More stares. I sat down and gave him a teta and he calmed down. The procession started to the rhythm of *Las Mañanitas*. Everyone was now singing happy birthday in Spanish to la virgen and here I was nursing my son, sitting next to old ladies who looked just like my abuelita. And of course, the second I heard the music and saw the statue being carried on the shoulders of the Mexican men, and I thought about my abuelita who used to scold me as a teenager for not going to church every week, I started to cry. Why did I have to be melodramatic?

Mexico in New York didn't have to be an emotional interlude. It was a part of everyday reality. And I didn't have to force Raul Ariel to do things à la Mexicana anymore. He was going to grow up with it because now he lived in a place where Mexico was everywhere.

Halfway through the mass I looked at my watch. It was almost noon and I had an aerobics class I wanted to take. La virgen or exercise, I thought to myself. Hmmm. I excused myself as I quickly maneuvered my way out of the pew, bumping into viejitas, young Mexican moms, a Puerto Rican family, my architect friend, and a group of vatos, gangster wannabe-look alikes wearing red, white, and green bandanas, the colors of the Mexican flag.

I rushed out to Amsterdam Avenue, flagged down a livery cab, jumped in, rushed home, ran up the five flights of stairs, put a sleeping Raul Ariel into his bed for his nap, tied my tennis shoes, and ran to the gym. It was time for my Sunday step class. And it was the day of la virgen in New York City.

DOMINICANA

I have a friend who is the perfect hostess. Her house is always impeccable, her daughter well dressed and well behaved, her cooking absolutely scrumptious. She can whip up a full spread for twelve people in an hour and a half. I tell her she is our very own Martha Stewart-Lopez-Perez!

But I am not.

It was four days until that all-important Christmas holiday when Gérman and I looked at each other and said, "So what are we going to do for Raul Ariel?"

Christmas had never been a big deal when I was growing up because we almost always spent it in Mexico. There, our tradition was to have a late dinner of tamales and pavo on the evening of the Twenty-fourth, Noche Buena, then stay up late and go to midnight Mass, and the next morning exchange a few small gifts.

Mom would always say to me, "Your Christmas present is this trip to Mexico to see your cousins." And so we never asked for nor got much in the way of big gifts.

Gérman and I didn't do much to celebrate Christmas, either. We just never got around to it when we were childless. The most we did was go to the central post office and answer a Letter to Santa. We would buy an anonymous child a big box of clothes and send it off in the mail.

Growing up, Christmas was about being with my family in Mexico. Now that we had Raul Ariel, I thought it would be nice to make Christmas in our house more about our time together than about toys, as well. And I had grand illusions that in the future, I wanted Raul Ariel to celebrate Kwanza when he got older as well as a night of Hanukkah and the lighting of the Menorah, the way I did with my friends when I was younger. But at this very moment, none of that really mattered. It was four days before Christmas and we had no plans. We didn't even have a Christmas tree.

In the back of my mind I excused myself by saying "He's not even a year old. He won't even remember this event. We can get away with no celebration at all."

At the last minute we invited some friends, a filmmaker and a dancer who we hadn't seen in a year, to join us for the holiday in the country at Boca Chica. And on our two-hour-long drive, they convinced us that we had to do something special for Raul Ariel's first Navidad.

So here we were late on December 24, driving off to Connecticut, with plans to make our home into a winter wonderland but with nothing to do it with. It was just about six o'clock by the time we got to the Bethlehem exit on the highway. And there was a Kmart at the end of the road.

"Mis queridos amigos," I said, with a twist of irony. "If you want to make our little home into a place with holiday cheer we have no place else to shop at this hour except for Kmart. Is everybody game?"

So we turned into Kmart, locked the car with our two cats, Gachica and Pachuco, in the back, and headed for the store. Inside, the little drummer boy song was playing and the announcer interrupted the music. "Attention Kmart shoppers . . ."

Yes, I had become a Kmart shopper. I had never had any reason to go to one until Pampers had become the most expensive item on our shopping list. Kmart sold Pampers here in Connecticut for half the price they went for in the city. That's all we thought we would ever buy when we went for our first visit some months earlier. But then we started to stock up on twenty-four-roll packages of toilet paper, ten-gallon detergent jugs, reams and reams of paper towels, baby wipes, toothpaste, shampoo, and soap.

My mom was still a Kmart snob. When I told her we shopped there she said, "Fine. Just don't buy any clothes. You know they can't sell clothes that cheap unless someone is being underpaid."

So we didn't buy clothes.

"Attention Kmart shoppers," we heard again over the loudspeaker as we looked at one another and smiled that December evening. "All Christmas decorations are now half price! Take advantage of our Christmas Eve sale and stock up for next year's Christmas decorations. Everything is half price in aisle number ten.

I looked at Gérman and said, "Let's go!" This was our big holiday break.

We got some Christmas lights and some imitation crystal red bubbles, mistletoe, ornaments, and tinsel. We packed up our cart and made our way to the check-out line. There we were at Kmart fifteen minutes before closing time on Christmas Eve, surrounded by Christmas season misfits in a craze of last-minute bargain hunting. And hey, like it or not, we were just part of that misfit crowd. I knew if I thought about it too much I would get depressed. (What were we doing here when the rest of the family was making tamales in my tía's kitchen in Mexico City?)

Raul Ariel was laughing, oblivious to everything, of course. It helped me to laugh at myself. On line at Kmart on Noche Buena in the heart of gringo-landia. What my life has come to!

We packed up the car and drove off into the darkness and left Kmart behind. The night was beautiful. The tradition in the small towns around Bethlehem was to line the country roads with candles in brown paper bags. I thought that was a New Mexico tradition I had read about in *Los Farolitos of Christmas,* Rudolfo Anaya's children's book. It was a story of a little girl who made luminarias to help her father, a soldier returning from war, see the road on his way home on Christmas Eve. But here the luminarias were lighting up the long driveways of huge homes with white picket fences.

It was us and the luminarias and Kmart in Connecticut on this Christmas Eve.

By chance or by fate, I thought as we made our way to our cottage, this Dominican–Mexican–New Yorker family was making this tiny section of wasp-landia our own. Before moving to New York almost twenty years ago, I had seen images of these New England towns only in the movies. I never imagined that I would be spending my weekends here, never imagined that my own son would grow up thinking that these rolling hills, old farms, big houses, and country fairs would be his.

On our weekends up to Boca Chica we would drive along the gorgeous tree-lined country roads of Litchfield County, listening to Milton

Nascimento, or Pablo Milanes, but the pickup trucks around us had bumper stickers that read I LISTEN TO 92 COUNTRY FM. Inside our car, we'd be blasting protest songs from Cuba or sexy songs from Brazil. My memories of all of that music took me to my yearning for Latin America. Raul Ariel, I imagined, will hear those songs when he gets older and think of Connecticut and imagine cows grazing and apple picking at Maroh farms.

It wasn't all so peachy keen. That fall we had invited some friends to spend the weekend. She was white and he was black and from Costa Rica. We were at a hardware store doing some shopping and we all sensed that we were being watched by hawk eyes. I had never felt that before but I knew sooner or later it was bound to happen. As we walked out, a middle-aged man looked at us and said haughtily, "So, you've come up for a weekend to look at the fall colors?"

"No," I said matter-of-factly. "We live here."

The man looked startled, tripped over himself, and bumped into his own car. "You live here?" he asked incredulously.

"Yes, over by the lake," I said, and we walked away.

The man nervously put the keys in his car and drove off.

That Christmas weekend when we went out for our afternoon drive so Raul Ariel would take his nap and Gérman and I could have some uninterrupted quality time to talk, we made a turn into a street about a mile behind our house. I looked around and suddenly it didn't feel like we were in small-town Connecticut, but instead this was a burgeoning suburban housing complex. I was stunned!

"Oh my God. Suburbia has made it to our Bethlehem. I gasped. "This can't be. The houses all look alike, the gardens are all perfectly tended. Yucky, mediocre, middle America is hiding out in the backyard of our sweet Connecticut Boca Chica paradise. It's the end for Bethlehem!"

Gérman looked at me and shook his head, smiling.

"Malu, you've got a lot of nerve talking about preserving Bethlehem. You're the one who's forcing change in this town. You are the yuppie, New Yorker, Latino and outsider. Now you can't all of a sudden want to control this place, too. You can't be the one who stands and says it's all got to stay the same."

Yes, this new mishmash of weekend getaway New Yorkers, old money Wasps, and middle-America suburbia was the future for this

small town. For Raul Ariel, this place would only be known as Boca
Chica, his purple-and-yellow house in the woods.

Two days after Christmas in Connecticut we took off for the Dominican Republic. Gérman was meeting with collectors and setting up
a show there for next year. It would be Raul Ariel's first visit to the paradise of Papá.

We arrived at the airport at seven in the morning to a party scene.
Everybody is going home. Everyone is feliz. Kids are running around
screaming, grandmothers are sitting on overloaded luggage that has
been wrapped in plastic so it looks like huge pieces of hard candy. (The
plastic wrapping is so no one will slit the luggage open and steal something.) It's a party at the airport, but the airline wants to keep everyone
in line, literally and figuratively.

"You're going to have to turn down the volume," a security guard says
to a man carrying a huge boom box playing merengue. What a difference. In the airport in the Dominican Republic they're *hoping* some one
has a loud boom box for music because inevitably there is some problem with the airport sound system and the music is on the blink.

Gérman's homeland and mine couldn't be any more different. While
for me Mexico is family and memory, it's also the place where I often
feel the most pressure to conform to conservative traditions. But here
in the Dominican Republic, Gérman is friends with all of the artists,
writers, musicians, and bohemians. Here, all of Gérman's friends are
the families who are breaking with traditions and often criticized for
creating new ones.

For me, the Dominican Republic is a place where I assume a new
persona that lasts only for as long as our visit. Once I step foot off the
plane, I am no longer the journalist, the professional. Here, I am simply
"the wife" and now, "the mother." I have nothing I have to do, nothing to
prove. I am the famous painter's esposa and my son's Mamá. Y punto.

And here I am also the most relaxed.

In the Dominican Republic, time is elusive—the last thing you con-
cern yourself with. In New York, my life revolves around schedules, the
minutes and moments of work and freedom. Sometimes I get angry
with Gérman because of his poor sense of time (he's always late), but I
bless him for bringing us to this place where time means nothing, where

hours and hours can slip away and no one feels that they have "wasted" time by not doing anything.

The day we arrive there is an afternoon party to welcome us. We take off Raul Ariel's clothes and he crawls around naked in the grass, playing with the water hose under huge avocado trees, the spiky grass tickling his feet. Children, sun-bronzed sons and daughters of Gérman's friends, are everywhere, screaming, laughing. Chilled beer in hand, I bless this tropical paradise, so removed from Manhattan neurosis.

Then the CD player is flipped on and Gérman's friend turns up the volume. It's Stevie Wonder singing "You are the Sunshine of My Life." Then it's Bob Marley. Then it's The Who. Then it's Billie Holiday.

For the first time ever, Raul Ariel is so happy to be playing that he forgets he is hungry. And I can actually take my eyes off of him for a few moments knowing that there are so many kids with their nanas here that he will be taken care of. He is so involved with the other kids that he doesn't even seem interested in where I am. I get a little mother's pang—but only for a second. Then I take another frosty cerveza out of the cooler and snuggle up to Gérman.

He looks even more handsome here on this island. His skin almost instantly turns a darker shade of brown from the scorching Dominican sun. I love watching him here, he seems so in control, such an hombre. Never for an instant will anyone talk down to Gérman here as I've seen happen in New York, when people hear his thick accent. Here Gérman is treated like a prince.

And if we came to live here, I think to myself, that means I could live like a princess. A flash image pops into my head—I could be the lady of leisure here. I could spend my days taking my son to the beach lazying around with friends, no deadlines to crash, no grit, no grime, no dog-eat-dog rat race.

"Amor," I say, reaching over and putting my arm around Gérman's neck. "Maybe we should move here. I could write novels for a living."

But then like the Ally McBeal record-scratching dream-buster moment, Gérman says, "You would last a month. Maybe two. Just think what it would be like to be writing on your computer in our air-conditioned house surrounded by coconut trees and then, the electricity disappears. Not for ten or fifteen minutes but for six hours. No air-conditioning, no computer, no refrigerator, no TV. Nada. You'd be very unhappy very soon."

"Oh well," I say, taking a deep sigh, "it was a good dream for a few seconds."

The next morning, Gérman took us to visit Biemba, my surrogate grandmother. Bienvenida, Biemba for short, was my first college roommate's Dominican grandmother. Biemba was by far the coolest seventy-five-year-old I had ever met (she would even hang out at our parties and serve beer). After college, my roommate, Biemba, and I shared an apartment in New York, and Biemba came to love me like one of her own granddaughters. A few years ago she left New York, though, saying she wanted to be in her own country when she died. She moved in with her son who lived in a shantytown outside of the capital.

We drove for more than an hour and then turned into a barrio with dirt roads. The car waddled and dipped in and out of potholes. Raul Ariel giggled in the backseat. The air was tinged with the smell of garbage and outhouses. I saw children my son's age walking around barefoot and carrying broken plastic toys as their prized possessions. Bienvenida's house was next to the gallera, the cock-fighting ring, and people were lining up outside for the fight that afternoon. Merengue blared from huge bassy speakers and the block pulsed with music.

Down a dirt path, there's a one-room shack. I carry Raul Ariel who protests that he wants to be put down. But I can't let him crawl here. It's all dirt and the chickens and dogs have pooped everywhere. I approach the front door and find Bienvenida sitting in a broken rocking chair. She sees me walk in, fixes her glasses, and then lets loose a huge smile when she recognizes that it's me, her mouth like a perfect dark circle. (Her teeth are all gone.) She sucks in her breath and squeals and stretches her frail arms out toward me, just like she did every night back in New York when I would come home late from my waitressing job. "Oh, Maria! Oh, Maria! Y esa belleza de muchachito! Qué lindo!" Biemba's voice is faint. Her brown skin is hanging from her bones. I can tell she isn't eating well. My heart sinks.

I take Raul Ariel and prop him up next to her and he gives her a squeeze. Bienvenida's eyes light up. I look around and feel sad but I know there is no use in telling her she should move out. She has always said she came from poverty and had no problem living her last days of

life the way her life began, with hardly anything. There are faded photos
of Marx and Lenin, the Pope and Fidel, on the walls. A single lightbulb
hangs over the dusty TV set that is turned on every night so Bienvenida
can watch the news. She taught herself how to read and write as a child
and survived by selling candies on the street. She got to New York
decades later, and took care of raising my roommate. When she lived
with me she made me buy her three newspapers a day and always had
something to say about la política of this or that.

Raul Ariel played with some of the children from around the block
who had come to visit when they heard out-of-towners were at Bienvenida's house. I had brought a roasted chicken, rice, and beans and we
all ate together. Raul Ariel studied his new friends intently as they de-
voured the chicken, sucking on their fingers to catch every morsel. This
might have been their only meal of the day but they made sure to feed
Raul Ariel, treating him like a baby brother, putting rice in his hands
and tiny pieces of meat in his mouth. Raul Ariel was shining like the sun.

The next day was Raul Ariel's first birthday, and Gérman became the
Martha-Stewart-Lopez-Perez of the event, coordinating it all. He invited all of his friends to his favorite park that overlooked the ocean, ordered the cake (vanilla and pineapple with orange-and-white frosting),
assigned what everyone had to bring, and stayed up late to make party
hats out of posters of one of his paintings, the one of the blue goat. He
bought dozens of balloons and tied them to the trees. It was beautiful.
But I couldn't get the image of Bienvenida out of my mind. The contradictions of vacation ecstasy and the sadness of poverty and hunger were
weighing me down.

Raul Ariel was excited even though I knew he had no idea that we
were celebrating his first birthday. He just wanted to hold on to the balloons. He would grab one string in each hand and then try desperately
to walk, as if they could somehow hold him up. I blew out the candle for
him after we sang happy birthday in three different versions: The Dominican version, "Las Mañanitas" from Mexico, and then "Happy Birthday to You" in English to a merengue beat.

The year had gone by in a flash, I thought as I watched him playing
with his new friends. He wasn't the tiny six-pound papoose I had held
in my arms just twelve months before. His baby-fat cheeks were thin-
ning out and his arms and legs were long and supple now. He needed me

still but I knew that what he wanted now was also to be free from me—
to show me that he could venture out on his own, pushing his small toy
truck that supported him as he walked away. But he still would always
look back to see if I was watching him and I knew that my bond with
him was still there.

That night, after I nursed him to sleep, I turned him around and fit
him like a spoon against my body. I cupped my hand around his
chest and felt the beat of his heart against the softness of my palm I
closed my eyes and thought about the first time I heard his heartbeat,
when he was just seven weeks old and in my womb. We had come so far.
Here was my milagro son in my arms and I had become this person that
not long ago I had only imagined I could be—a mother. He was growing up. But so was I.

A couple of days later we took Raul Ariel for his first-ever visit to a
Caribbean beach. It was the day before Three Kings Day, and everyone
was getting ready for the holiday. Raul Ariel was sitting on my lap in the
car, looking out the back window when we came upon a big crowd of
women and children blocking traffic. I could see police officers and soldiers with long twigs in their hands. All of a sudden I see a soldier lift a
twig way above his head then bring it down, swiping against the legs of
a woman carrying a toddler in her arms. They were corralling people as
if they were a herd of cows, viciously swiping at the women and children who would spring back at the sting of the twig. They got the
crowds on the sidewalk and started pushing them to get back, raising
the twigs again and again, threatening to swipe at them one more time.

"Qué pasa aquí?" I said anxiously to Gérman.

"Oh honey, I'm sorry you have to see this ridiculous drama," Gérman
said from the front seat. "Every year the president gives out free bicy-
cles and toys for the Three Kings Day holiday and distributes them from
the presidential headquarters. But he only gives out a couple of hundred and so he ends up forcing the poor to fight among themselves to
get a shot at a bike. And then he sets the police and soldiers on them.
It's a horrible game they play and every year it's the same thing."

We drive by and I hold on to Raul Ariel even tighter. There were
children his age hanging on to their mother's waists, so scared they

weren't even crying. They were just in shock, seeing their mothers hit by soldiers with big guns on their belts.

The images of the mothers and the children replayed over and over in my mind for the rest of the day. But that same day Raul Ariel gave us all a huge gift. That afternoon, on the hot white sand of the Boca Chica beach, while musicians played merengue on the shore and vendors sold beer and fresh oysters and the rich and the poor swam together in the blueness of the ocean, Raul Ariel walked for the first time. And he walked and walked and walked, with his arms up, reaching for the sky.

Yes, this was a land of many gifts, I thought to myself as I looked out to the turquoise ocean. And this place of extremes was a part of me and now a part of my son. I was just going to have to figure out how to explain to Raul Ariel that beauty doesn't mean there is no sadness and that harshness doesn't mean there is no love.

MA-PA

After two weeks in the Dominican Republic, lazying around so much, we came back home rejuvenated, tanned, invigorated, and ready to work. Raul Ariel had grown up in a couple of ways—he was walking, he had eaten ice cream and candy for the first time in his life, and he was now watching television. (Gérman and I decided it would be limited to *Sesame Street*—the show we agreed was the most nonracist, nonsexist, and nonclassist. I think we enjoyed it more than Raul Ariel did.) He had gotten his first haircut in the Dominican Republic (screaming the whole time) and now wisps of brown curls hung delicately over his dark eyes. I was also nursing him less, beginning a month and a half process of weaning. And upon our return, we had gone through another few days of crying-it-out to get him to fall asleep on his own again (he was taking forever to nurse to sleep). All very big things for this little niñito.

Life settled into an extended period of pleasure. Gérman was painting with an intensity that I hadn't seen in the past year. He had finished a series of blue paintings on the theme of oceans and migrations. Now he had begun a red-and-orange phase on the theme of women. He was putting the finishing touches on a painting of a woman dangling a house on a fishing pole. Underneath was a man holding the house on his shoulders.

I had asked and been given until May to start my new job (and they had even agreed to a four-day work week) so I was savoring this extended leave. I was writing at the library every day and invigorated. I had the best of both worlds: I was my own boss, I made my own hours, I worked every day, but I was home by four in time to play with Raul Ariel for a long while before his bedtime. I was doing what I wanted, when I wanted to do it, and how I wanted to do it. And as a mother I was feeling like I knew what I was doing, too. I wasn't that fumbling neophyte who felt awkward in the park anymore. Raul Ariel and I were a team now, like buddies, and I had become one of those guerrilla moms in the playground—stocked with food and toys and prepared for any disaster.

As we moved into spring and New Yorkers came out of their winter apartment caves en masse and made the city come alive again, I noticed that my barrio was going through its own unbelievable transformation. In the year since the shooting of the little boy a block away, the late-night catcalls of the dealers had softened almost to the point of silence. The familiar kids who were drug lookouts on all four corners of my block had vanished. The long line of addicts standing around the corner to buy their crack had been replaced by a long line of university students trying to rent tiny apartments that were now going for exorbitant rents. The garbage was gone from the streets and the broken sidewalks were filled in with fresh cement.

Everyone was happy about this, but in the bodegas I would overhear people talking about how the mysterious overnight fix-up of the barrio happened at the same time that the color of our neighborhood was slowly lightening. Guys on the front stoops thought it was all fine. Now they had all different shades of women to stare at.

The ultimate sign of change in the barrio (and never in my wildest dreams did I expect to see this) was the hip new coffee bar that opened up around the corner. I yelped about how we were on the verge of being just one more yuppified community. But when I needed a quiet, convenient place to write and didn't feel like making the trek to the library, there I was. Sitting at the counter eating a croissant sandwich with my laptop and notes sprawled all over. The neighborhood old-timers wasted no time in making it *their* coffee bar as well—the grease-covered corner mechanics who fixed cars on the sidewalk would traipse in ("Oye, chico, dáme un latté por favor!"), the women from the salon next door would dash in with their hair in huge pink curlers, and the homeboy tough guys revealed their softer side playing chess at small tables while the college students next to them read Nietzsche.

As the months passed, my days once again moved into countdown mode. As full moon passed to full moon, I sadly recognized that I would soon leave my predictable domesticity and would have to relinquish controlling my own time. And there was no way to get out of it this time. But there was part of me that was ready to get back to my reporting. I was ready to do stories, ready to learn TV, and ready to wear something other than what had become my permanent library uniform—overalls and a baseball cap.

The last weeks before starting my new job, I was besieged again with worries about being a working mamá and, almost as if in preparation for my work return, Raul Ariel had once again gotten even closer with Paty, his babysitter. And even though I was lucky to have a nanny who was so loving and patient, I couldn't help but feel, ridiculous as it sounds, competitive with her. Then I thought about Gérman's women friends in the Dominican Republic and my tías and primas in Mexico. They all had nannies taking care of their kids. But they didn't seem to suffer all these conflicts.

Only later would I realize that these women with nanas (even my grandmother had a nana for my own mamá) were fine with it, because even though they had nannies, these mothers still had absolute control over how their children were being raised. They may not have been holding their kids every hour of every day, but they were the ones holding their own houses from the fishing poles like in Gérman's painting. Ellas manejan sus casas—they *drive* their houses—they are the ones who give orders minute by minute, they have the play-by-play of their home operation down to a science. They were in control of it all. But soon I was going to see that I couldn't drive my house and hold down my job at the same time. Yes, I had an image of having it all. But something was going to have to give.

On a warm spring day in early May I woke up, made everyone breakfast, got myself ready, took the subway, and officially went back to work. I didn't have a spring business suit so I wore my black bell bottoms and a button-down cotton orange shirt and my long hair loose and flowing. I wanted to make a statement from the get-go that even though

I was working in television, I was not going to change who I was, what I looked like, or how I dressed.

So, of course, I didn't exactly fit in. This was not the low-key world of public radio. I was working for a company that had hundreds of employees and a huge hierarchy. And power dressing meant something here. I knew eventually I was going to have to bite the bullet and buy a couple of suits, even if it killed me.

My first weeks on the job, I called Gérman every couple of hours. "Did Raul Ariel take his nap?" "What did he eat for lunch today?" "Make sure he wears a sweater outside." "It's time for his snack. There are apples in the fridge." "Why don't you have Paty take him to the library today since it's raining." "He can have a play date with Loma this afternoon." "There is chicken for his dinner." "Make sure his diaper is changed often." And on and on and on, every couple of hours, day after day. Gérman asked me if I had forgotten that I used to be out of the house for hours even before I went back to work at the office. "So, why do you suddenly have to call me now all of the time?"

"Because this is *different,*" I said.

"How?"

"Because now I'm at the office!" It was lame, I knew it, but I just had this urge to make the umbilical cord long enough to somehow stretch from Thirty-fourth Street all the way uptown.

In fact, it was different. I couldn't leave my office whenever I wanted, I often had to work late and got home after Raul Ariel was asleep, and I was under pressure as the new employee on the block.

One day after three weeks on the job, I came home and Raul Ariel screamed "Viva México!" when he saw me.

"When did he learn how to do that?" I asked Paty, as I plopped myself down exhausted on the sofa after a long day.

"Oh, like three days ago. Big Bird taught him. Big Bird sings a song about Mexico with mariachis who are a bunch of Chicano kids from New Mexico," she said.

My son is learning about Mexican culture through gringo television and I'm not here to see it. I sighed and smiled and gave my muchachito a big hug. But it was true. He was growing up in ways that I was not going to be around to witness.

Ceci would call me at the office and I would tell her about my days. I'm setting up this interview, we're going here for a shoot, I'm working on a script, and so on. "And I have the whole evening down," I said to her, "timed and calculated to function in clocklike precision."

She was curious about our bedtime ritual and I told her we had made it into one of the special moments that Raul Ariel and I could share, at least on most days. I explained to Ceci that we read three books (that he would choose), then turned out the lights and said good night to Yemanya, Oschun, Obatala, and La Virgen de Guadalupe, Tonantzin. And then we would whisper buenas noches to everyone in the family, his abuela and tocayo, his tíos and tías and primos, all of his madrinas and padrinos, and then we'd say good-night to the moon, to the playground, to the swings and the sandbox and anything else Raul Ariel had played with during the day. I would call him all of my favorite names— mi rey, mi cielo, mi vida, mi amor, mi bello, mi gordo, mi flaco, and honey—and then squeeze him tight and kiss his face and neck and fingers and eyes. I would tuck him in tight, just like Mom used to do for me, and then in the same way she did every night, I would walk away and say "Que sueñes con los angelitos." He would cry for two minutes and then be down and I would scramble to throw on my lycra and twice a week, be out the door for my gym class.

She would listen in amazement to my stories and then tell me about her days with her baby, all alone.

"I'm exhausted! She's so demanding and I have so much house cleaning to do. And then I have a little play date in the park and I'm going to try to squeeze in some phone calls for some freelance work while she takes her nap, and then I have to make dinner and rock her to sleep for half an hour," she would tell me. "You're a superwoman, Malu."

"No, you're the superwoman," I would say to her. "I don't know how you're able to do the baby and the house and your gigs, all alone with no help." She was doing it alone. I always had backup with Gérman and Paty. She was on her own from eight in the morning till eight at night. Her husband always worked late.

"I don't know how our moms did it," I said. "Alone with four kids and the house always impeccable."

"Yeah, I'm staring at a huge pile of laundry I have to fold and it's been there for two days. Do you ever remember seeing piles of laundry sitting around your house unfolded for more than an hour?" she asked exasperated.

"Never," I say, nodding my head. "Never. The laundry was always done and folded in a second."

"No wonder we feel like we can't get things right," said Ceci sighing. "Our mother's were superheroes. Extraterrestrials! Mothers, new immigrants, wives, housekeepers, chefs. We'll never be able to be like them."

"Yeah, but we are destined to try and try and try. Está cabrón," I said and hung up quickly. I had to write a script before I left the office that day.

After six weeks on the job, riding home in the subway one evening and feeling exhausted, I took out my notebook and began to scribble this word: *angustia*. That was the word that captured how I was feeling now that I was back at work. I was starting to feel like Gérman was beginning to resent my long hours and even worse, I was beginning to sense another mommy-rejection phase coming on from Raul Ariel. And the pressure to prove myself in my new job was also a part of the mix.

To make things even worse, the next week I was going to be traveling across the country for four days. I didn't even know how I was going to break it to Gérman. Already in the past week he had been stuck with the evening bedtime chores for four days because I was working late and he was falling back on meeting his own deadline for finishing his paintings for an important upcoming show. But on the subway that evening, I came up with the perfect solution. I got home, put Raul Ariel to sleep, and over dinner I asked Gérman if he wouldn't like to go down to the Dominican Republic while I traveled to Seattle and Chicago next week on business.

I made it seem like this was a great thing for Gérman and Raul Ariel to do, but in essence I was trying to find a way to lessen my own guilt. I figured if Gérman went "home" while I traveled, this would lessen his resentment toward me. Anything to lessen the guilt, became my motto.

A week later, I helped pack Raul Ariel's bag, putting all of his outfits in separate Ziploc baggies and labeling them with the days he should wear each outfit. The morning they left, I held back my tears and hugged them both, and then watched as they drove away in a taxi.

That night, Gérman called me at home to check in. I was sure he was going to tell me that Raul Ariel was missing me frantically, that he had cried the entire plane trip over, that he wasn't eating, and that he hadn't stopped asking for me. Wrong. The news was that he was sleeping peacefully, had played during the whole plane ride, and was in general having the time of his life, had he asked about me? No.

Just wonderful, I said to myself glibly.

The next day I flew to the Latino journalists conference in Seattle and for two days I played the role of a free woman. I stayed out late, had wonderfully stimulating conversations with my colleagues, drank one and half light beers (all I could handle), and danced (alone, when no one would ask me).

I didn't feel guilty at all. But I did feel strange.

I felt like I was having too much fun. And for more than a few seconds, I realized I wasn't thinking about my son or my husband, and not having them in my head made me feel unsettled. How could I not be thinking of them? Had I forgotten them? Obviously I had. Dios mío!

But I was also happy hanging out with my friends. How could I be happy and not be thinking about my family, the family that I had so longed to create? Malagradecida! Ungrateful! Mala madre!

Thankfully Ro was at the conference and after a breakfast meeting I went up with her to her room and I confessed to her how I was feeling. I told her about Gérman's undercurrent of resentment about me being away so much for work.

"Nena, your husband may get upset at you because of your work but remember, he married you knowing this was the kind of person you were. He loves you and he believes in what you are doing," she said as she put on some wonderful red lipstick. I never tired of telling her how gorgeous and sexy she was. "And about that guilt? Olvídalo nena! It's a waste of time. You are here and they are there y se acabó! I bet they are having a great time and not thinking about *you* every minute of the day."

"Well, as a matter of fact, that's exactly the problem," I said and threw myself on the king-sized bed. "Sometimes it feels like Raul Ariel has forgotten about me entirely. The more I'm away, the more he seems to withdraw."

"You know, he is probably pulling away from you not because he doesn't love you but because he is sad that you are gone. But it's not as if he is going to stop loving you, nena. I mean, I'm away from my kids a lot and at first they were angry with me but now they're cool about it. And I came up with my own way of dealing with my separation from them when I go on business trips."

"What? You buy them gifts? You bribe them with trinkets, you mala madre?!" I said laughing. I got up and went to the mirror to try some of that red lipstick on myself.

"Whenever I go away on a trip, at the end of the day, when I get to the hotel, I order dinner and a beer and I pull out the hotel stationery. And then I write my kids a letter. I tell them about what I did that day, what is going on in my life, why I'm on the trip, what's going on in the world. Sometimes I just write them a few lines if I'm tired. But I always tell them that even though I was away from them, that I love them and that I think about them all the time. And then I put the letter in an envelope, date it, and then I take it back home with me. And at home, I have a box for each of my kids filled with these letters and one day, when they are older, I'm going to give them the box. I don't know if it's going to make them love me more, or forgive me for being away from them, or make them angry to see how often I wasn't around. But it is a special thing I am doing for them. From Mamá para sus hijos. Con amor."

"Damn, Ro, you are so smart. Why can't I be more like you?" I said and we left for the conference luncheon looking like two single women with happening red lipstick on.

That night, I wrote my first love letter to mi hijo. I told him how much I loved him and how much angustia I had for being away from him and how I was going to try to be the best mom that I could but that he needed to know que la mamá que le tocó was a periodista and so he needed to understand that I had stories to tell, not only for him, but for hundreds of people as well. And that being a journalist made me very happy. But that nothing made me as happy as hearing the words *Mamá* come out of his mouth. Afterward, I felt much much better.

Two day later, when I arrived back in New York, everyone was asleep when I walked in. I washed my face and got in bed and wrapped my arms around Gérman and breathed in deep. His hair was tinged with the smell of the ocean and his sweat smelled like the earthy musk of Santo Domingo and I dozed off in his scent. The next morning when I went to get Raul Ariel out of bed at six in the morning, and he smiled and hugged me, I thought my absence from my son was forgiven. Everything was fine until he saw his father come down from bed and then I heard Raul Ariel call him something that pierced a hole deep into my exhausted and travel-weary corazoncito.

He called his father "Mamá."

What?

Raul Ariel said it over and over again. "Mamá, Mamá!" and he stretched out his arms to Gérman. We looked at each other in shock.

"No, Raul Ariel," Gérman said gently. "Yo soy tu papá. Ella es tu mamá!"

"Mamá," he said again, holding on to Gérman's huge shoulders.

I got into the shower, turned on the water, and started to cry. But I can't cry, I say to myself, and try to stop, I'm supposed to be on the air today!

On the subway to work, gazing into nowhere, I think about who I can talk to about this. I was too embarrassed to tell my mother, or Sandy, or Ceci, or Ro, or Graci, or anyone. Forget calling my tías or my primas. I would be the laughingstock of Mexico. Nothing could be more shameful.

To make things worse that first day back at the office I had to work late. I was doing a piece on what African American women thought about the legacy of Dr. Betty Shabazz, the widow of Malcolm X, who had just died. This was an important story, a chance to put thoughtful and eloquent Black women on national television. But what about my son? I had to be there to put him to bed this very first night back together. I had to try to salvage being his mamá and not his papá.

I called Gérman and told him to keep Raul Ariel up until I got there. I finished the piece and then, thinking I would get home faster, jumped in a cab. But the traffic gods decided to punish me and instead of getting home in my usual fifteen minutes, the cab ride was an interminable forty-five minute slow hike. By the time I arrived home, running up all five flights of stairs, Raul Ariel was exhausted and cranky, and when Gérman handed him to me he began to wail.

Uno no gana! You never win!

Here I am, forcing my child to stay up late in order to prove something (that I love him?) and then I take him away from his father and rush the bedtime ritual. This is supposed to be strengthening our bond?

He finally fell asleep after a half hour of rubbing his back. He was so worked up and exhausted that he couldn't wind down, and by that time, I'm sure it didn't matter to him who put him to bed.

Gérman was upset with me as well. "It was stupid to keep him up just so that you could see him. Poor little muchachito."

Rub it in, why don't you, I said to myself. That's what you get for having a husband who is a real co-parent. He gets to have opinions about everything.

Before I had my baby, when I would see dads walking with their strollers down Broadway, I would look at them and think "How nice." My feminist side would applaud them. But I had forgotten how severely disconnected my feminist side was from my mujer side. I never imagined I would have such convoluted feelings about my own husband's relationship with *my* son. Real mujeres have children who know the difference between moms and dads. And dads were not supposed to be moms! Y ya!

The next day, Raul Ariel called me Mamá a few times. A sign of progress. But he still called Gérman Mamá, too.

That night, after I put Raul Ariel in bed and Gérman was in the kitchen, I called Dr. Mark and confided in him what was happening.

"It's only natural for Raul Ariel to want to be comforted by the person he sees the most during the day," he told me. "And what's important is that Raul Ariel knows that he is being loved, which he is."

"I know that Mark. But the problem is that it is just not supposed to be this way."

"Maria, there is no way it's supposed to be anymore, It's all uncharted territory from here on in. And besides, do you want to raise your kids the same way your mom and dad, wonderful as they may be, raised you?"

"No, but that is my point of departure."

"Exactly! Departure. Say adiós to it baby, 'cause that ain't what's happening in the future. I know you know that. That is what your whole life is about."

"Yeah, you're right, I said, and took a deep breath. I could hear Gérman in the kitchen making our favorite meal—queso frito, yucca and
plántanos maduros, and ensalada. I do have the absolutely best husband and man in the world, I think to myself. I said good-bye to Mark
and hung up.

Gérman, as usual, was calm. He was standing over the boiling hot
oil, slipping in the thick slices of cheese at just the right moment. I was
convinced that making Dominican fried cheese was an art. The yucca
and sweet plantains were boiling on the back burner. I reached up, put
my hand on his wide shoulder, and bent his full lips down to reach mine.
I always dreamed of having a man with lips like these, thick and wavy.
They exuded sexiness just by being there, doing nothing.

"The food smells great. Thanks for cooking, Papito."

"I want you to know, honey, that I love taking care of you and Raul
Ariel. It may bother you that he calls me Mamá, but it shows that he
loves his dad and knows I am here for him. I didn't feel that way about
my own father. And even though this sounds crazy, I want you to know
that we will never be without a roof over our heads. If we ever needed
it, I could build us a house. With my bare hands."

What a strange thing to be saying, I thought. It came out of nowhere.

"Well, I don't think a tornado is going to rip through Manhattan and
tear off our roof. But you never know. They did find wild wolves roam-
ing in the Bronx, so anything is possible," I said chuckling.

"No, Malu, you don't understand. You see, when you come from an
island you need to figure out a way of being able to get off the island if
something was ever to happen. That's why I taught myself to build
things. So that I could save my life if I had to. You know. The war and all
that taught me those things."

There were rare moments when Gérman would go back to his memories of the war. I would never know what would trigger it and I would
never stop him from talking about it. So that evening I pulled back and
just listened.

The year was 1965. A leftist had been nominated for president of the
Dominican Republic but the ruling party wouldn't let him take power.
People took to the streets. In the Dominican Republic it's called La
Revolución. Gérman was nine years old when the United States sent in

forty thousand troops on an aircraft carrier called the U.S.S. *Intrepid* to patrol his tiny island. And I don't think that Gérman could have ever imagined that same boat would be docked only a few miles away from where he would end up living as an adult. The *Intrepid* sits in the Hudson River, and we drove by it every time we took the West Side Highway downtown. Gérman also never could have imagined that his own brother-in-law (my sister's husband who served in the navy) would have been stationed on the boat years later, but those were the circles of life.

Hundreds of people died during La Revolución. Gérman lost people who he knew from his neighborhood.

"At least we survived, amor," Gérman said to me as we set the table together. "You have to be able to find the positive side of things. Otherwise you'll die of sadness."

It was because Gérman survived these things that I felt he was rooted to the earth in a way that I could never be. And it was because of his rootedness that I attached to him and wrapped myself around him like ivy to a tree. I forgot about the mami-papi confusion momentarily and gave thanks that my son would grow up having a father like Gérman. I could never imagine what it would be like to have a dad who was solid like a rock, who was unfazed by anything—exhaustion, physical pain, poverty, violence, or any insecurity. I was the queen of high drama in our household, but Gérman made me feel as though there was nothing we could not survive. Gérman was going to give to Raul Ariel the real definition of macho. The machismo that means strength without bullying, love without possession, and responsibility without abuse.

For three long months, during the height of the war, Gérman and his mother, grandmother, and brother couldn't leave their home because there was gunfire on the streets. They had to live locked up in their house (his father was away in the army), and for three months straight, all they had to eat were eggs and plátanos, except on the days when his grandmother killed Gérman's pets for food. His dog, rabbit, and chicken were slaughtered so the family could eat. (Gérman says he cried and cried when that happened and silently pledged to never eat meat again.) He spent his days locked in one closet, his grandmother and brother in the other, and his mom would shuffle between the two,

crawling across the floor to reach them. At night they would sleep under the beds. They could only whisper to each other. Sometimes the
rebels used their backyard to set up camp. He would listen as they tried
to calm wounded fighters. He would listen until the dreadful moaning
would stop. He knew then that someone had just died in the place
where he used to play canicas and good cop, bad cop.

Three months of war teaches a child that he can't always get what he
wants. That his life may depend on how silent and still he is able to be.
I never had to wait that long for anything as important as that.

During the day, Gérman tells me as we eat dinner slowly, he would
play with tiny paper soldiers cut out from leftover scraps of old newspaper. He would roll some paper into little balls and knock down the
soldiers from the enemy camp. They had no electricity, no fans, no open
windows. I can't imagine what the heat must have been like locked in a
closet, in the summer, in the Caribbean. That's why Gérman gives
thanks for the things I take for granted. That's why he savors every day
that we use our air-conditioning. I remember him saying once that he
would always be grateful for "esa máquina que enfría la casa." I tended
to complain about the noise it made and the bills it rang up.

We sit with our empty plates in front of us. I am enthralled by my
husband's stories, by his clear eyes and his strong voice. I sit on his lap
and put my hands on his forehead. I run my fingers through his hair and
massage his head gently. I am sad I never got to meet Gérman's mother.
She died one month after we met. I am sad Raul Ariel will never feel
her strong arms holding him tight.

I wrap my arms around his neck and kiss him lightly. I gently lay my
lips on each one of his eyes. They are salty and moist.

"When you live through something like a war you realize that every
single day you have on this earth is a blessing. I come from having nothing, absolutely nothing. The fact that I have you and my son and a house
and my paintings are all gifts. I don't need anything else in this life to be
happy. In fact, if I ask for more it's almost like I'm being greedy. I am so
lucky already. I am so full."

As Gérman and I talked I thought about how much of the time I'm
not satisfied. How much more I want in life. How impatient I am. How
demanding I can be. How upset I can get just because my son calls his

father Mamá. As long as he loves his father, I think, who cares what he calls him?

My son was lucky enough to have a father who would teach him the invaluable lessons from his own life. And while I was obsessed with my memories of how I grew up, of my identity, or my woes of not fitting in, Gérman's memories—of surviving a war, an abusive father, poverty—made him stronger. And while I had romantic memories of my childhood that I wanted to re-create for my son, Gérman wanted to create a new definition of family, one that had nothing to do with how or where he was raised. Gérman embodied the newness that Dr. Mark was talking about. And for Gérman, newness meant discovery and joy, not trepidation or longing for the old.

"My father never carried me, never hugged me, never took me out except for once to a baseball game and we were rooting for different teams," Gérman said to me as I began to clear the table. "I want Raul Ariel to know that his father's arms are strong enough to carry him or to build him a house. I want him to see that with my hands I can create beauty on a canvas or feed my newborn son with a tube on my pinky finger." He paused for a second and then continued. "I'll never forget being able to feed him on those nights when he was just days old. You gave me that closeness to my son, that regalo, that bond that many fathers are never given the chance to make."

The part of me that felt threatened and upset by a son who called his father Mom started slowly to disappear. We finished cleaning up the kitchen and took a nice long shower together. I was glad the weekend had arrived—glad to be connecting with my family again.

And I hoped my beeper wouldn't go off the whole weekend long. Luckily, it didn't.

On Saturday I took Raul Ariel to the Central Park Zoo and watched him laugh at the barking seals. We walked over to the carousel and rode in circles for three long rides. We sat on the curb and watched the skaters zoom down the park road. And then we danced to the congas at the rumba when they sang for Yemanya. By the end of the weekend, Raul Ariel had stopped calling Gérman Mamá and instead gave us both a new name—"Ma-Pa." How fitting. It was the perfect way my son had decided to teach me about learning to live with the reality of a different kind of family—a family with parents who were equal partners and equally in love with their son and with each other. And with their work.

I was getting into a groove. It was summer now, which meant a slow news period, so I got a chance to work on some feature stories. I was enjoying my new job immensely and was feeling less threatened by the new medium—television. I missed NPR, but here every story idea I came up with they loved. I felt like I was doing important work again.

My two selves were more intertwined now. My gringa self had everything under control. My Latina self felt like I was loved and loving. I was in balance. Or so I thought.

I was in charge of the mornings. I would wake up every day with Raul Ariel at 6:30 and we would play for a few minutes in his little loft bed that I was small enough to squeeze into. I'd get under the covers and play peek-a-boo and then we'd throw Beanie Babies at each other. Gérman had painted the wall of the loft bed blue like the oceans and had made carvings on the door that were a combination of Native American and Taino designs. There was a man with a sun for a head and a woman with a crescent moon as hers. There were elongated horses and a boat with stars above it. The sides of his bed were padded with cloth of an African animal print. I love Raul Ariel's bed as much as mine.

After our playtime, I would make Raul Ariel some breakfast and then take his high chair inside the bathroom with me while I showered. And he kept me company while I did my makeup. Then Paty would arrive and before I would leave for the subway, I would give him kisses all over his face (including besos de ojos—eyelash kisses) and he would wave at me from the window as I made my way down the street.

In the evenings, I was often getting back in time to do the bedtime ritual as well. I'd bathe him and then we'd get into bed and read books together. We read books about piñatas, and flying abuelas, and pelitos, books about Elmo, Curious George, Babar, and his favorite—a Virgen de Guadalupe pop-up book. After saying good-night to all of his santos and familia and padrinos, I would sing "Gracias a la Vida" to him and kiss him good-night. Things between Raul Ariel and me were getting on smoothly and he was back to calling me Mamá. But with Gérman, it was a different story.

By the end of the evening we were so exhausted, we weren't up for long, intimate discussions about things. We talked about work and schedules and about Raul Ariel. Our conversations during the day revolved around my calling and doing my military checkup of what was going on in my household. Did he sleep? How long? What did he have for lunch? Did he play with any friends? How long was he at the park? Et cetera, et cetera.

"One day it would be nice if you asked about how I was doing," Gérman said to me one afternoon when I was calling from the car on our way to do a shoot.

"I do care about you, honey. I love you," I said, and then paused. "Anyway, can you have Paty make the chicken for Raul Ariel's dinner? I'll see you later."

The space between Gérman and me was getting thicker and icier as every day went by. And the less we talked the more bricks Gérman laid in the impenetrable wall he knew how to build around himself. Gérman could be the sweetest, gentlest man in the world but, learning the trick to protect himself from his father, he could also be the hardest. And when he felt like he was being overlooked or taken for granted, he would withdraw so deeply into his shell that it would take Herculean efforts to draw him out.

But now I just didn't have the energy to focus on Gérman. It felt as if it had become all about managing my job and my son.

I was trying to "drive" my house in manual transmission, shifting the gears from my office miles away by phone. I was manejando mi casa, just as I had seen my mother and tías do it. It was the only way I knew how.

Finally, after two weeks of the frigidity in the house, Gérman and I talked.

"How do you think it makes me feel when all you do is give me orders about what to do with my son? Don't you think I know what I am doing? I am the one who is here at home with him every day! And I am sacrificing my own work so that one of us is here and so that Raul Ariel is not being raised by a nanny. You don't take my work seriously only because I don't have to get up and go to an office every day! Maybe I should rent a studio and that way you could give all your orders to the babysitter and I won't be in the middle!"

"We don't have the money for you to rent a studio," I said dryly, now retreating into my own shell. Couldn't Gérman see that my taking control, if even from afar, was a way in which I was cutting him some slack so that he *could* work? I did what I did so that Gérman would have *less* responsibility. And of course I supported his career. I fell in love with him because of his art.

"You treat me as if I am some kind of employee and not the father that I am!" he raised his deep voice and started wagging his finger at me. I hated when he did that.

"Don't yell at me. I don't think you are anyone's employee," I snapped.

"Then why don't you give me some credit and stop trying to overrule everything I say about what should or shouldn't be done with our son," he growled. "And why don't you give me just a little bit of love along with recognition. You come home and never ask me how my day was—as if I've been sitting around having the time of my life. It's not easy being at home!"

"And how come you never ask me how *my* day was?" I blurted out. "You think it's easy having deadlines all over the place and managing office politics and having to answer to several different bosses who are constantly judging me?"

It dawned on me that these were the typical arguments that working couples with kids always had. But there was one huge difference. I was sounding like the typical husband who complained of the stress of the nine-to-five. And Gérman sounded like the typical wife who felt like her work at home wasn't of value—with the caveat that I still thought I had the right and the need to be the mother from afar.

"Let me ask you something," Gérman said as he stood up. "Do you trust me in raising our son?"

"Yes," I mumbled.

"Really? You are always making decisions about what he should do and when. You are always telling me what he should wear. You are always deciding where he should be and with whom. You decide how often he naps and for how long. And you try to force me to follow those rules even when you're not here! It's illogical for you to do that! Why can't you just let go? Carajo!"

I froze. Gérman was asking me to basically give up being my son's mother. That was impossible! Mothering was managed by the women in the household. Even if it's from afar, las mamás siempre tienen el control. There was no other way to do it. Las mamás mandan! Mothers always give orders and maintain order!

Gérman wanted me to give up being the only kind of mother I knew how to be. If I gave that control up then what would be left for me to do?

And so the wall went up between us again, this time higher and thicker.

Thank God, I had planned weeks before for a three-day getaway with Raul Ariel to Chicago. The family wanted to see the baby and I would get a chance to see Ceci and her daughter as well.

In Chicago, Raul Ariel once again basked in the security of being surrounded by his familia. We went to the aquarium and to the children's museum. We visited my sister and her family in the suburbs and they took Raul Ariel for his first visit to a mall. They had tickle fights and played my sister's piano. Ceci and I got together and we took photos of our kids hugging each other.

But my argument with Gérman hung over me like a black cloud. And I didn't feel my family could help me understand how to handle this role-reversal issue. Even though my sister was a working mom, her husband also worked outside of the home and she still "drove" her house and her husband let her. And Mom never had to deal with this. Nor did Ceci.

So I kept quiet.

One night when the kids were all asleep, my sister and her husband and my parents and I sat in the living room and talked.

Since I couldn't talk about what was happening with Gérman I brought up a topic out of the blue. I had never asked my father what he thought about the fact that he had a namesake. I figured this was as good a time as any to bring it up.

"Well," he said, "he *is* Raul. But he's not Raul Hinojosa. He's Raul Perez-Hinojosa."

AAAAAGGGGGGGRRRRRRHHHHHH!

The most impossible man to please! I didn't even want to follow through on that conversation. I knew it would inevitably lead us to the whole why-did-we-leave-Mexico-thirty-five-years-ago conversation once again.

Instead my sister asked Mom and Dad about their retirement plans. Dad, after major prodding by Mom, had finally agreed to stop working at the end of the next year. They announced that they had decided not to go back to live in Mexico after all.

Wow. It was as if the chapter on Mexico had come to a close. Just like that. They were never going back. None of us was ever going back.

"Increíble!" I said to my parents. "That is a big deal. So now you are gringos for real and forever." I laughed.

"I may have lived in this country for thirty-five years, mi'jita, and I may be a U.S. citizen, but I know what I am. I am a Mexican. I am what I always have been. A Mexican living in the United States."

"Dad. You're never going back. You can call yourself an American now. Puh-leeze!"

Silence.

And then I turned to my father and said, "Dad, was it really such a bad thing to bring us all here? Would you really prefer to have all of us be just like our cousins in Mexico? When will you ever admit that coming to this country was a good thing? When will you ever allow me to feel fine accepting the Latina gringa that I am, that we all are? That you are, too? When, Papi? When?"

My sister and Mom both take deep breaths as I stare at my father. In the back of mind I say to myself, Why do you continue to push this whole American-Mexican thing with Dad? Why can't you learn to just let it go?

Papi took off his glasses and rubbed his eyes. He slowly reached into his back pocket and pulled out his perfectly folded white pañuelo. He wiped his nose and sniffled.

"You know, Malulis, there's an interesting story about how we ended up in this country. I've never told this to anyone except your mom and she probably has forgotten because I said it only once, thirty-five years ago."

Papi leaned his head back on the sofa and closed his eyes as if this would help him go back in time. "It's been thirty-five years since these words have crossed my lips.

"When I was considering whether or not to come to the United States, I called your tío Pancho, my uncle who was the only one in my whole family who had ever lived in the States. He was an artist, a bohemian, and he went to live in New York City for three years. I respected him. And when we were faced with having to leave Mexico, I told him that I wasn't sure about my decision, that I wasn't sure I wanted to leave my great country, my home, mi país, to come to the States just for a job. For me, leaving and taking this new job meant I would have to give up my Mexican citizenship. And I didn't know how I could do that and still be who I was raised to be . . .

"But, your tío Pancho sat me down and told me this. 'In the United States, you don't have to give up being who you are. You will always be a Mexican, wherever you end up living. In America, you can be anyone you want to be without sacrificing your Mexicanidad. That is the beauty of the States.' And right then and there I knew my mind was made up. We would come here and we would raise you like Mexicans, which is all we knew. I just never imagined that you would all, including your mother, take it upon yourselves to become who you wanted to be. I thought somehow I could control it and make you still be like your mother and me. But you have all become who you wanted to be."

Papi lifts his head and then says slowly, "And I *am* proud of you. All of you. I am proud of who you have become."

That night, alone in my bed, I rewound the conversation and played it back in my head over and over again, as I stared at Raul Ariel sleeping soundly next to me. My father had told me he was proud of who I had become. Proud of his daughter the gringa Latina. Just with that one word I felt as if my life meant something. It sounded ridiculous but I guessed in many ways this is what I had been wanting to hear for so long. That Dad was orgulloso to have a daughter who had done something important with her life, in this country. Even though he didn't say it exactly, I felt as if he was giving me his blessing, too, for being a mom and having a career. That was who I had become in his eyes. A gringa Latina working mamá.

Be who you want to be, I said to myself, as I laid my head down next to my son's. This is who I want to be after all.

But then I thought about Gérman. He wants me to be a *different* kind of mother. And he wants to be a *different* kind of father. Great. So I've got Dad finally accepting me and a husband who wants to change me. Dad is distracting himself from Mexico but I feel as if Mexico's definition of mothering is so close it's choking me.

Gérman wants me to stop being a typical Latina mamá who needs to be on top of her casa to feel as if she's in control. He wants me to become someone else. Someone I don't think I know how to be.

It feels frightening to think of giving up the fishing pole. It feels scary to give up the reins of my household and give them to my husband, the man who is holding the house on his shoulders. It feels strange to look at my husband and completely trust that he *can* raise our son and run our home. It feels strange to see myself as a mother—a woman—who can take on other roles.

It takes some of us many years to realize the simplest of things. I wasn't going to be like my mom or Ceci's mom or my primas or any of the women I knew from New York. I was going to be a New York-type-A-Mamá-Mexicana-Domini-Mex-workaholic-abrazos-giving-gym-addict-reporter-order-giving-work-in-progress-madre-mother-mom-mami. And this mami would have days when it all seemed to fit together like a puzzle and other days when she felt like she was losing it and was a rompecabezas herself. And it would be forever changing and each change would make her shudder pero ni modo. Así se hace y ya.

We fly back to New York, Raul Ariel and I, and he screams the entire two-hour plane ride. The flight attendants just about spit on me. The guy sitting next to me said out loud he would have given anything to not be on that flight. I didn't care. I gave him my best it-is-what-it-is look, shrugged my shoulders, and turned back to my screaming baby.

Gérman was waiting for us at the airport and I gave a soft smile that let him know my guard was down. The miniguerra was over. Raul Ariel dove into his arms.

That night, when we got home, we put Raul Ariel's favorite CD on and we all started dancing in the middle of the floor. The rainbow of masks from all over the world looked down at us, Gérman's paintings glowed red and orange in the background, and the candles and incense on our altar warmed the room like a burning fireplace. The music was DLG, Dark Latin Groove. Raul Ariel held two maracas in each hand and his face was like a rayo de sol, jumping up and down, holding on to Ma-Pa with one hand and his other Ma-Pa with the other.

Epilogue

At night, when I would lay in bed with Raul Ariel (yes, now I was back to getting in bed with him and staying with him until he fell asleep—sacrilege!—but it filled my heart nonetheless and on other days bothered me to no end) my hands would reach under his pajama top and I would rub my palms against his warm smooth skin. I would rub his legs rhythmically, up and down, up and down, just as Mami had done to me to ease my "growing pains." I had developed my hands into those of a sobadora. (Maybe not such a good sobadora, but I knew my now three-year-old son loved it.) Sobándolo, I would put him to sleep. After a few minutes he would doze off and then start snoring gently, just like his father.

I had come to terms with the fact that I would not be able to (nor did I know that I would always want to) play with my son seven days a week. But when we did do things together, I would plant myself right next to him and like my Hasidic friend Rebecca, tried to make him feel that at that moment in time, nothing could be more important than him. And there were never-ending abrazos and besos, and I-love-you's, a quick kiss on the lips while he watched Elmo or a round of eyelash kisses before dinner.

And yes, like my mother before me, I began to feed my son by hand. On days when I was home in time for his dinner, I would sit next to him at the table and delicately place each tiny piece of chicken or noodles right into his mouth, like a bird feeding her young.

•

It was late in the summer of 1997 and Gérman had a show opening in downtown Rio de Janeiro. We decided this would be a great opportunity to take a second honeymoon, especially since our first one had been a bust—we went to Brazil and crime was so out of control I couldn't even show off my cool new Aztec-design wedding band. I had my mom and dad come and stay with Raul Ariel and I flew down to meet my husband for our first-ever leave away from our son, who was nineteen months old.

The night I was supposed to fly, my flight was canceled and I was forced to fly to Buenos Aires and then make a connection to São Paulo and Rio. I finally arrived twenty-four hours later, ran into the airport bathroom after landing, took out the minidress I had bought to wear for the opening, touched up my makeup, and, like Cinderella, Gérman whisked me straight off to his opening where we arrived just in time for caipirinhas.

We walked the streets of Copacabana and relished the sight of sun-bronzed men and women in tiny bathing suits. The sensuality was so thick it seeped into our pores. You couldn't peel me off of Gérman. We made love the way we hadn't been able to as newlyweds. We knew each other so well. We had had a son together. I whispered to Gérman one night in Rio to forget about the protection. And he did.

I didn't think about my new job, I didn't think about not having any space for a new baby, I didn't think about anything except for the hunger for Gérman, I felt so intensely right then.

"Que sea lo que la diosa mande," I mumbled into his ear and then felt him deep inside of me and I knew.

A month later the little pink strip confirmed it.

Seismic fights like the one we had had not long ago about me redefining my mothering style still occurred. Just not as often. And I pulled back even more from "driving mi casa." It wasn't easy but I stopped calling in from the office so often, and when I did call I would always ask Gérman how he was doing first. And I didn't have to ask for details about Raul Ariel. Gérman now volunteered the information. We would have long periods of tranquility. And then I would end up having to travel on business for four days in a row and everything would get out of whack and we'd have discussions and then we'd grumble at each other for a few hours and then we'd move on. We realized it took too much time and energy to get and stay in fighting mode.

A month after I got back from Brazil, I walked into my boss's office and cried when I told her I was pregnant. Yes, I had become a grown woman, but it felt like it would take forever to dismiss that timid little girl in me. I felt foolish. But my boss just gave me a wide smile and said "Congratulations! Now we can share stories of being mothers of two!"

My daughter would be born the next year on Cinco de Mayo, after fifteen hours of labor and one and a half hours of pushing and then, finally, a cesarean. But my dream had come true. I had experienced labor. I had lived through those real-woman pains.

We named her Maria Yurema Guadalupe de los Indios: *Maria* in memory of Gérman's mother, *Yurema,* because she was made in Brazil (Yurema is the name of an aphrodisiac plant and a religious belief system that combines Indian and African traditions—we didn't know any of this when we chose the name—we just liked the way it sounded— *zzhhu-reh-mah*—so sensual); *Guadalupe*, because Mom insisted she have a Lupe somewhere in her name; and *de los indios,* because she was born a brown baby.

After Yuyu (her nickname) was born, I took six months off and spent the summer afternoons with my two children in the playgrounds of Central Park and Riverside Drive. I told people I never imagined I would love being a mother so much. And I did. But this time I was ready and anxious to go back to work.

At the office I was busier than I had ever been and I felt torn as much and as often as I did before. And I discovered that it never goes away. Ever.

I told Ro that I felt as my love intensified for my children so did my love for my work. I couldn't exactly explain it and I certainly didn't feel this way all of the time, but when I did, I felt invigorated by both parts of my life. Feeling torn became a part of my emotional makeup bag. I realized it would stay with me until a day that I might become my own boss and work for myself. But I knew, I understood, I needed, to always have my work.

I still tried to control things. I still gave orders. But when Gérman would tell me to stop I would. It was easier now. Sometimes I didn't. This control-caca was a part of me—whether we liked it or not.

One of the many nights when I missed putting Raul Ariel to sleep, my son turned to Gérman and said, "Mamá está busy, verdad, Papá?" Mom is busy, right?

"Yes, Raul Ariel," he said to him. "Now you know what the word *busy* means." He hugged him and kissed him and said, "Mami will be busy many days, but you know she loves you."

"Sí, Papi, I know that," he said, and told my husband he was going to go to sleep. "Y no me molestes porque voy a soñar con los angelitos!"

FOR THE BEST IN PAPERBACKS, LOOK FOR THE

In every corner of the world, on every subject under the sun, Penguin represents quality and variety—the very best in publishing today.

For complete information about books available from Penguin—including Puffins, Penguin Classics, and Arkana—and how to order them, write to us at the appropriate address below. Please note that for copyright reasons the selection of books varies from country to country.

In the United Kingdom: Please write to *Dept. EP, Penguin Books Ltd, Bath Road, Harmondsworth, West Drayton, Middlesex UB7 0DA.*

In the United States: Please write to *Penguin Putnam Inc., P.O. Box 12289 Dept. B, Newark, New Jersey 07101-5289* or call 1-800-788-6262.

In Canada: Please write to *Penguin Books Canada Ltd, 10 Alcorn Avenue, Suite 300, Toronto, Ontario M4V 3B2.*

In Australia: Please write to *Penguin Books Australia Ltd, P.O. Box 257, Ringwood, Victoria 3134.*

In New Zealand: Please write to *Penguin Books (NZ) Ltd, Private Bag 102902, North Shore Mail Centre, Auckland 10.*

In India: Please write to *Penguin Books India Pvt Ltd, 11 Panchsheel Shopping Centre, Panchsheel Park, New Delhi 110 017.*

In the Netherlands: Please write to *Penguin Books Netherlands bv, Postbus 3507, NL-1001 AH Amsterdam.*

In Germany: Please write to *Penguin Books Deutschland GmbH, Metzlerstrasse 26, 60594 Frankfurt am Main.*

In Spain: Please write to *Penguin Books S. A., Bravo Murillo 19, 1° B, 28015 Madrid.*

In Italy: Please write to *Penguin Italia s.r.l., Via Benedetto Croce 2, 20094 Corsico, Milano.*

In France: Please write to *Penguin France, Le Carré Wilson, 62 rue Benjamin Baillaud, 31500 Toulouse.*

In Japan: Please write to *Penguin Books Japan Ltd, Kaneko Building, 2-3-25 Koraku, Bunkyo-Ku, Tokyo 112.*

In South Africa: Please write to *Penguin Books South Africa (Pty) Ltd, Private Bag X14, Parkview, 2122 Johannesburg.*